LANGUAGE AND LITERACY SERIES

Dorothy S. Strickland and Celia Genishi, SERIES EDITORS

The Administration and Supervision
of
Reading Programs

SECOND EDITION

Edited by
**Shelley B. Wepner
Joan T. Feeley
Dorothy S. Strickland**

International
Reading
Association

Teachers College
Columbia University
New York and London

The list on pp. 26–27 originally appeared in *Standards for Reading Professionals* (pp. 28–29), 1992. Reprinted with permission of the International Reading Association.

All photographs were provided by the team of Andrew Clayton and Kozo Nozawa

Published simultaneously by Teachers College Press, 1234 Amsterdam Ave., New York, NY 10027 and The International Reading Association, 800 Barksdale Rd., Newark, DE 19714

Library of Congress Cataloging-in-Publication Data

The administration and supervision of reading programs / edited by
   Shelley B. Wepner, Joan T. Feeley, Dorothy S. Strickland. — 2nd ed.
      p.   cm.
   Includes bibliographical references (p.) and index.
   ISBN 0-8077-3415-2 — ISBN 0-8077-3414-4 (pbk.)
   1. Reading—United States. 2. School management and organization—
United States. 3. School supervision—United States. I. Wepner,
Shelley B., 1951–   . II. Feeley, Joan T., 1932–   .
III. Strickland, Dorothy S.
   LB1050.2.A36   1995
   428.4'07'12—dc20   94-39965

ISBN 0-8077-3414-4 (paper)
ISBN 0-8077-3415-2 (cloth)
IRA Inventory Number 158

Printed on acid-free paper
Manufactured in the United States of America

02 01 00 99 98 97 96   8 7 6 5 4 3 2

Again, to our parents, our first role models and supervisors:
Carole and Bernard Markovitz
Theresa and Ed Stollmeyer
Evelyn and Leroy Salley

Contents

Foreword

A few years ago, I was an external evaluator for the reading program at a university in New Jersey. In that position, I was invited to observe some of the reading classes being conducted, one of which was on the organization and the supervision of the reading program. In that class, the young professor apologized for the photocopies of the text she was using. After class we both bemoaned the fact that there was absolutely no current texts in print that covered the subject matter in the course. I was particularly concerned because a significant portion of my professional life had been spent as a reading supervisor. How awful that there were no good books in print focusing on the preparation of professionals for the administration and supervision of reading programs.

"Why don't you write one?" asked the young professor.

"Why don't you?" I replied.

Well, several years have passed and I'm pleased to see that the young professor, Dr. Shelley B. Wepner, did accept my challenge, and along with her colleagues, Drs. Joan T. Feeley and Dorothy S. Strickland, produced an excellent volume on the administration and supervision of reading programs. I was thrilled, for now I too was teaching a course with the same name, and this book would be my basic text. In fact, the book was so good that I immediately abandoned any plans to bring out a volume of my own. Thus, for the last five years, *The Administration and Supervision of Reading Programs* (1989) has been the text for all my students seeking reading supervision certification. It has been an excellent guide for them as they plan programs for their own districts.

This new edition is organized with the same major divisions as the first volume, with each major section dealing with the knowledge areas necessary for administering reading programs. The first section provides a comprehensive overview of the major components of any reading program and serves as an organizer for the rest of the book.

The second section discusses program development and organization from the pre-elementary through high school level. A particularly unique and relevant aspect of this section is the chapter on pre-elementary programs, a component often overlooked in describing reading programs. This new edition provides readers with insights into comprehensive reading/literacy programs at all levels.

The third section deals with all the activities necessary to implement a successful reading program: program assessment, staff development, selection and use of materials, and community outreach. This section is one of the most significantly changed from the 1989 edition; it contains material on observing in the child-centered classroom, portfolio assessment, and other cutting-edge topics of the past five years.

Finally, the last section of this volume focuses on the relationships of reading with other parts of the curriculum and other school personnel. Discussion centers on the interrelationships between reading, writing, and learning and the importance of technology in literacy instruction. Some attention is also given to working with special needs students and students from diverse populations.

Undoubtedly, this edition, like the last, will continue to be a basic text in my class and in countless others across the country. The material included in this work provides an important source of recent and relevant research on the organization of reading programs. Furthermore, already practicing supervisors and coordinators have in this volume a handy reference that will provide a bench mark against which they can measure their own programs.

In short, Drs. Wepner, Feeley, and Strickland are once again to be congratulated for providing the educational research community with a readable, research-based volume on an often neglected aspect of the field of reading.

Jack Cassidy
Professor of Education
Millersville University
President of I.R.A., 1982–83

Preface

The second edition of *The Administration and Supervision of Reading Programs* is offered as a practical and readable text for those who supervise reading programs. We sent a survey to the readers of our first edition to solicit their input on ways to revise the original text in order to continue to provide current information about realistic concerns. As a result of their input, we have added new chapters and topics, deleted others, and made major revisions to existing ones. Although similar information may be found elsewhere in a variety of sources, there still are very few coherent texts written specifically for specialists, administrators, and supervisors. Accordingly, we have attempted to bring together state-of-the-art information for this audience.

As with the original text, this second edition aims to help preservice and inservice reading specialists, supervisors, and administrators understand how to organize and supervise reading programs for pre-K through grade twelve. Sound theoretical principles and practices for effective reading supervision in today's schools are offered through examples, observations, and research.

The four parts are written with these goals in mind. Part I provides an overview of reading supervision by describing effective reading program components and the personnel responsible for program implementation. Part II presents guidelines for developing reading programs at the pre-elementary, elementary, middle school, junior high, and high school levels. Part III describes five critical areas for program implementation and evaluation: reading material selection and use, classroom observations, staff development, assessment of reading programs, and community outreach. Part IV explores four areas that need to be interconnected with comprehensive reading program development: connecting reading, writing, and learning using technology, providing for diverse student populations, and dealing with special needs students. The book closes with a discussion of the connections made throughout and a look toward the future in reading supervision.

The strength of this book continues to come from our authors, some of whom have changed since the first edition in order to discuss the topics suggested by our readership from the first edition. By working in the schools in a variety of capacities over the years, our authors have created new visions about delivering reading and writing instruction that they share with us here. We believe that their individual contributions create a unique chorus of harmonized ideas for supervising reading programs. We hope that your sentiments echo ours.

We would like to thank Dorothy Rowe, principal, and the staff and students of School 26, Paterson, NJ, and Erika Steinbauer, principal, and the staff and students of Cherry Hill School, River Edge, NJ, for allowing us to photograph them in their schools. We also gratefully acknowledge the following people for enhancing the quality of the book: Jean Sawey, typist; Andrew Clayton and Kozo Nozawa, photographers; Carol Collins, Development Editor, Teachers College Press; Sarah J. Biondello, Executive Acquisitions Editor, Teachers College Press; and all the administrators, supervisors, and teachers who have shared their ideas with us.

Part I

OVERVIEW

Part I sets the stage for this book by providing a structured overview of the components needed for reforming school reading programs, and the personnel needed to create this climate for change.

Chapter 1 provides specific guidelines for implementing three essential elements—curriculum, instruction, and assessment—in any effective reading program. A process for change, including principles and policies for implementing such change, is also provided. Chapter 2 describes the evolving nature of the roles and responsibilities of reading personnel: reading specialists as teachers, reading specialists as consultant/ coordinators, and reading supervisors. Other school personnel are described, particularly in relation to their roles on site-based management teams. In combination, these two chapters provide a comprehensive picture of how reading program components are interwoven.

1 Effective Reading Program Development

RITA M. BEAN
University of Pittsburgh

The past several decades have seen numerous efforts to restructure or reform school reading programs. Some of these efforts have been spurred by dissatisfaction with student performance in reading, others by research findings that have provided educators with additional information about how to create, implement, and assess instructional programs in reading. Still other restructuring plans have evolved through the efforts of teachers who have been encouraged to become directly involved in decisionmaking in the schools (see Chapter 2). Developing a school reading program is an important task required of those in leadership positions. It necessitates a deep knowledge and understanding of reading acquisition, reading research, and reading instruction. It also requires an ability to create an atmosphere for change, and thus an understanding of the dynamics of leadership and the change process. In this chapter, we provide a framework for thinking about the essential elements of a school reading program and discuss a process model that promotes teacher empowerment and can be used to initiate and implement change in the schools.

FRAMEWORK OF A SCHOOL READING PROGRAM

Although individual teachers may work effectively in the classroom with students, their individual efforts do not constitute an overall reading program. The effective school reading program must be based on a broad, comprehensive view of reading; it requires a vision of what reading is, and demands a concerted effort that involves all professionals in the schools working toward a shared vision. These professionals include teachers, administrators, and support personnel such as reading specialists, counselors, and librarians. The development of a reading program also requires communication with parents and a knowledge of the community in which the school is located.

To establish an effective program, professionals must assist in the selection of literacy goals and have the competency and commitment to develop instructional plans that will help students achieve those goals. The framework described in the following sections provides a model for thinking about goal identification. It includes three essential elements of any school reading program: curriculum, instruction, and assessment. Although some scholars would subsume instruction under the broad rubric of curriculum, I consider each as a separate entity for the purpose of discussion and elaboration. The framework is graphically portrayed in Figure 1.1.

Curriculum

The reading curriculum is the plan for guiding learning in the school; it provides the ideas for charting the directions for the classroom. The curriculum includes the goals and philosophy of the program and the student outcomes identified as important. These outcomes include the understandings, skills, and attitudes that a school wishes students to achieve. Materials that facilitate achievement of school goals are also included in the curriculum. Although a written curriculum exists in most schools, there is also the "actualized" curriculum that occurs in the classrooms on a day-to-day basis. Although there should be consistency be-

Figure 1.1   Essential Elements of an Effective School Reading Program, K–12

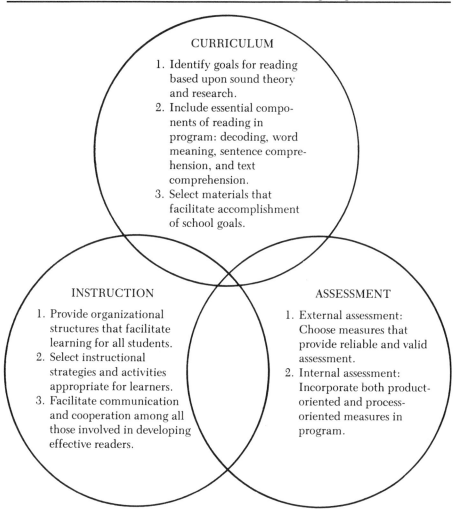

CURRICULUM

1. Identify goals for reading based upon sound theory and research.
2. Include essential components of reading in program: decoding, word meaning, sentence comprehension, and text comprehension.
3. Select materials that facilitate accomplishment of school goals.

INSTRUCTION

1. Provide organizational structures that facilitate learning for all students.
2. Select instructional strategies and activities appropriate for learners.
3. Facilitate communication and cooperation among all those involved in developing effective readers.

ASSESSMENT

1. External assessment: Choose measures that provide reliable and valid assessment.
2. Internal assessment: Incorporate both product-oriented and process-oriented measures in program.

tween the written and the actualized curriculum, at times this is not so. For example, although the written curriculum may call for daily experiences with sustained silent reading, a particular teacher may not schedule such an activity because of felt exigencies, such as helping students prepare for an upcoming standardized test. Teacher beliefs may also influence whether and how a particular goal or objective is presented in the classroom. Teachers who object to a specific approach or practice may choose to deemphasize or ignore a specific goal. Described below are guidelines that professionals involved in the development of reading curriculum might wish to consider.

1. *The school must decide upon goals for reading instruction based upon a sound definition of the reading process.* Harste (1989) suggests that a balanced reading curriculum is based on four areas of knowledge: our understanding of language (reading and writing), language learning, successful language users, and the evolution of literacy. In setting goals, all involved — from school administrators and teachers to school boards and parents — must understand how their views or beliefs about each of these areas of knowledge influence the school reading program. For example, if reading is viewed as a skill, instruction will tend to be organized as a set of tasks presented in an organized, sequential fashion. If reading is viewed as an interactive process, the curriculum will be organized as a set of experiences provided for students. The ideas and goals of the curriculum and, of course, the subsequent instruction will be different, depending on the beliefs held by the group.

Thus, as professionals set goals and identify student outcomes, they should reflect upon their own beliefs about the four areas of knowledge. They should also consider the research of the past several decades that has led to important understandings about the reading process (Anderson, Hiebert, Scott, & Wilkinson, 1985; Barr, Kamil, Mosenthal, & Pearson, 1991; Pearson, 1984). Experts agree that reading is not simply a hierarchically arranged set of subskills easily taught and tested, but rather a complex activity requiring the coordination of a number of interrelated sources of information (Anderson et al., 1985). Five generalizations generated from research and discussed in *Becoming a Nation of Readers* (Anderson et al., 1985) provide important considerations for planning a reading program. They state that reading: is a constructive process, must be fluent, must be strategic, requires motivation, and is a continuously developing skill (pp. 9–16). A curriculum based upon these generalizations limits or discourages what Winograd and Greenlee (1986) call the reductionists' view of teaching reading, which tends to overemphasize skills and views the teacher as a manager of materials. Rather, these generalizations suggest an emphasis on providing students with many different purposes for reading, and with a variety of texts. They stress the importance of self-monitoring and motivation in the reading program. The importance of a K–12 reading program is apparent when one understands that becoming a reader is a lifelong pursuit requiring much practice and refinement, particularly in this technological society with its sophisticated demands of the adult reader.

One of the other contributions that research has made to practice is the understanding of the interrelationships among the language arts. The relationship between reading and writing is especially important; in fact, evidence indicates that writing promotes ability in reading, and that the most effective programs are those that enhance integration of the formal language skills of reading and writing in the school curriculum (Anderson et al., 1985; Stotsky, 1983; Tierney & Shanahan, 1991; Wittrock, 1983).

2. *The school curriculum should provide for the essential components of reading, identify the foci at various levels, and specify the means for articulation.* As mentioned previously, reading is a complex process that requires integrated use of multiple skills; yet there is still a need to identify the components of reading so that specific goals and instructional activities can be selected. As stated by Calfee and Drum (1986), the identified components should be simple, yet coherent. The framework selected should have a sound theoretical base and at the same time be one that classroom teachers can use effectively. Often, basic frameworks or conceptual plans can be obtained from departments of education at the state level (e.g., California State Department of Education, 1987; Cook, 1986; Lytle & Botel, 1988), and from reading methods textbooks or basal reader manuals. These plans may serve as a guide for discussion and as a basis for program development, but may need to be modified to meet the specific characteristics of a school district. In fact, a review of various plans will reveal the use of different terminology for similar components (e.g., *word attack* for decoding, *word meaning* for vocabulary, study skills separate from comprehension), and there may be differences in how various elements of reading are sequenced.

Any model one adopts or develops, however, should include the following literacy components: word meaning, word analysis, comprehension and appreciation of narrative text, and comprehension and ability to use expository text. Further, within each of these components, there should be evidence that (1) there is provision for learning of strategic behaviors, that is, students are learning to learn; (2) writing is an integral part of each component; and (3) there is an awareness of the importance of developing student interests and attitudes toward reading.

Articulation of activities and experiences, K–12, needs to be addressed by those involved in developing a reading program. Although there is no one correct sequence of how reading experiences and skills should be organized, each school should develop a broad plan that illustrates where in the curriculum various understandings, skills, and attitudes would be addressed. Otherwise, students may receive little or no experiences with various aspects of reading (e.g., no introduction to any study strategy), or they may receive the same experiences again and again.

Some issues that schools need to address include:

- What skills and knowledges are important at the emergent literacy stage that will enable students to move successfully into a more formal reading program?
- When and how much phonics should be introduced? Which phonic elements should be introduced first? How much attention should be devoted to phonics after second grade (especially for those who have not been successful)?
- What should be the focus of the elementary school reading program (literature, or skills, or both)?
- What should be the focus of the middle school reading program (literature-based or content-based)?
- When and how do students get experience in reading content materials?

Answers to these and other questions specific to one's own school district will help curriculum developers identify the foci at various levels of schooling and provide ideas for effective articulation.

3. *Materials should be chosen to help schools achieve their reading goals.* In an effective school reading program, materials should reflect the curriculum, goals, and objectives of the school. Too often, materials determine and drive the curriculum; they influence both activities and the content that students learn (Duffy, Roehler, & Mason, 1984). Although the basal reader is still used extensively as the predominant material and approach to reading at the elementary level, recently there have been many efforts to expand reading programs to include many more experiences with literature or trade books (Gambrell, 1992). Teachers have become much more knowledgeable about the availability and advantages of various types of reading materials.

In addition to experiences with narrative text, however, the program should include opportunities for students to read expository materials, including texts used in the content areas. Further, various supplemental books and nonprint materials such as films, records, maps, and charts add other dimensions and encourage students to view reading as a communication tool. The availability of technology (e.g., computer software, interactive videodisc) for classroom reading programs leads to the need for careful scrutiny of these materials.

To help schools select materials appropriate for the curriculum, various guidelines and evaluation suggestions have been developed. A series of guidelines, *Guide to Selecting Basal Reading Programs* (1987), developed by the Center for the Study of Reading, is an important aid for evaluating basals. Various sources also exist that provide criteria for assessing and using computer software in the reading program (Kamil, 1984; Scott & Barker, 1987; Wepner & Feeley, 1993).

The three guidelines discussed above provide a skeletal outline for what needs to occur in any school reading program. Although it is essential that school personnel spend time thinking about *what* it is they want students to learn, it is also imperative that they think about *how* the curriculum will be delivered, that is, how instruction will take place.

Instruction

Any discussion of instruction needs to include a description of the learning activities, strategies, and organizational arrangements that help teachers meet the needs of individual learners. Although a teacher working with an individual student must have an excellent understanding of the reading process and reading methodology, this task is simple compared to the responsibility of providing instruction for 20 or more students whose range in reading performance may be wide. Thus, any reading program must provide experiences that enable each student to grow and learn in an environment that promotes risk-taking and guarantees success (Harste, 1989). This means that students who are performing at accelerated rates are challenged and encouraged to continue their learning. At the same time, students who are experiencing difficulties with the grade-level curriculum need to receive specialized reading instruction that will help them to succeed and progress. One of the important tasks of the professional responsible for a total reading program is to promote communication and congruence between the special programs in schools and the classroom reading program. In this section, three major guidelines are discussed.

1. *The organizational structure must provide for student differences in background, performance, and ability.* The recent shift from the basal to literature-based, process-oriented approaches has influenced organizational and grouping decisions (Barr, 1992). In the past, the primary means of organizing reading instruction was ability grouping, because it was thought to help teachers adjust the pace and level of instruction to a

smaller range of student abilities. These groups, once formed, tended to become permanent arrangements, resulting in concerns about the negative effects of such grouping. Further, researchers found qualitative differences in the instruction experienced by high and low reading groups that were detrimental to the students in the low groups (Allington, 1983; Gambrell, Wilson, & Gantt, 1981; Hiebert, 1983). Other researchers indicated that although ability grouping might be helpful to the advanced child, it was not necessarily helpful to the slow child (Kulik & Kulik, 1982). There was also concern that ability grouping might have harmful effects on the social and affective development of children, especially those in the low ability groups (Esposito, 1973; Rosenbaum, 1980).

Some of the new approaches that encourage whole class instruction, followed by small group experiences and teacher feedback, are suggested as a means of addressing concerns about ability grouping. Barr (1992), for example, discusses the advantage of prereading instruction, in which a comprehensive discussion about a particular topic enables students of all abilities to read and understand a particular selection. She also describes the teaching strategy commonly used in a literature-based approach, in which the teacher reads and rereads a story aloud to all the children in the classroom. Students are then encouraged to read the story aloud in unison or with partners. These two approaches, along with other organizational structures such as cooperative grouping, research groups, and peer tutoring, may be helpful to schools interested in providing for individual needs of students. (Other helpful resources for those interested in providing for individual needs of students can be found in Chapter 15.)

2. *Select instructional strategies and activities appropriate for learners.* In this general overview chapter, I identify five critical points from research and theory that school personnel need to consider as they develop their reading program.

First, those involved in designing or selecting instructional activities need to consider the variables that contribute to success in reading, given its interactive, constructive nature. These variables include the reader, the text, and the context. Readers approach experiences with varying experiences and knowledge; they will handle some assignments better than others and will need more assistance with some than others. Further, the text material will affect students' ability to be successful. Material that is written in a clear, logical, and consistent manner should enhance understanding. On the other hand, material that is not well organized or coherent, what Anderson and Armbruster (1984) call inconsiderate text, may necessitate more teacher direction and intervention. The context for reading also influences students' performance. Context includes many factors, such as purpose for reading, classroom atmosphere, reading group composition, and interactions with the teacher.

Teachers should take these three factors — reader, text, and context — into consideration in deciding how much and what kinds of instruction are necessary (for example, the amount of prereading preparation, which vocabulary words to teach and how extensively, the degree of guided reading, the types of follow-up to text reading). In order to do this, teachers must have an excellent understanding of the reading process and how it affects instruction. They must be able to identify the what, why, and how of reading instruction (Michigan Reading Association, 1984):

- *What* is being read? Is it a poem, a story, a newspaper?
- *Why* are the students reading? For information? For enjoyment?
- *How* should students read? What strategies do students need to use to accomplish the task? Should they study or skim?

Second, time must be provided in the classroom for reading practice. Research points to the importance of independent reading, both in and out of school, identifying it as one of the best ways in which to improve reading performance (Allington, 1984; Leinhardt, Zigmond, & Cooley, 1981). Thus, in any school reading program there must be opportunities for students to read on a daily basis.

Third, composing should be an integral part of the reading program. As mentioned previously, research evidence supports the connection between these two formal language skills. The notions of comprehension and composition as "two sides of the same basic process" (Squire, 1983) is an important concept for the curriculum developer. Students should participate in experiences that help them see the relationship between the reading and writing process (i.e., being an audience for someone else's writing, and writing for an audience). Both reading and writing can, in fact, be used in the classroom as tools of learning (Rowe & Harste, 1985).

Fourth, students should also be given opportunities to become independent and to self-monitor their literacy progress. From kindergarten on, students need experiences that help them to realize that reading is a task that relies on what readers bring to it and their purpose for reading, as well as on the type of materials or text. All lessons can be planned to help students monitor their reading and to reflect upon what they have learned.

Finally, the climate in a school must be conducive to the development of students as readers. Not only should the classrooms contain all sorts of reading materials, but there should be an atmosphere in the school that promotes reading as an enjoyable and necessary part of life. There should be opportunities for teachers to read to their students, even in the upper grades, and motivational programs that encourage student reading.

3. *Promote congruence between reading programs in the schools.* There has been a great deal of criticism about the separate systems of education provided for students who experience difficulties in learning, especially those who are Chapter 1 or special education students (Allington & McGill-Franzen, 1988; Ysseldyke, Thurlow, Mecklenburg, & Graden, 1984). Much of this criticism has revolved around the pullout arrangements that are the prevalent models for compensatory education. Although there are many concerns about pullout models — including scheduling, loss of instructional time because of student movement, and possible stigmatizing of participants — one of the major concerns has been the nature of the instruction; that is, the fact that the remedial and developmental programs are not congruent (Johnston, Allington, & Afflerbach, 1985). Low-achieving students have had to handle the demands of two different classroom settings, approaches, and teachers. Thus, various educators (Johnston et al., 1985; Kennedy, Birman, & Demaline, 1986) recommend greater congruence between the remedial reading program and the classroom reading program. Walp and Walmsley (1989) discuss the need for three types of congruence: procedural, instructional, and philosophical. Procedural congruence deals with the structure and organizational plans for operating the remedial and classroom programs. Instructional congruence focuses on the similarity between the content and methods of the remedial teacher and the classroom teacher, while philosophical congruence relates to the beliefs held by teachers.

To promote collaboration and congruence, there must be communication among all those involved in reading instruction. An important aspect of building the school reading program is developing a climate in which such cooperation and communication can thrive among all professionals who are involved in helping students become effective readers. Teachers, whether specialists or classroom, can no longer work in isolation. All professionals need to learn to work as members of a team to plan for the needs of students. Teachers in fact recognize the need to learn new strategies as they experiment with various models that promote full inclusion of students and collaboration with other adults (Bean, Trovato, Hamilton, Golembesky, & Rice, 1992).

Assessment

The school reading program generally includes two broad categories of reading assessment: assessment designed for external accountability and assessment designed for instruction, or internal assessment (Calfee & Hiebert, 1991). Both are important. External assessment deals primarily with accountability issues. Results from these measures are generally used to portray the relative standing of groups of students. Often these results are used to make judgments about the school reading program (how well are we teaching comprehension as compared to others in the nation?). Internal assessment is used by the classroom teacher to make decisions that affect daily lessons and is closely linked to the curriculum and the instruction that occurs in the classrooms.

External Assessment. Most often, conventional standardized measures are used to provide information about the reading performance of students to important constituents: parents, board members, and school administrators. Test scores from these standardized instruments are also used to make initial grouping decisions, provide information that serves as a basis for referral for additional assessment, and provide information about the general strengths and weaknesses in the reading program. However, at the present time, there are many concerns about the limitations of such instruments (Shephard, 1989; Worthen & Spandel, 1991), as well as efforts to develop alternative assessment instruments and strategies (Herman, Aschbacher, & Winters, 1992). Since one of the responsibilities of developing a reading program is to determine the measures by which to assess its effectiveness, curriculum leaders must understand exactly what a conventional standardized test can and cannot provide. There must be a close match between the content of any standardized test selected and the curriculum and instruction of the school (Farr & Carey, 1986).

Using standardized measures as the sole criterion for assessing the effectiveness of a school reading program tends to be very limiting and shortsighted. These results ignore skills, habits, and attitudes that are important aspects of the reading program. As stated by Cuban (1983), "improved test scores are simply not enough. . . . How can the broader, more complex and less easily measured goals of schooling be achieved as we improve test results?" (p. 696). Further, these instruments have been criticized by scholars as being too limited in what they assess (Resnick, 1987; Worthen & Spandel, 1991). The recent efforts at state levels to reform reading assessment by developing tests that are based on an interactive model of reading, rather than a skills-based model, are indications of the major interest in developing better external measures. Further, information other than standardized test results can provide important and revealing data. Indicators such as numbers of books checked out from the library or results of reading attitude inventories should be considered by those developing, implementing, and evaluating reading programs.

Internal Assessment.   The conventional standardized measures that generally serve as external measures do not appear to be very useful to teachers in planning and modifying classroom practice (Salmon-Cox, 1982). Moreover, at the present time there is a great deal of interest in classroom assessment and its role in helping teachers plan for instruction. Such assessment should be dynamic and adaptable to the always changing nature of the classroom. Results should help the teacher establish goals for the year as well as assist in day-to-day planning. Teachers have a number of informal measures that they can use to assess the progress of individual students in their classroom. These measures may be product-oriented and assess student outcomes. Criterion-referenced tests, workbook sheets, and end-of-unit tests in basals often serve this function. Measures that focus on process, that is, how students are performing (e.g., oral reading, think-alouds), should also be used.

Internal measures should be authentic; that is, they should include opportunities for students to demonstrate their ability to perform real literacy tasks. Students, therefore, can be observed as they read orally; they can be asked to write in response to a selection of narrative prose; or they can be asked to recall the most important ideas from a content selection. Teachers can use all of these measures to develop portfolios to document students' growth over time (Tierney, Carter, & Desai, 1991).

These types of assessment, which are closely related to instruction, provide an efficient and effective means of helping teachers plan their daily lessons. As teachers observe and interact with students during a lesson, they can assess a student's degree of success in applying various strategies and the amount of teacher guidance needed to assure success. As Johnson (1987) suggests, the expert teacher is an "evaluation expert" who can describe the extent and quality of a child's literacy development (p. 748).

Curriculum, instruction, and assessment form the essential core of the reading program. They provide the framework for developing, implementing, and evaluating any program. Yet these elements do not occur instantaneously, nor are they easily achieved. Sizer (1985) states it well: "A good school does not emerge like a prepackaged frozen dinner stuck for 15 seconds in a radar range; it develops from the slow simmering of carefully blended ingredients" (p. 22).

PROCESS FOR CHANGE

The reports from commissions and individuals during the past several decades have all described the need for school restructuring and school improvement efforts, and indeed many new reform movements have been initiated at district and state levels. Large-scale staff development notions such as teacher centers, career ladders, mentoring, and coaching are being tried and tested singly or in combination in districts across the country. At the same time, schools continue in their efforts to update, modify, and change their reading programs. But too many of these efforts, which start with much enthusiasm and excitement, fall short of reaching their mark. We have learned that the change process is a complex one that is more "rolling" than linear (Joyce, Wolf, & Calhoun, 1993). Specifically, changing behaviors involves collective, innovative action and constant assessment of this action (Joyce et al., 1993). The following principles are useful in thinking about and planning changes in school reading programs.

1. *Change is systemic and as such, there must also be a process for change that involves all constituents.* Fullan and Miles (1992) indicate that working systemically means focusing on "the development and inter-relationships of all the main components of the system simultaneously — curriculum, teaching and teacher development, community support systems, and so on; and . . . on the deeper issues of the culture of the system" (p. 751). In other words, even changing only one aspect of the school program — its reading program — involves a host of different issues and many individuals with differing perceptions of how reading should be taught. Thus anyone involved in a leadership position must be sensitive to the complexity of bringing about long-lasting change.

There are many different ideas about how to apply knowledge about change processes to curriculum development. The school change process described below is an adaptation of various models that have been generated by scholars in the field of curriculum planning (Doll, 1986; Glatthorn, 1987).

Step 1: *Identifying a need for change.* As part of any process for curricular change, an initial step is reviewing the current program to determine where there is a need for change. Information should come from school sources such as test data, teacher interviews, or observation of classrooms; it can also come from published information about current trends or research findings.

Step 2: *Diagnosing the situation.* As part of developing an awareness of a need for change, there is a need for knowledge about the current status of reading instruction in one's own school. For example, How do teachers in our elementary school teach reading? What are the reading strengths of students as a whole and where do they appear to have difficulties? One useful activity at this stage is to ask teachers to describe and assess their own reading curriculum. Various strengths and weaknesses of curriculum as well as perceptions and beliefs of teachers can be identified through this effort.

Step 3: *Considering alternative courses of action*. At this stage, teachers and others (consultants, parents, administrators) can investigate various ideas, materials, and approaches that will enable the school to make changes. Teachers may attend various conferences; educational consultants may be asked to make presentations at the school. Teachers may also be given suggestions of professional articles about specific innovations (e.g., Reading Recovery, whole language) to read and discuss.

Step 4: *Implementing the ideas*. Before there is full-scale implementation, pilot-testing may be necessary to validate the effectiveness of the identified changes. Further, there may also be a need for providing staff development for all teachers so that they understand how to implement the specific changes. Too often good ideas that are placed into curriculum guides or district manuals are not implemented into the daily teaching repertoires of the classroom teachers. Often this is caused by inadequate preparation and training for the teachers who will actually implement the change. According to Joyce et al. (1993), "a curriculum change in a major area probably requires ten to fifteen days of training rather than the one or two that are often provided now" (p. 32).

Step 5: *Evaluate the change*. There should be formative evaluation throughout the first four steps just described that documents how well the change *process* itself is progressing. In addition, a process for determining the effect of the changes should be identified. Step 5 calls for specific attention to assessing the success of the change (Does it make a difference?) and the degree to which the innovation has become institutionalized (Are teachers using the ideas?). Too often, the effects of new programs are minimal; they never become an integral part of teachers' repertoire.

In addition to the need for a change process that is systemic, the process must also be conducted in a humane and understanding manner. In their Concerns-Based Approach to change, Hall and Hord (1987) discuss the importance of understanding how teachers perceive change and adjusting the process to teachers' needs and point of view. This aspect of the change initiative is a critical one to consider in school curriculum changes.

2. *The school, rather than the individual, is the key unit for effective change* (Goodlad, 1984; Lezotte & Bancroft, 1985). By focusing on schools as the units for change, supervisors or other change agents work

with a critical mass necessary to generate ideas and sustain enthusiasm for change. Moreover, the learning that can occur in group activities appears to be important for initiating and sustaining change. However, a school does not exist as an island isolated from other schools (at the same level or different levels) in a district. Often, in initial phases in a change process — where goals are being determined or questions about the general philosophical bases for the reading program are being discussed — representatives from all schools in a district may need to be involved. The key, however, is working with a group of professionals who have the same concerns and interests and who, therefore, can be directly involved in decisionmaking and committed to the agreed-upon initiative.

3. *Collaboration is a key to success in school improvement.* Collaboration means more than the fact that all constituents play a part in helping to make decisions about change; they must also be responsible and share authority for basic policy decisionmaking (Hoyt, 1978). Most individuals involved in change or reform efforts are aware of the importance of involving all actors in the process: teachers, principals, resource persons (reading specialists, librarians, and so forth), and community representatives (including students). The role of principal as instructional leader has received enormous support during the past several decades. Although the reading supervisor may be given the primary responsibility for initiating change in the reading curriculum, it is paramount that the principal be an integral part of the change process, both in the initiation and implementation phases.

Moreover, if one involves parents at early phases of school change, there is greater likelihood of community support and understanding. Recently, the selection of various textbooks has created dissension in some districts across the country. The involvement of community representatives can help a district avoid such controversy; more importantly, it can help those involved in school change select goals and activities that address the values and expectations of the primary stakeholders — the parents and students.

The notion of involving all constituents is commonly accepted; however, collaboration is somewhat more difficult to achieve. It emphasizes (1) the central importance of people in an organization, and (2) people working together as equals to solve problems. Collaboration can occur between any number of individuals or groups: university and school; grade-level and content teachers; foundations and school districts; teacher organizations and school districts. Some examples of collaboration are:

- collaboration between universities and schools to assess the effectiveness of a new approach to teaching middle school reading;

- collaboration between content teachers and reading specialists to develop more congruence between programs;
- collaboration between community library and elementary reading teachers working on a joint program for summer reading.

4. *Staff development efforts must be an integral part of any change process.* As stated previously, too often good ideas never become a reality in classroom practice. There are too many examples of "one-shot" inservice programs that provide initial enthusiasm, but no more. Yet one very important finding from the Huberman and Miles (1984) studies is that commitment follows competence. That is, individuals are more willing to maintain and practice certain innovations if they have the competence to do them well. Thus, staff development must be ongoing and intensive in order to provide continuing support and feedback to teachers (see Chapter 9). The clinical model of supervision (Acheson & Gall, 1987) provides one such model for staff development. Observations become a means of helping teachers identify areas where they wish to improve or change. Ongoing support is provided beyond any initial training to ensure continued implementation and usage of the desired innovations.

The four principles described above illustrate the need for intimate involvement of the classroom teacher in both generating ideas for change and in implementing change in the classroom, and acknowledge the importance of the teacher as a decisionmaker in creating excellent learning experiences for students. The cyclical nature of the change process is also evident. As stated by Fullan and Miles (1992), "change is a journey, not a blue print. . . . One should not plan, then do, but do, then plan . . . and do and plan some more" (p. 749).

SUMMARY

The development, implementation, and evaluation of a well-balanced reading program (K–12) is an exciting and challenging task that requires the cooperation and collaboration of all concerned. In this overview chapter, we describe the three essential elements of an effective reading program — curriculum, instruction, and assessment — that can be used as a framework for conceptualizing the reading program. For each of the three elements, specific guidelines are described. Because implementation of any program is essential to its success, a process for change is described, and principles and procedures for implementing such change are suggested.

REFERENCES

Acheson, K. A., & Gall, M. D. (1987). *Techniques in the clinical supervision of teachers*. New York: Longman.

Allington, R. L. (1983). The reading instruction provided readers of differing ability. *Elementary School Journal, 83*(5), 548–559.

Allington, R. L. (1984). Oral reading. In P. D. Pearson (Ed.), *Handbook of Reading Research* (pp. 829–864). New York: Longman.

Allington, R. L., & McGill-Franzen, A. (1988). *Coherence or chaos? Qualitative dimensions of the literacy instruction provided low-achievement children*. State University of New York at Albany. (ERIC Document Reproduction Service No. ED 292060).

Anderson, R. C., Hiebert, E. H., Scott, J. A., & Wilkinson, I. A. G. (1985). *Becoming a nation of readers: The report of the commission on reading*. Washington, DC: National Institute of Education.

Anderson, T. H., & Armbruster, B. B. (1984). Content area textbooks. In R. C. Anderson, J. Osborn, & R. J. Tierney (Eds.), *Learning to read in American schools* (pp. 193–224). Hillsdale, NJ: Lawrence Erlbaum Associates.

Bean, R. M., Trovato, C. A., Hamilton, R. L., Golembesky, B., & Rice, D. (1992, May). *Chapter 1 programs in Pennsylvania: A focus of inquiry*. University of Pittsburgh, Technical Report.

Barr, R. (1992). Teachers, materials and group composition in literacy instruction. In M. J. Dreher & W. H. Slater (Eds.), *Elementary school literacy: Critical issues* (pp. 27–50). Norwood, MA: Christopher-Gordon Publishers.

Barr, R., Kamil, M. L., Mosenthal, P., & Pearson, P. D. (Eds.). (1991). *Handbook of reading research, Volume II*. New York: Longman.

Calfee, R., & Drum, P. (1986). Research on teaching reading. In M. Wittrock (Ed.), *Handbook and research on teaching* (pp. 804–849). New York: Macmillan.

Calfee, R., & Hiebert, E. (1991). Classroom assessment of reading. In R. Barr, M. L. Kamil, P. Mosenthal, & P. D. Pearson (Eds.), *Handbook of reading research, Volume II* (pp. 281–309). New York: Longman.

California State Department of Education. (1987). *English-language arts framework*. Sacramento: California State Department of Education.

Cook, D. M. (1986). *A guide to curriculum planning in reading*. Madison, WI: Department of Public Instruction.

Cuban, L. (1983, June). Effective schools: A friendly but cautionary note. *Phi Delta Kappan, 64*(10), 695–696.

Doll, R. C. (1986). *Curriculum improvement: Decision making and process*. Boston: Allyn and Bacon.

Duffy, G. G., Roehler, R. L., & Mason, J. (1984). *Comprehension instruction: Perspectives and suggestions*. New York: Longman.

Esposito, D. (1973). Homogeneous and heterogenous ability grouping: Principal findings and implementations for evaluating and designing more effective educational environments. *Review of Educational Research, 43*(2), 163–179.

Farr, R., & Carey, R. F. (1986). *Reading: What can be measured?* (2nd ed.). Newark, DE: International Reading Association.

Fullan, M. G., & Miles, M. B. (1992, June). Getting reform right: What works and what doesn't. *Phi Delta Kappan, 73*(10), 745–752.

Gambrell, L. B. (1992). Elementary school literacy instruction: Changes and challenges. In M. J. Dreher & W. H. Slater (Eds.), *Elementary school literacy: Critical issues* (pp. 227–240). Norwood, MA: Christopher-Gordon Publishers.

Gambrell, L., Wilson, R., & Gantt, W. M. (1981). Classroom observations of task-attending behaviors of good and poor readers. *Journal of Educational Research, 74*(6), 400–404.

Glatthorn, A. A. (1987). *Curriculum leadership*. New York: HarperCollins.

Goodlad, J. I. (1984). *A place called school*. New York: McGraw-Hill.

Guide to selecting basal reading programs. (1987). Champaign, IL: Center for the Study of Reading.

Hall, G. E., & Hord, S. M. (1987). *Change in schools: Facilitating the process*. Albany: State University of New York Press.

Harste, J. C. (1989). *New policy guidelines for reading*. Urbana, IL: National Council of Teachers of English.

Herman, J. L., Aschbacher, P. R., & Winters, L. (1992). *A practical guide to alternative assessment*. Alexandria, VA: Association for Supervision and Curriculum Development.

Hiebert, E. H. (1983). An examination of ability grouping for reading instruction. *Reading Research Quarterly, 18*, 231–255.

Hoyt, K. (1978). *A concept of collaboration in career education*. Washington, DC: U.S. Office of Education.

Huberman, A. M., & Miles, M. (1984). *Innovation up close: How school improvement works*. New York: Plenum Press.

Johnson, P. (1987, April). Teachers as evaluation experts. *The Reading Teacher, 40*(8), 744–748.

Johnston, P., Allington, R., & Afflerbach, P. (1985). The congruence of classroom and remedial reading instruction. *Elementary School Journal, 85*(4), 465–477.

Joyce, B., Wolf, J., & Calhoun, E. (1993). *The self-renewing school*. Alexandria, VA: Association for Supervision and Curriculum Development.

Kamil, M. L. (1984). Computers, literacy, and teaching reading. In J. F. Baumann & D. D. Johnson (Eds.), *Reading instruction and the beginning teacher: A practical guide* (pp. 262–272). Minneapolis: Burgess Publishing Company.

Kennedy, M. M., Birman, B. F., & Demaline, R. (1986). *The effectiveness of chapter services*. Washington, DC: Office of Educational Research & Improvement, U.S. Department of Education.

Kulik, C. C., & Kulik, J. A. (1982). Effects of ability grouping on secondary school students: A meta-analysis of evaluation finding. *American Educational Research Journal, 29*, 415–428.

Leinhardt, G., Zigmond, N., & Cooley, W. W. (1981). Reading instruction and its effects. *American Educational Research Journal, 18*, 343–361.

Lezotte, I., & Bancroft, B. (1985, March). Growing use of the effective schools model for school improvement. *Educational Leadership, 42*(6), 23–27.

Lytle, S. L., & Botel, M. (1988). *PCRP II: Reading, writing and talking across the curriculum*. Harrisburg: Pennsylvania Department of Education.

Michigan Reading Association. (1984). Reading redefined: A Michigan Reading Association position paper. *The Michigan Reading Journal, 17*, 4–7.

Pearson, D. (Ed.), (1984). *Handbook of reading research*. New York: Longman.

Resnick, L. B. (1987). *Education and learning to think*. Washington, DC: National Academy Press.

Rosenbaum, J. E. (1980). Social implications of educational grouping. In D. C. Berliner (Ed.), *Review of research in education* (Vol. 8) (pp. 361–401). Washington, DC: American Educational Research Association.

Rowe, D. W., & Harste, J. C. (1985). Reading and writing in a system of knowing. In M. R. Sampson (Ed.), *The pursuit of literacy: Early reading and writing* (pp. 126–144). Dubuque, IA: Kendall/Hunt.

Salmon-Cox, L. (1982). Teachers and standardized tests: What's really happening? *Phi Delta Kappan, 63*, 631–634.

Scott, D., & Barker, J. (1987, May). Guidelines for selecting and evaluating reading software: Improving the decision making process. *The Reading Teacher, 40*(9), 884–889.

Shephard, L. A. (April, 1989). Why we need better assessments. *Educational Leadership, 46*(7), 4–9.

Sizer, T. R. (1985). Common sense. *Educational Leadership, 42*(6), 21–22.

Squire, J. (1983, May). Composing and comprehending: Two sides of the same basic process. *Language Arts, 60*(5), 581–589.

Stotsky, S. (1983, May). Research on reading/writing relationships: A synthesis and suggested directions. *Language Arts, 60*(5), 627–643.

Tierney, R. J., Carter, M. A., & Desai, L. E. (1991). *Portfolio assessment in the reading–writing classroom*. Norwood, MA: Christopher-Gordon Publishers.

Tierney, R. J., & Shanahan, T. (1991). Research on the reading-writing relationship: Interactions, transactions, and outcomes. In R. Barr, M. Kamil, P. Mosenthal, & P. D. Pearson (Eds.), *Handbook of reading research, Volume II* (pp. 246–280). New York: Longman.

Walp, T. P., & Walmsley, S. A. (1989, February). Instructional and philosophical congruence: Neglected aspects of classroom coordination. *The Reading Teacher, 42*(6), 364–368.

Wepner, S. B., & Feeley, J. T. (1993). *Moving forward with literature: Basals, books, & beyond*. Columbus, OH: Merrill/Macmillan.

Winograd, P., & Greenlee, M. (1986, April). Students need a balanced reading program. *Educational Leadership, 76*, 442–451.

Wittrock, M. C. (1983, May). Writing and the teaching of reading. *Language Arts, 60*(5), 600–606.

Worthen, B. R., & Spandel, V. (February, 1991). Putting the standardized test debate in perspective. *Educational Leadership, 48*(5), 65–69.

Ysseldyke, J. E., Thurlow, M. L., Mecklenburg, C., & Graden, J. (1984). Opportunity to learn for regular and special education students during reading instruction. *Remedial and Special Education, 5*, 29–37.

2 Evolving Roles and Responsibilities of Reading Personnel

SHELLEY B. WEPNER
NANCY E. SEMINOFF
William Paterson College of New Jersey

Ms. C., a reading specialist in a K–6 suburban school, has been using trade books with her small groups of below-average readers for as long as she has been teaching. Identified by adults and children alike as the teacher with "problem" children, Ms. C. decided long ago that she was not going to subject her students to the basal materials that had failed them in the first place. Even though she walks around with the echo of her principal's admonishment to "get her students to pass the standardized test," she knows that she has to help her students learn to enjoy using print.

Books that contain characters with whom her students can identify are her tools for improving their academic psyches. She spends her time away from school reading books alone and with her own children, to identify which ones she can share with her students.

Ms. C. introduces a different book to each group of students about every two to three weeks. Her students' skill development is an integral part of what happens daily with her books. As you might imagine, Ms. C.'s students like coming to her class. Although their invisible labels, such as reading disabled, still shadow them, their spirit for learning to read is remarkably high.

In order to move beyond her image as just the "reading repairperson," Ms. C. runs a reading incentive program throughout the school to encourage all the students to read. She works closely with the PTA to purchase various items to present to students when they read a certain number of books. She has transformed her once dreary, closetlike classroom into a colorful carnival atmosphere where reading events occur.

Her unquestionable success with students and their parents has given her the courage to work with small groups of teachers to get them to see beyond the basal. Ms. C. meets informally with them during their preparation and lunch periods to suggest books to use and to show them how to weave skill development into literature-based reading. So far, she has teachers from two grade levels experimenting with trade books.

Although Ms. C.'s district competes in a standardized test race that her principal supports, she knows enough about literacy development to feel confident about what she is doing. Her nonthreatening, easygoing personality helps her to penetrate beyond her own classroom.

*   *   *

Mr. D. is a reading specialist in a suburban-rural middle school. Like Ms. C., Mr. D. has a principal whose knowledge about literacy development is derived from an introductory reading course taken 25 years ago. When Mr. D. was first hired as the school's reading specialist, the principal scheduled every one of his teaching periods with a different group of students, who were to use the fourth and fifth grade basals imported from the elementary schools.

It took Mr. D. one day to quietly rebel against his assigned schedule and allocated materials. He explained that he had been hired to be a reading specialist, not only a remedial reading teacher, and that a portion of his day was to be spent serving as a resource to teachers. The principal agreed to release him from one of his teaching periods. Mr. D. then explained that he could not possibly use fourth and fifth grade basals with seventh and eighth grade students who perceived themselves to be academic misfits. The principal explained that while Mr. D. would have to use these materials to satisfy the districtwide mandate, Mr. D. could use his own combination of materials for the majority of the instruction.

Although Mr. D. did not have the ideal situation, he knew that with time he could penetrate the system with his own ideas. He quickly infused all types of materials into his curriculum. He introduced SQURT (Super Quiet Uninterrupted Reading Time) to his students, allowing them to read material of their own choosing, even automobile and romance magazines, during this time. He worked diligently to get his students, some of whom were reading at the second grade level, to read for longer periods of time. He used the basal sparingly, and with apologies each time he did so. By the third quarter of Mr. D.'s first year, his students had actually started reading some print selections on their own.

In the meantime, while wearing his resource hat, Mr. D. used his evenings and weekends to identify ways to help his fellow teachers. In addition to putting weekly reading ideas into everyone's mailbox, he would work with small groups of teachers to resolve reading-related problems. For example, when a team of sixth grade teachers expressed to Mr. D. that they did not know how to help their students take notes, Mr. D. provided them with strategies to use. As word got around that Mr. D. was a credible, reliable source of information, more teachers invited Mr. D. to help them strengthen their reading programs. His most memorable moment occurred when a once-skeptical eighth grade science teacher asked for some techniques for introducing the science text.

Today, Mr. D. spends almost half of his day working with teachers to help them with the process of reading across the curriculum. He demonstrates lessons in teachers' classrooms, and he works with students along with teachers while they are using content-area texts. When he works with his small groups of students, now fewer than before, he is very often using the same texts that his fellow teachers are using in their classrooms.

*   *   *

These two reading specialists see themselves as pivotal in helping teachers to abandon tired forms of past practice in favor of more current and useful techniques for teaching reading. Their graduate-level preparation in reading has given them the necessary background to work competently with teachers to help them make important changes in their literacy practices. And, although it is not immediately obvious, they also have had an impact with their administrators and parents on alternate ways to promote literacy.

Many schools are not fortunate enough to have reading specialists who have evolved into resource persons for their teachers, or to have reading specialists at all. Yet they may have building principals and districtwide reading personnel who promote effective literacy programs. Because schools need to cultivate an atmosphere that supports reading and reflects current research, it is important to know the personnel responsible for the schools' reading programs. What are their evolving roles and responsibilities? What impact can reading personnel have on site-based management of literacy programs? These two questions form the basis of this chapter.

OVERVIEW OF READING PERSONNEL

An enriched reading program has administrators, reading specialists, classroom teachers (both elementary and content-area), parents, librarians, auxiliary personnel, school board members, community members, and students working closely together to develop and implement a cohesive, systemwide program at the elementary and secondary levels. Reading personnel's responsibilities shift as one examines elementary and secondary responsibilities. At the elementary level, reading personnel work with classroom teachers, who are responsible for both content-area and developmental reading instruction. At the secondary level, they work with teachers who are responsible primarily for content-area instruction through appropriate instructional strategies (Peters & Seminoff, 1982).

According to the International Reading Association's (IRA) 1992 *Standards for Reading Professionals*, reading educators need to have in-depth knowledge of the reading process; philosophies and theories of reading instruction; and language development, cognition, and learning. With this knowledge, reading personnel can work with others to:

- create a literate environment
- organize and plan for effective instruction
- demonstrate knowledge of instructional strategies
- demonstrate knowledge of assessment principles and techniques
- communicate information about reading
- plan and enhance programs (pp. 11–12)

Even with these standards, there still is little agreement about the role of reading personnel (Cassidy & Rickelman, 1989). This is partially due to the varied competencies required for reading specialist certification in different states, differences in graduate program offerings for reading personnel, and the different emphases placed on the roles of reading personnel by local school boards and administrators (Fuccello, 1987; Weisberg, 1986). For example, reading specialists "can spend all day with students, no time with students or any assignment in between" (Cassidy & Rickelman, 1989, p. 4). Some may be responsible for working closely with teachers; others may not. Reading consultants in one district may spend more time working directly with students than reading specialists in a neighboring district.

Nevertheless, reading personnel contribute significantly to reading programs, be they specialists, consultants, supervisors, or teachers. When prepared properly, persons in these categories have the competencies needed to help elementary and secondary teachers and administrators acquire current understandings about reading (Eltink, 1990). It is important, though, that the roles and responsibilities of reading personnel be clearly identified, so that ultimately a common language can be in use within the profession.

READING SPECIALIST'S ROLES AND RESPONSIBILITIES

The designation of *reading specialist* has shifted in the past few years. In 1986, IRA listed five distinct roles of the reading specialist: diagnostic/remedial specialist, developmental reading/study skills specialist, reading consultant/reading resource teacher, reading coordinator/supervisor, and reading professor. In 1992, IRA listed only three roles: teacher or clinician, consultant/coordinator, and teacher educator/researcher. In this chapter, only the first two descriptions from the 1992 standards will be explored, the teacher/clinician role (referred to hereinafter as reading specialist) and the consultant/coordinator role.

As Teacher/Clinician

The reading specialist in a teacher or clinician role, according to the 1992 IRA standards, does the following:

- Teaches developmental reading and/or study skills at the secondary/college level.
- Provides reading services to students in reading/learning disability, compensatory, or special education programs (e.g., inclusion programs, Chapter 1, regular education initiatives, mainstream programs).
- Provides specialized reading instruction, assessment, and remediation services to students at one or more of the following levels and settings: preschool, elementary, middle school, secondary, college, or adult in public, private, or commercial schools or reading resource centers or clinics, in cooperation with other professionals.

- Has primary responsibility of teaching reading, writing, and language. (pp. 28–29)

Contrary to IRA's focus on the reading specialist as one whose primary focus is teaching, Ms. C. and Mr. D. are examples of reading specialists in two different districts who have release time to confer with other classroom teachers, order materials, and lead staff development sessions. In some districts, reading specialists are totally responsible for helping content teachers incorporate reading into teaching.

Research findings (Bean, 1979; Cohen, Intili, & Robbins, 1978; Hutson, 1982; Woods & Topping, 1986), as well as our own observations and personal experiences, support our belief that reading specialists who serve in a resource role help teachers to become better instructors of reading. This can be accomplished by meeting regularly with classroom teachers, engaging in demonstration teaching, providing inservice sessions accompanied by periodic follow-up consultations, suggesting materials and concomitant instructional strategies, coordinating materials selection committees, participating on curriculum committees, assisting in establishing, modifying, and evaluating program goals, and serving as a liaison between the community, district, and school (Smith, 1989; Tutolo, 1987). The more that reading specialists perform in this capacity, the better they will be able to serve as schoolwide leaders in promoting literacy. Obviously, the role of the reading specialist is affected by many factors: the size and type of school, institutional policy and practice, the personality of the individual specialist, financial conditions or priorities (Bean & Eichelberger, 1985), and statewide practices.

Clarification of reading specialists' roles and responsibilities is more likely to occur when reading specialists, principals, classroom teachers, and reading professors communicate more effectively about reading specialists' competencies and available services. Rupley, Mason, and Logan (1985) found that while reading professors' perceptions closely matched the overall impressions of reading specialists and administrators, reading professors nonetheless retained some anachronistic notions—for example, that reading specialists still were giving vision and hearing tests. Similarly, administrators believed that reading specialists seldom taught a regularly scheduled remedial reading class and seldom taught in more than one school.

State departments of education must insist that reading specialists be consulted and invited to participate in decisionmaking as new legislation is enacted and implemented. Reading professors must work in school settings or, at the very least, communicate with people who are teaching, to keep abreast of changing role responsibilities. Administrators must confer with reading specialists at the building, district, college, and state level to ensure that they are sufficiently informed in order to provide optimal leadership in program development. This enhanced communication will help to eliminate existing and potential misconceptions between the various stakeholders about reading specialists' services.

Reading specialists also need to better understand how to implement the resource role within school and district parameters. Robinson and Pettit (1978) and Hammond (1987) suggest ways in which to give meaningful assistance to both elementary and content-area classroom teachers. Moreover, in Hammond's (1987) compendium of ways to successfully develop the resource role, she suggests learning how to speak the language of the teacher, whether it be the generalist, the science teacher, or the mathematics teacher (as Mr. D., from the opening vignette, is doing).

As Consultant/Coordinator

In contrast to the teacher or clinician position described above, the reading specialist as a consultant/coordinator administers the reading program. IRA's (1992) description of the consultant/coordinator role lists the following responsibilities:

- Includes reading and language arts consultants who administer reading, language arts, bilingual, and/or ESL programs in schools or other institutional settings.
- Serves as a resource in the area of reading or literacy education for teachers, administrators, and the community.
- Provides leadership and supervision in the area of reading or literacy in cooperation with other professionals.
- Directs organization, management, and assessment of school, district, or institutional reading or literacy programs.
- Provides professional development opportunities and programs.
- Coordinates reading and literacy-related programs.
- Provides leadership in reading, writing, or language instruction. (p. 29)

Whereas the reading specialist (i.e., teacher/clinician) usually teaches, even if only for a few periods a day, the reading consultant/coordinator spends all or most of his or her time working with teachers, administrators, and the community on the reading program for one school, a few schools, or the entire district, depending on the assignment.

For example, the second author of this chapter spent nine years as a reading consultant, and was responsible for overseeing several buildings in the K–12 reading program in a large urban district. In this role, Nancy shared techniques and materials with teachers, worked with students for a period of time so that teachers would better understand how to employ certain reading and writing strategies, tested students new to the district to assist teachers in matching materials to students' needs, interacted with the building principals about students' reading progress, worked with other consultants to plan schoolwide or districtwide staff development programs, edited a districtwide newsletter, and served on materials selection and curriculum committees. In addition to working closely with elementary classroom teachers, Nancy developed activities and lesson plans, replete with related handouts, for secondary teachers so that they would understand how to guide students through print material about content-related concepts. Nancy also worked with both groups of teachers to help them plan topical or thematic units.

As a reading consultant, Nancy was there to enhance the effectiveness of the teachers with whom she worked. Nancy was the person with the goods, such as classroom sets of books, magazines, and other instructional materials that she was able to get from publishers. Nancy was not a threat to teachers, but rather a resource person who was coordinating the reading program in her territory.

Not unlike the reading specialists described above, Nancy served as a mentor to classroom teachers. Unlike the reading specialists, she was responsible for coordinating and developing the literacy program on a larger scale, and as a full-time job.

READING SUPERVISOR'S ROLES AND RESPONSIBILITIES

In contrast to the reading specialist/teacher or clinician and the reading specialist/consultant/coordinator as defined by IRA, the reading supervisor coordinates and appraises all facets of the reading program, including teacher observations and evaluation. A reading supervisor possesses many of the skills of the consultant/coordinator plus the supervisory skills and certification to observe teachers officially.

As with reading specialists and reading consultants, reading supervisors provide specialized help and service to teachers, both individually and in groups. For example, Ms. L., a reading supervisor in a medium-size district, is in charge of meeting weekly with a committee of elementary classroom teachers to help implement a literature-based program, by resolving some of the disparities in teaching philosophies and by establishing an appropriate list for book selection. However, because she cannot devote adequate time to all teachers in the district, she depends on reading specialists such as Ms. C., from the opening vignette, to work directly with the teachers in her building. Ms. C., with the support of Ms. L., has been helping the teachers in her building understand how trade books can be used effectively for reading instruction. She also is there daily to provide materials and strategies and to assist teachers with issues related to instruction and assessment.

In developing a reading curriculum, reading supervisors need to determine what is to be taught, by whom, when, where, and in what pattern. They need to build into their plan a cyclical procedure for assessing the district's program needs, revising or reconfirming goals, developing a coherent plan, and implementing and evaluating this plan. Reading supervisors also need to organize instruction, both developmental and remedial, at the elementary and secondary levels. With developmental programs, this entails dealing with conflicts between the self-contained and departmentalized advocates, a major concern in itself in terms of teacher commitment and involvement. It also involves an understanding and appreciation of different grouping patterns within and between classes. With remedial reading programs, it means being able to establish credible entrance and exit criteria after devising a suitable adapted program. Furthermore, reading supervisors must make sure that students, staff, space, and materials are coordinated (Harris, 1975). In addition to designing, organizing, and evaluating the reading curriculum, reading supervisors are responsible to and for the teachers. With both elementary and secondary teachers, reading supervisors must disseminate information and materials, usually through staff development and teacher observations. This means that supervisors must know what teachers need before planning to assist. Reading supervisors should have enough reading expertise to know how to evaluate teachers' instructional strengths and weaknesses and enough supervisory expertise to predict what individual conferencing and staff development strategies will work with the teachers.

Two other responsibilities are inherent in the supervisory role: budgeting and community outreach. Supervisors need to know about all facets of program development in order to be able to forecast annual budgets for personnel and nonpersonnel expenses such as materials and supplies, staff development, and equipment. With community outreach, there should be a continuous free flow of information, whether through face-to-face communication, news media, or specialized school publications (Burg et al., 1978), so that the community is aware of the reading program and the parents appreciate what goes into developing diversified reading experiences for students. There must also be outreach efforts to get parents involved so that eventually they are part of the district's decisionmaking process (see Chapter 11).

THE ROLES OF OTHER SCHOOL PERSONNEL

The Principal

In effective schools, principals have five broad instructional and leadership areas: working with teachers, working with students, creating a school atmosphere, providing policy leadership, and building community support. Successful reading programs are characterized by principals' leadership, direction, and support in these five areas (Mottley & McNinch, 1984). Principals who create a "reading climate" (Finn & McKinney, 1986) in their schools share mutual concerns with teachers about the reading program (Prince & Conaway, 1985), provide needed staff development (Nufrio, 1987), get involved with and celebrate students' literacy activities inside and outside the school (Siu-Runyan, 1990), and promote awareness of the school's reading program within the community (Moss, 1985).

Although principals may assume different leadership roles, they nevertheless need to be interested in and aware of the school's reading program. In one study of two schools with high achievement scores in reading, the principals did indeed play very different roles; however, the teachers from both schools followed similar schoolwide policies and practices to promote reading. While both principals were extremely supportive and knowledgeable about the reading program, one chose to be involved with every facet of the program while the other managed from a distance, using other faculty as program coordinators. However, because there was no real differences in the level of the principals' interest, students from both schools performed similarly on the reading achievement tests, and teachers from both schools were equally satisfied with the programs' progress (Hallinger & Murphy, 1987).

Unfortunately, many principals still have not received sufficient preparation for teaching reading or developing reading programs (Nufrio, 1987). Because of their lack of reading program expertise, many principals rely upon classroom teachers, reading specialists, reading consultants/coordinators, and other central office staff to provide the major ideas for decisionmaking, as in the experiences of Ms. C. and Mr. D. While it is important to value staff participation and decisionmaking, it is also important for principals to know enough about reading to evaluate the effectiveness of reading instruction (Prince & Conaway, 1985) and to supervise their staff in reading. Even if they are not experts, they must acquire enough knowledge of the reading process and of methodology for teaching reading in elementary and content-area classrooms to communicate intelligently with their staff.

Some of the best schoolwide independent reading programs emanate from principals (Cowan, 1991; Martinez, 1991; Sanacore, 1988, 1989). One principal has students read to him every time they receive a "Reader of the Month" or "Reader of the Week" certificate (McCarthy, 1983). Another principal who created all types of buttons related to reading gives them out to members of the school (students, teachers, secretaries, custodial staff) every time they complete a book. Principals, as the educational leaders of schools, make the difference in creating a community that values reading (Barnard & Hetzel, 1986).

The Teacher

All self-contained classroom, content-area, and special needs teachers are key contributors to a sound reading program. They need to provide appropriately planned instruction by stimulating, extending, and reinforcing learning. They should create effective reading environments and model appropriate reading behavior. They need to demonstrate effective reading techniques by reading aloud, encouraging independent reading, facilitating student interaction, and communicating realistic student expectations. Content-area teachers, in particular, need to help students acquire content-related reading skills. Teachers also should participate in their own staff development for professional growth and effective instruction. IRA's 1992 standards identify the necessary competencies for early childhood, elementary, middle school, and secondary school teachers.

Other Stakeholders

The Local School Board.   School boards should be informed continuously by superintendents or their designees so that the members of the board are able to make knowledgeable decisions concerning curriculum, staffing, and budget (Cook, 1986). The school board's endorsement, both privately and publicly, of the strides made in the district's reading program is important in helping the district to reach its program goal. To do so, members need to be apprised of the current and anticipated progress so that they are adequately informed about all facets of the program.

The State Department of Education.   State department of education personnel oversee the statewide implementation of curriculum and instruction. Specialists (those responsible for specific areas such as reading or science) or generalists (those responsible for all curricular areas) assist teachers by providing leadership in creating action plans, disseminating information, offering staff development, suggesting materials, and participating in assessment decisions. Some also spearhead statewide textbook selection committees. Although not directly involved at the local district level, state supervisors can help to move local districts forward with literacy education.

The State Board of Education.   State boards create the policy and standards that affect curriculum and assessment within local districts. For example, if a state board adopts standardized assessment for selected grade levels, this drives the curriculum, which, in turn, determines student outcomes. Awareness of the role of the state board of education is important in understanding how curricular decisions are made. Informed educators can have a voice in determining educational policy by participating in statewide task forces and statewide professional organizations.

INTERACTION OF VARIOUS ROLES
WITH SITE-BASED MANAGEMENT

Since many schools are in the throes of shifting to site-based management of programs, personnel, budget, and students, it is important to better understand how these skills come into play as reading educators and other professionals interact.

A concept borrowed from business and higher education, site-based management (also referred to as school-based management and school-site management) shifts decisionmaking about program development from administration to professional consensus. With the central focus on shared decisionmaking, site-based management "professionalizes" the teaching occupation by granting more authority to teachers (Timar, 1989). In higher education national accreditations, the accreditation is of the faculty; therefore, decisions about curriculum, class scheduling, faculty promotions and budgeting of allocated funds are recommended by the faculty through collegial consensus. Site-based management allows K–12 personnel to exercise similar actions.

Although there are a wide variety of site-based management practices, one or more of the following conditions usually exist: (1) some choices about staffing; (2) discretionary budget for materials or staff development; (3) some type of mechanism for teachers to get involved; (4) the writing of an annual performance report; and (5) parental involvement (David, 1989). Along with these conditions, teachers and administrators must have time during normal operating hours to learn to work collaboratively and effectively as accountable professionals. This time should allow for each professional to examine existing bureaucratic rules and develop skills in consensus decisionmaking (MacPhail-Wilcox, Forbes, & Parramore, 1990).

Let's look at how site-based management works. As you may recall from the opening vignette, Mr. D. spends nearly 50 percent of his day helping content-area teachers with instructional strategies. Even though he feels that he has enlightened some of the teachers about the relationship between the reading process and content-area instruction, he continues to be frustrated with the eighth grade social studies program. Only one generic social studies text is used for all the students. While it contains all the necessary "facts," it is too difficult for the average and below-average students to read. The result is that each social studies teacher virtually ignores the text, lecturing to students daily from an individual knowledge base. Consequently, students really are not using any print material to support content-related concepts.

The social studies teachers need to be better educated about the use of print and how to identify appropriate materials — trade books, magazines, pamphlets, computer software, and databases. The site-based management team needs to think about staff development, instruction, curriculum, textbook selection, and budget. Now that Mr. D. is part of a site-based management team with the principal, vice principal, content-area teachers representing each discipline, support personnel representatives, and a parent representative, he can work collectively with other interested parties to develop a plan of action.

The team approach of site-based management is greater than the sum of its independent professional roles. While each member brings a different perspective, the collaborative "think tank" focus provides a forum for solidifying ideas that might not have been generated independently. The principal, in providing the leadership for the school, can help to anchor ideas with the reality of, for example, budgetary allocations. The vice principal, assigned to assist the principal with the school's operations, can help to facilitate the program's implementation in the context of numerous other curricular endeavors.

The content-area teachers provide varying levels of instructional expertise. The social studies representative can learn and grow from the content-area teachers representing other disciplines, and vice versa. The reading consultant/coordinator and reading supervisor, with their district perspectives on curriculum and instruction across and between grades and content areas, can serve as liaisons between the instructional staff and the administrative team. Because a reading consultant or supervisor typically serves as the district's point person for publishers' materials and statewide initiatives, she or he provides yet another dimension to the change process.

Mr. D., well grounded as the reading consultant or supervisor in content-area instructional strategies and materials, yet familiar with teachers' instructional strengths and weaknesses, can help the team to understand the feasibility of its recommendations. Mr. D. can support change on a daily basis through demonstrations and observations. Support personnel — special education teachers, guidance counselors, and resource teachers — serve to communicate to the team how any suggested changes will impact on special needs instruction. At the same time, they can learn about alternative instructional techniques that would better serve their student population. A parent representative brings to the table the community's response to their children's education and serves as a community liaison to promote broad-based understanding. Concurrently, the team helps to educate the parent about the whys and hows of school-based decisions.

What are some of the areas addressed by this site-based management team for the eighth grade social studies program? Once Mr. D. and others inform the entire team of what is happening with the eighth grade social studies program, the team assesses what has to be done in order to create a different approach to teaching and learning social studies. Essentially, the team decides that the social studies teachers need to help students to understand content and concepts rather than to regurgitate facts. For example, while studying the political and economic differences between communism and capitalism, students should have opportunities to work in groups and role-play, so that they can make decisions about safety and risk factors involved in working together or in going off on one's own (an idea contributed by students from the Pingry School in Martinsville, NJ). Trade books, magazines, era-based newspapers, and software should be used as major supplements to the text, so that students can read about and experiment with social issues from varying perspectives.

The team realizes that a yearlong staff development plan is needed to help the social studies teachers (1) see for themselves how their own learning is affected by different techniques and materials; (2) use their staff development experiences to revise their philosophy about social studies instruction; and (3) create an alternate instructional model that promotes critical and creative thinking. A staff development plan is created in concert with the social studies teachers, with input from the students and the community. While the team meets on a regular basis to create this plan, individual team members also are pursuing ideas outside the regular team meetings. The principal and vice principal plan for the release of teachers during the day and/or financial compensation. The reading consultant/coordinator or supervisor identifies personnel (e.g., eighth grade social studies teachers from a different school) and consultants (e.g., social studies experts and media specialists) who can help the social studies teachers with the needed philosophical/curricular/instructional changes. She or he also works closely with Mr. D. to organize group meetings, individual conferences, and lesson demonstrations. The eighth grade social studies teachers meet together as a group to discuss existing problems for the team to address. They also meet with Mr. D. to determine the instructional areas in which they need the most assistance (e.g., questioning techniques, or selection and use of trade books). The school's support personnel meet with the team representatives to create their own wish list of instructional accommodations for their students. The parent representative works closely with the principal and vice principal to survey parents about concerns and recommendations for social studies instruction, and to solicit parents' willingness to volunteer to be guest speakers or classroom hosts for special events.

Since the staff development plan represents the collective thinking of the school's various constituencies, rather than the arbitrary decisionmaking of an administrator from the central office or a teacher in a self-contained classroom, the team's efforts to ensure its success become more critical. Teachers are assuming administrative responsibilities in order to have more direct control of what happens to themselves and to their students. Administrators are relinquishing some of their power so that the highs and lows of change are shared by all those involved in the process. Together, this group is validating the notion that a school's power to make decisions autonomously promotes the best instructional practices for students.

CONCLUSION

Of particular importance to reading personnel is the creation of a community of literacy advocates: administrators, teachers, and students who value the importance of general and content-area literacy. Although clear-cut directions for assuming instructional or supervisory positions in reading cannot be offered, certain trends that reflect current research and societal needs help to define our respective professional missions. We firmly believe that reading personnel need to become an integral part of the school's activities, whether through site-based management or their own resource initiatives, in order to truly help teachers promote literacy in their classrooms. As with Ms. C. and Mr. D., reading personnel need to see every challenge as an opportunity to learn and grow with their colleagues.

REFERENCES

Barnard, D. P., & Hetzel, R. W. (1986). *Principal's handbook to improve reading instruction* (2nd ed.). Lexington, MA: Ginn.

Bean, R. (1979). Role of the reading specialist: A multifaceted dilemma. *The Reading Teacher, 32,* 409–413.

Bean, R. M., & Eichelberger, R. T. (1985). Changing the role of reading specialist: From pull-out to in-class programs. *The Reading Teacher, 38,* 648–653.

Burg, L. A., Kaufman, M., Korngold, B., & Kovner, A. (1978). *The complete reading supervisor: Tasks and roles.* Columbus, OH: Charles E. Merrill.

Cassidy, J., & Rickelman, R. J. (1989). The importance of specialists in reading!? *The Reading Instruction Journal, 32*(2), 3–7.

Cohen, E. G., Intili, J. K., & Robbins, S. H. (1978). Teachers and reading specialists: Cooperation or isolation? *The Reading Teacher, 32,* 281–287.

Cook, D. M. (1986). *A guide to curriculum planning in reading.* Madison: Wisconsin Department of Public Instruction.

Cowan, L. L. (1991). Some principals would do anything to get kids to read. *Executive Educator, 13*(3), 13.

David, J. L. (1989). Synthesis of research on school-based management. *Educational Leadership, 46*(8), 45–53.

Eltink, M. A. (1990). Concerns of practicing reading specialists. *Journal of the Wisconsin State Reading Association, 34*(4), 7–10.

Finn, C. E., Jr., & McKinney, K. (1986). Reading: How the principal can help. *Principal, 66*(2), 30–33.

Fuccello, J. (1987). [National survey of reading supervisor/reading specialist roles in the schools.] Unpublished raw data.

Hallinger, P., & Murphy, J. (1987). Schools show improvement in reading skills. *AARSIC Abstracts, 2*(4), 2–4.

Hammond, L. (1987). A compendium of wisdom for the reading specialist: 18 sources, annotated. *Journal of Reading, 31,* 118–123.

Harris, B. M. (1975). *Supervisory behavior in education* (2nd ed.). Englewood Cliffs, NJ: Prentice Hall.

Hutson, B. A. (1982, December). *A multifaceted view of the roles of the reading specialist.* Paper presented at the Annual Meeting of the National Reading Conference, Clearwater, FL.

International Reading Association. (1992). *Standards for reading professionals.* Newark, DE: Author.

MacPhail-Wilcox, B., Forbes, R., & Parramore, B. (1990). Project design: Reforming structure and process. *Educational Leadership, 47*(7), 22–25.

Martinez, M. G. (1991). What principals can do to promote voluntary reading. *Principal, 70*(3), 44–46.

McCarthy, J. (1983, June). Paperback pizzazz. *News for Administrators, 3*(2), 1.

Moss, R. K. (1985, March). *More than facilitator: A principal's job in educating new and experienced reading teachers.* Paper presented at the National Council of Teachers of English Spring Conference, Houston, TX.

Mottley, R. R., & McNinch, G. H. (1984). The principal and the reading program. *Reading World, 24*(2), 81–86.

Nufrio, R. M. (1987). *An administrator's overview for teaching reading.* (ERIC Document Reproduction Service No. ED 286 287)

Peters, C. W., & Seminoff, N. (1982). Advocating a comprehensive reading program at the secondary level. *Michigan Reading Journal, 16*, 6–8.

Prince, J., & Conaway, B. D. (1985). The principal's effect on the school reading program. *Small-School-Forum, 6*(3), 1–3.

Robinson, R. D., & Pettit, N. T. (1978). The role of the reading teacher: Where do you fit in? *The Reading Teacher, 31*, 923–927.

Rupley, W. H., Mason, G., & Logan, J. W. (1985). Past, present and future job responsibilities of public school reading specialists. *Reading World, 24*, 48–60.

Sanacore, J. (1988). Schoolwide independent reading: The principal can help. *Journal of Reading, 31*, 346–353.

Sanacore, J. (1989). Needed: The principal's support in creating a positive professional attitude toward independent reading in the schools. *Reading Research and Instruction, 28*(4), 73–79.

Siu-Runyan, Y. (1990). Supporting principals. *Journal of Reading, 33*, 546–548.

Smith, J. A. (1989). Reading specialists can enhance classroom reading instruction. *Journal of Reading, 33*, 56–57.

Timar, T. (1989). The politics of school restructuring. *Phi Delta Kappan, 71*(4), 165–175.

Tutolo, D. (1987). *The changing role of the reading specialist.* Paper presented at the Annual Meeting of the Association of Teacher Educators, Houston, TX.

Weisberg, R. (1986). [Survey of state policies in reading specialist training and reading instructional practices.] Unpublished raw data.

Woods, A. R., & Topping, M. H. (1986). The reading resource specialist: A model. *Journal of Reading, 29*, 733–738.

Part II

PROGRAM DEVELOPMENT

Literacy development is both similar and different across grade levels and contexts. It is similar in that the basic principles of language and learning hold true throughout. It is different in that the application of those principles will differ depending on what is developmentally appropriate at each level. Part II focuses on the various settings for which administrators and supervisors must plan and carry out reading programs. It offers suggestions for responding to the differing instructional needs of students as they progress through school.

Pre-elementary school programs are becoming increasingly common in the public schools. Their presence has provided a variety of challenges and opportunities for administrators. Chapter 3 describes a series of awareness workshops focused on young children's literacy learning. The workshops could be implemented in any elementary school. Key topics include: how young children learn to read and write and the implications for instruction; instructional strategies that support what is known about how young children learn literacy; ways to merge instruction with assessment; and methods for evaluating the early childhood literacy program.

A set of guidelines for developing a successful elementary reading program is the focus of Chapter 4. Included are suggestions for becoming better informed about learning to read and reading instruction, ideas for curriculum development, tips for organizing and scheduling the day, and suggestions for including literature and the development of skills in a meaningful context. Ideas for assessment and parent involvement are also included. The guidelines are accompanied by many concrete examples for implementation.

Middle and junior high schools tend to vary greatly from district to district. Confusion about the nature of these programs is frequently manifested in uncertainty about what is appropriate reading instruction at this level. Chapter 5 helps to clarify the goals of middle school and junior high programs. It describes the reading development of preadolescent and adolescent students and offers guidelines for developing reading programs for children of this age. Numerous programs commonly found at this level are examined.

"The high school literacy teacher's most important role is to encourage an active response to reading, creating a classroom community where readers and learners support each other in the making of meaning with text." This statement from Chapter 6 suggests that attention to reading should be so pervasive that it becomes a natural part of every discipline and every lesson in which print materials are used. Suggestions for achieving this goal in every high school classroom form the core of Chapter 6.

Broadly interpreted, the principles and guidelines presented in each chapter may be applied to all the others. This is reassuring for administrators, supervisors, and teachers, since it means that the essence of sound, effective reading instruction remains the same for children at any level.

3 Pre-elementary Programs: A Model for Professional Development

DOROTHY S. STRICKLAND
Rutgers University

Pat Murray looked around at her new office and contemplated the challenges before her. She would have to draw on everything she had learned during her past 20 years of teaching and supervising early childhood programs. Although she was confident she knew a great deal, she wasn't so sure it would be enough. Her new position at Clinton Hill School District was that of Director of Early Childhood Education. She knew that it was her master's degree in reading, however, that had really convinced the recruitment committee that she was right for the job. The superintendent

41

had made it very clear that he planned to make their new early childhood initiative a model language arts project. Now she sat in a dusty, non–air-conditioned office on a hot September day. Her desk was still empty inside. On top were dozens of commercially prepared teacher's manuals shared with her by teachers throughout the district and almost a dozen legal pads filled with notes she had gathered from interviews with teachers and administrators. Pat was beginning to find out what she was really in for.

CLINTON HILL: A STORY OF CHANGE

Clinton Hill Township is a midsize community of about 75,000 that sits on the fringes of a large urban metropolis. Long characterized as a very stable, homogeneous, working-class community, Clinton Hill is presently undergoing change in a variety of ways. More and more of its young married couples and professionals are settling in other parts of the state. They are being replaced by working-class families from the city center and recent immigrants seeking a better life in "the suburbs." The demands of working with culturally diverse populations with seemingly new and different needs have been met with some resistance and bewilderment in the district's six elementary schools, two middle schools, and high school. But, to its credit, the district has decided to take action and the early childhood initiative is key to its overall plan.

Pat reviewed her notes. What had she learned so far? First, no comprehensive early childhood curriculum guide had ever been developed. Several years ago, a booklet entitled *Effective Activities for Readiness in Kindergarten* had been prepared by a committee of teachers. For the most part, however, the 14 half-day kindergarten teachers and four Head Start teachers had worked pretty much on their own, using the teacher's manuals from published materials as their primary resource for professional guidance. Interviews and classroom observations revealed a wide disparity among teachers in philosophy and practice. This year, four kindergartens had been extended to full-day programs. Over the next three years, full-day scheduling would be expanded to all kindergartens throughout the district. Plans were also under way for two additional Head Start programs.

Pat considered her role in terms of both long- and short-term goals. Long-term, she would plan a combination of activities, including attendance at workshops, both in and outside the district; cross-visitation by teachers to observe good teaching strategies in and outside of the district; a school-based, professional lending library of books, articles, videotapes, and audiotapes of articles and lectures; the start of a similar lending library for parents; and the introduction of voluntary study groups in which teachers would read and discuss professional materials and children's literature on a regular basis. She hoped that some teachers eventually might even become involved in teacher research projects.

For the short term, Pat planned a series of what she called Awareness Workshops. (See Chapters 9 and 12 for other approaches.) These had already been budgeted, in the form of pay for substitutes, to allow four inservice days for the pre-elementary teachers. Additional money for supplies and speakers had been obtained through a grant from the State Department of Education. Pat decided to spread the four full-day sessions over a period of two months. The purpose was to start a dialogue about current practices as well as to offer some concrete possibilities for change.

In the interest of curriculum continuity, Pat insisted that all first grade teachers and elementary supervisory staff join the pre-kindergarten and kindergarten staffs as part of these sessions. Because substitute money had not originally been allocated for the first grade teachers, each was able to attend only two of the sessions. Pat decided to stagger their participation so that several first grade teachers attended each time. Principals were also invited, and most attended. She also invited the staffs of local "feeder" day care centers and the "kindergarten room mothers" ("head" parent helper in each classroom) to attend if they desired.

This chapter is a description of those staff development sessions. It is intended to provide readers with key content about pre-elementary literacy programs, as well as a framework for sharing that information through a professional development plan.

The Workshop Plan

Two weeks before the first workshop, flyers were distributed describing the purpose of the series and listing the topics for each session, with brief descriptions of program content. The topics focused on child development and emergent literacy:

1. How young children learn to read and write and the implications for instruction.
2. Instructional strategies that support what is known about how young children learn literacy.
3. Merging instruction with assessment of language and literacy.
4. Evaluating the early childhood literacy program.

Deciding on a location for the workshops presented a major problem, since Pat refused to use an auditorium setting. She hoped to provide a more informal and collegial atmosphere by using a room with tables, such as a cafeteria or all-purpose room. After being refused every cafeteria in town, she finally arranged to use a large room with tables at the Board of Education building. While parking was a major problem, it was worth the trouble to set the tone she wanted to achieve.

General Procedures for All Workshops

One week before each session, participants were given a brief article to read. A three-by-five card was stapled to each article. Participants were asked to respond, on the card, to some aspect of the article. They were also encouraged to comment in the margins or use a response log if they wished. The three-by-five card was set as a minimum response.

Each session started with a warm-up activity, during which participants at each table introduced themselves, selected a leader for the day, and proceeded to share their reactions to the article and respond to each other's comments. The group leader was responsible for keeping the conversation going and making sure that everyone participated. Pat circulated among the groups. The comfort of moving with coffee and Danish to a friendly discussion proved to be the perfect prelude to the more formal presentations with question-and-answer periods that completed the mornings. In the afternoons, participants were actively involved in hands-on activities and discussion groups. Each session ended with a time for reflection. Participants were asked to write down one thing they would take away from the day's activities and one thing they would leave behind, that is, "What have I learned that is new and that I will apply to my work, and what will I try to eliminate or rethink?" In the following sections, I will describe the content of each workshop.

TOPIC 1: HOW YOUNG CHILDREN LEARN TO READ AND WRITE

First Language Learning

Learning language is perhaps the most marvelous of all human accomplishments. In a very short period of time, very young children acquire extremely complex systems of knowledge and rules. Indeed, the rules of their language are internalized with such a high degree of proficiency that pre-kindergartners are able to use them to generate utterances they have never heard before. This feat alone is marvelous enough. But for educators, the most amazing aspect of first language learning is that children accomplish it without the benefit of lesson plans, skills checklists, or competency tests (Strickland, 1987).

Because language development is such a marvelous human accomplishment and because it is fundamental to every aspect of an individual's social and cognitive development, it has received considerable attention from educational researchers. By examining the conditions under which very young children undergo the remarkable acquisition of spoken language, we can deepen our insight into how we might shape the language curriculum of the school. The following key factors seem to be universally present when first language learning occurs:

1. *An atmosphere of success.* Children acquire spoken language in a warm, rewarding atmosphere. The nature of the learning environment is positive. Parents are delighted with whatever the child accomplishes. Moreover, they show it. Anxiety about first language learning is rare. Not only are the child's miscues or mistakes accepted, they become the content of family stories right through adulthood.

2. *Respect for individuality.* Children acquire spoken language in an atmosphere that conveys respect for the uniqueness of each individual. There is little temptation to mold the child to fit a group standard or method. Individual styles and approaches are generally respected. Parents are most apt to judge achievement in terms of what a child can do today that he or she could not do yesterday.

3. *Child-centered atmosphere.* During first language learning, adults and children frequently interact on an individual basis. The child is an active participant—curious about the environment, asking endless questions and demanding to know the answers.

4. *Meaningful, functional context.* First language learning is always related to meaningful activities, objects, and situations. If there is no meaning for the child, an idea or element of language is quickly discarded. Each new work or concept must find its place in the child's existing schemata or frameworks of knowledge. Adults act to help bridge the known to the unknown. Throughout, the adult uses language with the child to do something besides teach language.

5. *Holistic learning.* In first language learning, children are presented with the whole system of what is to be learned. Language is neither sequenced nor segmented into skills. All of the components of language are presented as they exist—as an interrelated, integrated whole. Yet children learn the rules of their language and apply them with ever-increasing facility in order to form new utterances they have never heard before.

The conditions of first language learning cannot and need not be prescriptively duplicated at school. Awareness of these conditions, however, has direct implications for pre-elementary curricula. A sound pre-elementary curriculum will be characterized by an atmosphere of success; respect for individuality; child-centeredness; a meaningful, functional context; and holistic learning. It will be important to keep these factors in mind as we consider the kind of curriculum that fosters language and literacy.

Language Learning at School

The literacy program at the pre-elementary level should be embedded within the framework of a developmentally appropriate curriculum. According to the National Association for the Education of Young Children (Bredekamp, 1987), a developmentally appropriate curriculum is one that:

1. Takes into account all areas of a child's development—physical, emotional, social, and cognitive factors.
2. Integrates all aspects of the curriculum so that children's learning does not occur in narrowly defined subject areas.
3. Includes curriculum planning based on teachers' observations and recordings of each child's special interests and developmental progress.
4. Emphasizes learning as an interactive process in an environment where children are encouraged to learn through active exploration and interaction with adults, other children, and materials.
5. Stresses learning activities and materials involving concrete, real experiences relevant to the lives of children.
6. Accounts for a wide range of interests and abilities.
7. Provides a variety of activities and materials with increasing difficulty and complexity.

Discussion Questions and Activities

What can be done with the physical environment of the classroom to support what we know about how children learn? What can be done with the affective environment? Create a map of how you might rearrange your room to better support children's emerging literacy. Share and discuss it with others. Share an idea related to today's topic that has worked for you.

TOPIC 2: INSTRUCTIONAL STRATEGIES

Establishing an instructional framework within which children can both learn literacy and learn through literacy is critical. The Reading/Writing Workshop in Figure 3.1 was offered as a model for teachers to adjust to their own grade levels. Teachers were asked to begin each day with a workshop of this type. (See Chapter 12 for more examples of reading/writing workshops.) It might take as little as 15 minutes or as much as 45, depending on the maturity of the students. Materials used in the workshop are selected to support several areas of the curriculum simultaneously: language and literacy development, social studies and science, mathematics, and basic concept development, such as sequencing, opposites, and so on. Following is a brief description of the four components of the Reading/Writing Workshop shown in Figure 3.1.

1. *Shared Reading* invites children into the reading process as the teacher models and the children participate to the extent that they can. It makes use of big books, charts, and predictable texts of all types. Materials are reread frequently and the materials are made available for children to "read" on their own with growing independence. Guided rereadings by the teacher allow children to master the text over time.

Figure 3.1   A Model for Reading/Writing Workshops
(Early Childhood Programs)

1. SHARED READING

> Read Aloud
> > *Demonstration*
> > *Participation*
>
> Response
> > *Discussion*
> > *Drama*
> > *Drawing/writing*
> > *Movement*

2. STRATEGY LESSONS

3. INDEPENDENT READING AND WRITING

4. SHARING

Each time a text is revisited, the mode of response can vary. Response may include discussion, drama, movement, independent writing, and shared writing, where the teacher guides the group in creating a written response. Rereadings are carried over into the home, as children are allowed to take home "little book" versions of the big books or copies of charts that the teacher has duplicated.

2. *Strategy Lessons* allow teachers to focus on a specific strategy or skill that is salient to the text. Most often, the strategy lessons are embedded within the shared reading activity. Children may recall specific details in the text, discuss the main ideas, note how the illustrations help carry the message, and so on. In texts where the same phrases, words, or initial consonants are repeated, they may be highlighted and discussed as patterns in the language. The key to the strategy lessons is not in the direct instruction of a predetermined, prearranged set of skills. It is in the teacher's ability to make use of viable literacy situations to provide ongoing development of literacy in a way that is planned and documentable. The lessons should have structure, but they must remain informal, joyful activities.

3. *Independent reading and writing* time should be provided each day. This may be included as a part of the independent, center-based activities. Occasionally, a specific period of time may be set aside during which all children may be asked to choose a book to read, or provided with paper and pencil to draw/write something of their choice.

4. *Sharing* personal literacy events integrates oral and written language. The sharing of reading may involve a child's telling about his favorite part of a particular book. These will frequently be books that have been read aloud in class and that the child has elected to "reread" on his or her own. The sharing of drawing/writing may involve the child's telling about a picture that he or she has created that may contain some attempts at writing. The recalling of other activities such as events during dramatic play or block play may also be shared.

Making the Most of Shared Reading

The use of enlarged texts, known as big books, has become increasingly popular for shared reading. Big books often contain humorous stories with predictable and repetitive language, causing even the most restless youngsters to become quickly engrossed. Largely inspired by the work of Don Holdaway (1979), big books offer teachers opportunities to help children develop concepts about print and an understanding of the reading process. Big books offer teachers an opportunity to develop the objectives of a reading program for young children in a whole language context. Figure 3.2 provides some examples of big book activities suggested for use

Figure 3.2   Some Tips for Shared Book and Chart Experiences

TEACHER	CHILD	OBJECTIVES
Before the Reading:		
• Asks children what they think story might be about, based on title and cover. Or, thinks aloud about what he/she thinks this story might be about.	• Uses clues from title and cover, together with background knowledge, to formulate predictions about the story. Or, observes teacher model the same.	• Using clues from text and background knowledge to make inferences and formulate predictions.
• Shows pleasure and interest in anticipation of the reading.	• Observes as teacher models personal interest and eagerness toward the reading.	• Building positive attitudes toward books and reading.
During the Reading (teacher reads aloud):		
• Gives lively reading. Displays interest and delight in language and story line.	• Observes teacher evoke meaningful language from print.	• Understanding that print carries meaning.
• Hesitates at predictable parts in the text. Allows children to fill in possible words or phrases.	• Fills in likely words for a given slot.	• Using semantic and syntactic clues to determine what makes sense.
• At appropriate parts in a story, queries children about what might happen next.	• Makes predictions about what might happen next in the story.	• Using story line to predict possible events and outcomes.
After the Reading:		
• Guides discussion about key ideas in the text. Helps children relate key concepts.	• Participates in discussion of important ideas in the text.	• Reflecting on the reading; applying and personalizing key ideas in a text.
• Asks children to recall important or favorite parts. Finds corresponding part of the text (perhaps with help of children) and rereads.	• Recalls and describes specific events or parts of text.	• Using print to support and confirm discussion.

Source: Strickland, D. (1988). *The Reading Teacher.* Newark, DE: International Reading Association.

before, during, and after the reading. Each is organized according to what a teacher might do, what the children would be doing, and the curricular objective that is being met (Galda, Cullinan, & Strickland, 1993, pp. 102–103).

Launching into Writing

The importance of treating writing as an integral part of a literacy program cannot be overstated. Listening, speaking, and thinking are also active ingredients. Oral language encounters provide data for written language and vice versa. Experimentation and development in any aspect of language must be seen as a multilingual event. Whether the child is listening to a big book, sharing in the reading or retelling of one, or attempting to write a story independently, literacy is supported. This new way of viewing early literacy has stimulated the introduction of writing into the curriculum at the pre-elementary level.

Karnowski (1986) offers guidelines for early childhood writing programs. She suggests that teachers determine what children understand about communication in general and writing in particular. In order for this to happen, children must be in an environment that will allow them to experiment with writing and to share with others their growing communication awareness. This also requires a teacher-observer who is informed by the growing body of information on communication and early writing. Such teachers will operate under a definition of writing that values scribble writing and invented spelling, recognizing that convention should never come before language expression. Karnowski describes concrete ways in which teachers can offer invitations to write throughout the day:

> Because young children often combine writing with other alternative communication systems, teachers should include tools in other areas of the classroom, as well as in the writing center. Writing tools in the music area encourage the writing of musical notes or words to go with a rhythm. Writing tools in the home-making area encourage the writing of shopping lists, phone messages notes, and reminders. Writing tools in the art center encourage children to write about their pictures, and writing tools in the block area encourage the labeling of structures and buildings. Writing flourishes in a social environment where young children are free to use oral language, art, music, and drama to explore and enhance their writing. (p. 60)

The Place of Phonics

Opportunities to point out patterns in the language emerge constantly throughout the day in early childhood classrooms. Big books and other picture books use alliteration, repetition, and various other types of language play for children to enjoy and explore. An early childhood classroom that indirectly invites children to read and write all day long, with adults and on their own, encourages them to try out what they are learning in informal ways. As teachers and children begin to informally call attention to letters, sounds, and words of interest to them, the children are helped to make the necessary connections regarding the patterns in our language.

Perhaps the best evidence of children's growing awareness of phonics is the invented spelling they produce as they attempt to write. Teachers who are acquainted with the various stages of spelling development will have a better understanding of what their students know about phonics. Gentry (1982) has outlined five stages that children move through on their way to becoming conventional spellers. They are very briefly described below:

Stage 1: Precommunicative Spelling. Typical of children ages 3–5. Children string scribbles, letters, and letterlike forms together, but they do not associate the marks they make with any specific sounds.

Stage 2: Semiphonetic Spelling. Typical of children ages 5 and 6. Children begin to demonstrate a rudimentary understanding of the alphabetic principle that links letters and sounds.

Stage 3: Phonetic Spelling. Typical of children 6 years of age. Phonetic spellers continue to make use of letter names as a link to represent sounds; however, they also use consonant and vowel sounds in increasingly refined ways.

Stage 4: Transitional Spelling. Typical of children 7 and 8. These spellers stop relying totally on phonological information and begin to use visual clues and morphological information as well.

Stage 5: Correct Spelling. By age 8 or 9, most children have mastered the basic principles of English spelling and are capable of spelling a large number of words correctly.

Discussion Questions and Activities

How would you describe the read-aloud program in your classroom? What opportunities exist for children to explore with writing materials on a daily basis? What role, if any, does phonics play in your instructional program? Share an idea related to today's topic that has worked for you.

TOPIC 3: MERGING INSTRUCTION WITH ASSESSMENT

Effective classroom assessment at any level is designed to enhance the quality of students' learning by gathering information about their performance relative to the goals of instruction. Assessment in early child-hood classrooms should reflect what is known about how young children learn to read and write. It should be based on information gathered from a variety of sources and real learning experiences. It should be an ongoing process, integral to instruction, and not take large amounts of time in preparation and instruction. For example, assessment during shared reading could take the form of an informal observation of the overall progress of the group. The items suggested in Figure 3.3 (Observation Checklist During Shared Reading) may be helpful in deciding upon a set of observational criteria.

At times a teacher might select an individual for special monitoring. For example, a teacher might want to assess the literacy development of a child who rarely participates in the group, or take a closer look at the literacy knowledge of a particularly advanced child.

Children's growing abilities and confidence with literacy can be monitored by saving samples of their drawing/writing over time and analyzing it for content and in terms of the stages of spelling development outlined earlier. See Figure 3.4 for examples of each stage of emergent writing.

Evidence of oral language competence can also be gathered as teachers listen critically to children's sharing over time. Figure 3.5 contains some criteria to keep in mind regarding oral language development. Emphasis should be placed on praising children when these criteria are evidenced, rather than specific lessons on their value or the castigation of individual children.

Discussion Questions and Activities

What kinds of informal observation techniques are you currently using to monitor children's literacy development? What aspects of literacy do you think are most significant for assessment purposes? Of oral language? How are you obtaining and using parents' knowledge of their children's abilities as a resource for planning? Share an idea related to today's topic that has worked for you.

TOPIC 4: EVALUATING THE EARLY CHILDHOOD LITERACY PROGRAM

In light of increasing public demands for stronger and more extensive pre-elementary programs, it is extremely important for teachers, administrators, and supervisors to work together toward program improvement. Administrators need to let teachers at this level know that their work and

Figure 3.3   Observation Checklist During Shared Reading

BOOK HANDLING AND KNOWLEDGE.
Students demonstrate an understanding of the following:
_____ Right side up of reading material
_____ Front and back of book
_____ Front to back directionality
_____ Title
_____ Author
_____ Illustrator

CONCEPTS ABOUT PRINT.
Students demonstrate an understanding of the following concepts:
_____ Print evokes meaning
_____ Pictures evoke and enhance meaning
_____ Left to right direction
_____ Sentence
_____ Word
_____ Letter
_____ Similarities in words and letters

COMPREHENSION AND INTERPRETATION.
Students demonstrate understanding of familiar books and stories through the
following:
_____ Discuss meanings related to characters and events
_____ Make and confirm reasonable predictions
_____ Infer words in cloze-type activities
_____ Remember sequence of events
_____ Compare/contrast events within and between books
_____ State main ideas
_____ State causes and effects
_____ Recall details

INTEREST IN BOOKS AND READING.
Students demonstrate their interest in books and reading through the following
behaviors:
_____ Show interest in listening to stories
_____ Participate in reading patterned and predictable language
_____ Engage in talk about books and stories
_____ Request favorite books to be read aloud
_____ View themselves as readers

As follow-up to shared reading, students:
_____ Voluntarily use classroom library
_____ Show pleasure in "reading" independently

COMMENTS ABOUT SPECIFIC CHILDREN:

Figure 3.4   Examples of Emergent Writing

A. Precommunicative Spelling: Scribbles made by "waiter" during restaurant game (Jon, 4.8)
B. Precommunicative Spelling: Drawing/writing combined (Terri, 4.10)
C. Precommunicative Spelling: Letter strings (Jason, 5.0)
D. Semiphonetic Spelling: Sign on bedroom door (Jason, 5.8)

the children they serve are every bit as important as any other program within a district. They must be sure to assign teachers to this level who have the training and experiential background needed to work with very

Figure 3.5   Oral Language Checklist

1. Uses language with increasing confidence. Note that this has nothing to do with the child's home language or dialect. The focus is on self-assurance, regardless of the language in use.
2. Organizes ideas with some sense of logic.
3. Has a sense of audience: looks at audience, speaks loud enough for all to hear.
4. Listens and responds appropriately to others.

young children. Administrators and teachers need to keep up with new developments in the field and adjust their programs accordingly. Professional cooperation among pre-kindergarten, kindergarten, and primary grade teachers must be fostered as a critical component of program continuity. All of the professionals involved should work together to design and implement a long-range plan for ongoing self-assessment and change.

Brainstorming activities, during which teachers and administrators worked together to set goals for the next three years, produced consensus on a list of items to work toward. Some of these items are listed below.

FUTURE GOALS

For Teachers:

1. Literacy will be made more visible and integral to all activities throughout the day. *Examples:* Dramatic play area will contain signs, environmental print, and materials for children to read and write; lists of children's names will be displayed and used purposefully.
2. More small group activities will be provided in which children work together on blockbuilding, dramatic play, and literacy. *Examples:* Children will engage in supermarket play area in which counting and reading environmental print on boxes, cans, and signs are integral; group books patterned after predictable texts will be created on a regular basis.
3. More opportunities will be offered children to select from a variety of activities. *Examples:* Throughout the day, including center time, there should be "invitations" for children to engage in literacy events such as handling interesting picture books on display (with covers facing children so that they are appealing) and browsing in a writing center where writing materials are made readily accessible.
4. Opportunities for children to express their imagination and creativity through a variety of means will be emphasized. *Examples:* Response to

literature may take the form of discussion, telling original stories, acting out parts of the story, moving like people, animals, or other creatures in the story, making collages, or engaging in other artistic media; there would be few, if any, times when children were asked to use commercially prepared worksheets or workbooks.

5. Teachers will observe children and document their development, literacy and otherwise, in some systematic manner. *Examples:* Making use of a checklist for observing children during shared reading; collecting samples of children's drawing/writing over time and making evaluative comments on the child's development.

For Administrators:

1. Show continued interest in and support of the early childhood program. *Examples:* Meeting regularly with the early childhood staff alone; supporting opportunities for external visits to conferences whenever feasible; stressing the importance of these activities with the central administration.
2. Place emphasis on the need for continuity of new directions and practices across grade levels. *Example:* Help teachers find a balance between prescribed similarity of practice and a shared vision from which similar practice evolves.
3. Work with teachers to initiate a parent involvement program and to articulate new practices to parents. *Example:* Support development of a coordinated reporting system to parents across pre-K through second grade.
4. Continue the dialogue in formal and informal ways. *Example:* Continue to read and bring to the attention of teachers materials relevant to their work, and conversely read and be willing to discuss materials distributed to them by teachers.
5. Help teachers rethink the current procedures for assessing and reporting children's literacy development. *Example:* Push at the district level for the elimination of standardized testing before third grade and work with teachers to help them develop informal, systematic assessment strategies and an appropriate instrument for reporting to parents.

Discussion Questions and Activities

What are some of the ways in which we can continue the dialogue we have started? How can we self-monitor our progress on the items we have listed? What system should we put in place to monitor them with our colleagues at the grade and school levels? What kind of professional development support is needed to help ensure progress? If we were to prioritize our wish list of professional development activities, what would we do first, second, third, and so on?

CONCLUSION

Pat Murray was more than gratified with the response to the Awareness Workshops. She felt confident that all of the participants had reflected on their current practice at least to some degree and that many would be inspired to change. She asked for time at the next supervisors' meeting for a debriefing on their views. She also met with the principals at their meeting to get their reactions and to discuss next steps. During these meetings, Pat was careful to point out the critical roles of the administrators and supervisors in the change process.

One of the great dilemmas of school administrators (and supervisors, to a lesser degree), whether they are assigned to the district level or are school-based, is that they can never hope to be expert in all the disciplines, developmental levels, and areas of concern for which they are responsible. Everyone concedes that this is true. It is possible, however, for administrators and supervisors to become well enough acquainted with each area under their supervision to become effective observers and questioners of those who are expected to have the expertise. Workshops such as Pat's can help to do this.

Literacy at the pre-elementary level is a highly important, issue-laden topic. It is a topic in which the public is increasingly interested and about which they are likely to have questions and opinions. For these reasons, it is essential that administrators and supervisors have sufficient background to serve as active, informed participants in its discussion. It is our hope that these administrators and supervisors take a true leadership role in an area in which change and controversy are likely to remain for some years to come.

REFERENCES

Bredekamp, S. (Ed.). (1987). *Developmentally appropriate practice in early childhood programs serving children from birth to age 8*. Washington, DC: National Association for the Education of Young Children.

Galda, L., Cullinan, B., & Strickland, D. (1993). *Language, literacy, and the child*. Orlando, FL: Harcourt Brace.

Gentry, R. (1982). An analysis of the developmental spellings in *Genius at Work*. *The Reading Teacher, 34*, 378–381.

Holdaway, D. (1979). *The foundations of literacy.* Sidney, Australia: Ashton Scholastic.

Karnowski, L. (1986). How young writers communicate. *Educational Leadership, 46,* 58–60.

Strickland, D. (1987). Whole language: What does it mean? How does it work? *Scholastic Teacher, 44,* 4.

Strickland, D. (1988). *The reading teacher.* Newark, DE: International Reading Association.

4   Elementary Programs

KATHRYN H. AU
Kamehameha Schools, Honolulu

The purpose of this chapter is to offer guidelines an administrator might follow in developing a successful elementary reading program, given the profound changes taking place in the field of reading and language arts. Supporting research is discussed, and practical examples are drawn from my experiences in improving language arts instruction with the Kamehameha Elementary Education Program (KEEP), a program based in Hawaii. KEEP operates in public schools with students of Native Hawaiian and other diverse cultural and linguistic backgrounds.

A key assumption in this chapter is that developing an effective reading program is not a simple matter of choosing the right textbooks or applying a formula. An effective reading program can only be developed through an interactive process, informed by current theory and research on literacy instruction, involving teachers, students, and parents. An effective reading program cannot be selected and installed; it must evolve through a grassroots effort at the building and classroom levels. With this perspective in mind, I offer eight guidelines for the development of an effective elementary school reading program.

GUIDELINE #1: BECOME INFORMED ABOUT CURRENT THINKING ON LEARNING TO READ AND READING INSTRUCTION

Throughout the nation, elementary school reading programs are in a state of transition. Many states, districts, and schools are moving away from transmission or skills-oriented reading instruction to more dynamic, holistic forms of instruction, termed constructivist or whole language approaches (Bird, 1989). The transition to a constructivist approach involves a lengthy process of change that appears to take teachers and schools from 5 to 10 years (Routman, 1991). Some teachers and schools have already made this transition, many more are in the midst of doing so, and others are just beginning the journey.

These changes in elementary school reading programs are being influenced by major shifts in the field of reading and language arts, spurred by research that shows the power of new forms of instruction (Au, 1993). Change has also been fueled by research documenting the weaknesses of conventional reading instruction. Studies suggest that skills-oriented, transmission forms of instruction have not brought large numbers of students to high levels of literacy (Shannon, 1989) and that an overemphasis on skills as opposed to real reading and discussion of text ideas is particularly damaging to low-achieving students (Allington, 1991). Furthermore, the conventional practice of organizing reading instruction with three fixed ability groups appears to lead to an ever-widening gap in achievement between students initially judged to be of high and middle versus low ability (Barr, 1984).

To overcome these and other problems, reading educators are adopting new ways of thinking. Having an awareness of these new ideas will enable administrators and supervisors to better support the change process. Recommended readings include Goodman's (1986) brief, readable account of the whole language philosophy, *What's Whole in Whole Language?*, and *The Administrator's Guide to Whole Language* by Gail Heald-Taylor (1989). *Becoming a Whole Language School: The Fair Oaks Story* (Bird, 1989) includes accounts of the change process written by a principal and a superintendent. Summarized below are new views in three areas: how reading is defined, how young children learn to read, and how reading should be taught.

How Reading Is Defined

Reading is now understood to be a highly complex process that goes far beyond the ability to identify words. At present the generally accepted definition is that reading involves a dynamic interaction among the reader, the text, and the social context in which reading takes place (Wixson et al., 1987). This definition draws upon research indicating that a text serves as a kind of linguistic blueprint from which the reader must construct meaning (Collins, Brown, & Larkin, 1980). The process of constructing meaning will not be identical for every reader or for every occasion of reading, because it is influenced by the reader's perspective and prior knowledge (Anderson & Pearson, 1984).

The current definition recognizes that the reading process is influenced by the social world surrounding the reader. Research shows that people's views of reading and literacy are influenced by the community in which they are raised. In some communities, for example, people believe that text has authority and should be interpreted literally, while in others people believe that text should be interpreted in terms of personal experiences (Heath, 1983). Also, people read and respond quite differently to text depending on the audience for their reading. For example, people read in one manner when reading a novel at home for personal enjoyment versus reading the same novel in preparation for discussion in an English class (Purves, 1985). In short, reading is a social process of considerable complexity and flexibility.

How Children Learn to Read

Many experts now believe that children learn to read by reading, that is, by being involved in the full process of reading (Smith, 1988). Children gain proficiency in reading and other abilities through a process of being assisted by other, more capable people (Vygotsky, 1987). At first children will be able to read only with the assistance of a teacher or other able reader. Gradually they will be able to take on more and more of the responsibility for reading, and the teacher will need to do less and less (Pearson, 1985). By gradually releasing responsibility for reading to the child, providing instruction and support only when necessary, the teacher can lead the child to independence in reading.

A substantial body of research shows that the process of learning to read begins at home, long before children enter kindergarten (Teale, 1987). For example, a child may pick up a storybook and, referring to the illustrations, tell the story in her own words. Although the child is not reading the text as an adult would, she shows her understanding that books contain stories, with clues to the story being provided by the illustrations. In her own way the child is approximating, or coming as close as she can, to the full process of reading. Holdaway (1979) and others describe the process of learning to read as one of successive approximation, in which children come closer and closer to reading proficiently by trying to read on their own. Skill instruction still has a place, but skills such as initial consonant sounds or the sequence of events are taught in the context of real reading, rather than for their own sake (Spiegel, 1992).

How Reading Should Be Taught

As mentioned above, current thinking about reading instruction is strongly influenced by the constructivist perspective. Constructivist approaches recognize the importance of the student's own efforts to construct meaning while reading and the holistic or unitary nature of the reading process (Flood & Lapp, 1991). In a constructivist approach, instruction proceeds from the whole to the part. That is, the teacher seeks to involve students in an authentic literacy activity and then provides the guidance and skill instruction the students require to complete the activity successfully (Au, 1993). Literacy learning is seen to take place in the social context of the classroom, and the teacher seeks to organize the classroom so that students share ideas about their literacy with one another and support one another's learning. In this way the classroom becomes a community of literacy learners (Cairney & Langbien, 1989).

The teacher encourages students to explore the functions of literacy, not just typical school functions but functions useful in the real world. These might include reading a newspaper for specific information or reading a novel purely for enjoyment. Instruction is student-centered, in the sense that the teacher develops lessons on the basis of students' needs and interests as literacy learners, establishing connections between new knowledge, skills, and strategies and students' existing background and abilities. The teacher emphasizes the process of thinking about text rather than attending only to the product or the correct answers. By emphasizing the thinking process, teachers foster strategies and attitudes that will be generally useful to students when they read. Finally, in constructivist approaches the teacher shows respect for students' cultural and linguistic backgrounds (Au, 1993). Diversity is welcomed for the variety of perspectives and range of knowledge that can be introduced by the students themselves in activities surrounding different works of literature and other texts.

In 1989, along with many schools and districts throughout the United States, KEEP began the process of making the transition to a constructivist curriculum framework. This process involved KEEP staff members and teachers in the study of recent theory and research in reading and the language arts and in considering the significance of these ideas for the literacy instruction of KEEP's students. Of course, the process of reading and learning is ongoing. Books that KEEP staff members and teachers have found especially valuable include *Transitions* and *Invitations* by Regie Routman (1988, 1991), *Understanding Whole Language* by Weaver (1990), *Living Between the Lines* by Calkins (1991), and *Lasting Impressions* by Shelley Harwayne (1992). Three journals (*Language Arts, The New Advocate,* and *The Reading Teacher*) have been a source of many informative articles.

GUIDELINE #2: DEVELOP A CURRICULUM THAT INCORPORATES A BROAD RANGE OF LITERACY OUTCOMES AND INSTRUCTIONAL ACTIVITIES

Administrators and supervisors often have the responsibility of seeing that the key ideas garnered from the professional literature are organized in a manner that guides teachers in their work with students in the classroom. In most cases, this means developing a curriculum framework, including suggestions for instruction and a system of assessment. A curriculum consistent with current thinking might take many forms, given the broad, general nature of constructivist and whole language theory. However, a constructivist curriculum should meet several requirements if it is to be both sound and practical. It should

- Respect the complexity of the reading process and of literacy.
- Be specific enough to guide teachers' thinking and instruction.
- Be subject to continual discussion, revision, and improvement.

The KEEP Whole Literacy Curriculum

Drawing upon constructivist and whole language ideas, as well as their experience in classrooms, KEEP staff members developed a new whole literacy curriculum (Au, Scheu, Kawakami, & Herman, 1990). The curriculum reflects the new definition of reading, as well as new ideas about how children learn to read and how reading might best be taught.

As shown in Figure 4.1, the curriculum is structured around six aspects of literacy: ownership, the writing process, reading comprehension, language and vocabulary knowledge, word reading strategies/spelling, and voluntary reading. Ownership of literacy, the overarching goal of the curriculum, refers to students' valuing of reading and writing in their own lives (Au, Scheu, & Kawakami, 1990). This goal makes it clear that students should have the will as well as the skill to use literacy both in and out of school. The writing process is seen as dynamic and nonlinear, involving activities such as planning, drafting, revising, editing, and publishing (Graves, 1983). Reading comprehension involves the ability to interpret text and to make connections between the text and one's own life. Language and vocabulary knowledge refers to the ability to understand and use appropriate terms and structures in both written and spoken English. Word reading strategies include the use of meaning, visual/graphophonic, and structural cues to identify words (Clay, 1985). Finally, voluntary reading means students' willingness to read books on their own.

Two of the six aspects of literacy, ownership and voluntary reading, are affective, demonstrating the importance of motivation as well as cognition in students' literacy learning. The writing process and reading comprehension are placed at the same level of importance, just below ownership, to signal that both are equally important. Recent research suggests

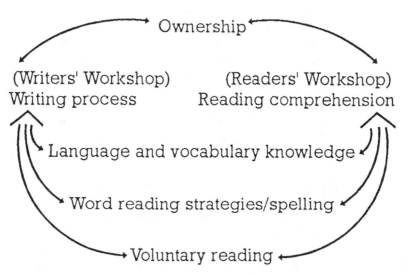

Figure 4.1   Six Aspects of Literacy in the KEEP Curriculum

that children's reading can be strengthened by writing process activities and vice versa (Blackburn, 1984). Giving writing the same degree of emphasis and amount of instructional time as reading is a definite shift from previous practice in elementary schools, where reading has typically received the lion's share of attention.

Instruction in the KEEP program is organized in two cycles, a writers' workshop and a readers' workshop, and both reading and writing take place during each workshop. (See Chapter 12 for detailed descriptions of the writing workshop and reading workshop.) During the writers' workshop students choose their own topics for writing, participate in conferences with peers and the teacher, and share their writing with the class as a whole. Often, books written and illustrated by the students are displayed in the classroom library.

During the readers' workshop students read, write about, and discuss literature. Teachers attempt to strike a balance between encouraging students to enjoy literature and teaching them the strategies, skills, and knowledge they need to be proficient readers. Guided discussions provide teachers with opportunities to teach students to comprehend and critically evaluate text. KEEP teachers learn to conduct small group, guided discussion lessons following the experience–text–relationship (ETR) approach for narratives (Au, 1979). In this approach teachers begin by having students talk about background experiences related to the theme of the story (E phase). Next, sections of the story are read silently and discussed (T phase). Finally, teachers help students draw relationships between story ideas and their own experiences (R phase). Teachers also learn to use the K-W-L (What do I KNOW? What do I WANT to know? What did I LEARN?) approach for developing students' ability to comprehend and take notes from informational text (Ogle, 1986).

Besides conducting small group discussion lessons, KEEP teachers promote reading development through

- Literature response logs, in which students write down their feelings and ideas about texts they have read.
- Projects, such as plays or movie rolls, that allow students to show what they have learned and to share literature with others.
- Research projects carried out by individuals or small groups.
- Reading aloud to students: teachers of younger children read picture storybooks, while teachers of older students read a chapter a day from novels.
- Sustained silent reading: the students and teacher read silently from books of their choice, perhaps for 10 to 20 minutes a day.
- Reading for homework: teachers ask their students to read for 15

minutes or more each evening in a book of the students' own choosing.

GUIDELINE #3: SCHEDULE AMPLE TIME FOR READING INSTRUCTION, BUT ALSO ENCOURAGE LITERACY LEARNING THROUGHOUT THE SCHOOL DAY

According to Goodlad (1983), the average amount of time set aside for reading/language arts instruction in the early grades is about 1 hour and 45 minutes. In the primary grades this is probably the minimum amount of time that should be allocated. Ironically, schools with a large proportion of students from low-income families usually schedule *less* time for reading instruction than other schools (Allington, 1991). The reason for this situation is not known, but certainly the students in these schools need and deserve ample time for reading instruction.

In primary grade classrooms in the KEEP program, approximately 2 hours is scheduled for the teaching of reading and writing. In the upper grades less time may be scheduled for literacy instruction per se, because students are taught reading strategies during the study of science, social studies, and other content areas. However, even when adequate time is allocated for reading instruction, as in KEEP schools, this time is often interrupted by pullout programs or special events.

Administrators can use their leadership to ensure that students receive the time for reading instruction they need. They can schedule assemblies for late in the school day, preserving the morning time for instruction. They can ask resource teachers, such as those in the remedial reading program, to work in the classrooms instead of pulling students out for instruction. Measures like these minimize disruptions to reading instruction and allow students with special needs to remain a part of the classroom community of readers.

Of course, adequate time for reading instruction is only part of the solution. Close attention must also be paid to what actually happens in classrooms during reading instruction time. This guideline about *quantity* of time must be considered along with other guidelines that speak to the *quality* of instruction.

Time for literacy learning can be increased if teachers look for natural opportunities throughout the school day when students can read and write. For example, students can keep math journals in which they write about the process they use to solve problems. Instead of taking home a teacher-prepared weekly newsletter, students can write letters to their parents telling about the week's events.

Especially in the upper elementary grades, teachers can emphasize reading comprehension and vocabulary development during content-area lessons. For example:

- In math class, children learn how to interpret word problems in terms of mathematical operations.
- In science class, children learn to follow step-by-step directions in setting up experiments.
- In a social studies class, children learn to critically evaluate the logic of a written argument.

Besides content-area lessons, other times when reading and writing can be highlighted for children are:

- During the planning of classroom projects, such as performing a play (students can write down materials needed for sets and costumes, mark their parts in the script, etc.).
- During classroom routines such as taking attendance (a student needs to be able to read classmates' names and to mark those who are absent).
- During excursions, when notes can be taken and signs read.

By highlighting reading throughout the day, teachers show students the situations in which they should be applying reading skills.

GUIDELINE #4: PUT LITERATURE AT THE HEART OF THE CLASSROOM READING PROGRAM

Another change in the elementary school reading program centers on the use of literature-based instruction. Formerly, students were taught to read not with literature, but with texts designed especially to teach them to read. The vocabulary in these texts was carefully controlled, and students were taught each new word before they encountered it in a story. Sentences were kept short, on the assumption that long sentences were harder to read than short ones. Unfortunately, texts written according to these guidelines often held little interest for students.

Literature-based instruction grows from the idea that students should be taught to read using authentic works of children's literature. The rationale for literature-based instruction is both affective and cognitive (Huck, 1990). Due to strong plots, engaging characters, vivid language, and other features, authentic works of literature have an inherent interest for most children. In addition, literature has a richness of ideas and themes for students to grapple with, and interpreting literary texts promotes reasoning and other forms of higher-level thinking.

Literature-based instruction draws on reader response theory (Probst, 1991). In early work on reader response, Rosenblatt (1978) highlighted the uniqueness of the individual's personal response to literature. She emphasized that meaning did not reside in the text or in the reader, but in what she called the *transaction* between the reader and the text. Every reader's response to a particular work of literature will be somewhat different, Rosenblatt argued, because of individual differences in knowledge, beliefs, and personal histories. As you can see, reader response theory is consistent with the constructivist perspective in recognizing the role of the reader and the reader's background knowledge and experience in the interpretation of text.

Changing the materials used to teach reading serves as a starting point for literature-based instruction. However, there must also be changes in the nature of reading instruction, including student outcomes, lessons, and the structure of interactions between teacher and students and among the students themselves. These changes are likely to be difficult for both teachers and students accustomed to seeking out a single "correct" interpretation to a text.

Teachers in elementary schools are using a variety of approaches to encourage students to respond to literature and to develop strategies for interpreting literature and making connections among different works. Often, teachers organize their students into small groups for the purpose of discussing works of literature. These groups may be called literature circles, literature study groups, or book clubs (McMahon, 1992; Short & Pierce, 1990). Students usually write in response to literature in preparation for meeting in these groups. The discussion may be led by the teacher or by the students themselves.

Often the initial barrier to literature-based instruction is the availability of trade books. Administrators can be instrumental in helping teachers obtain the funds to purchase trade books, perhaps by working with parent or community organizations.

KEEP supports teachers in literature-based instruction by assisting with the purchase of trade books, often multiple copies of a particular title. Usually, teachers work out the themes (survival, friendship, caring for the environment) and topics (volcanoes, the Civil War) they would like to explore with students. Then they decide upon the books that will work well with these themes and topics. If space permits, the books are kept in a common area so they can be shared among classrooms.

Administrators can facilitate communication among teachers at different grade levels so that teachers know the themes and topics taught at earlier and later grades. Administrators can help teachers sort out areas of overlap so that students have the opportunity to read different books and to explore different themes and topics at each grade. In some schools teachers agree on a list of core literature to be used at each grade level. In this situation teachers concentrate on the core titles for their own grade level, supplemented by books not on the list, and they do not teach with the core titles for other grades. Many teachers in schools with literature-based instruction favor a core literature list because they find it easier to plan units when they have an idea of the books their students have or have not read and discussed in earlier grades.

Another barrier to the implementation of literature-based instruction may be teachers' lack of familiarity with alternative forms of classroom organization. Frequently, teachers are accustomed to organizing reading instruction with three fixed ability groups or with whole-class instruction. These teachers often need considerable inservice and moral support before they gain the knowledge and confidence to organize their reading program around literature circles in which students are heterogeneously grouped. Inservice sessions may also be needed to give teachers the background to guide literature discussions and interact with students in a conversational manner around text ideas.

Administrators can help teachers gain the necessary background in a number of ways. One is by arranging workshops and other inservice activities. KEEP staff members arrange and conduct workshops, often featuring experienced teachers who have made the transition to literature-based instruction. KEEP teachers learn to conduct small group discussions about literature in a responsive manner (Au & Kawakami, 1984), accepting students' answers and encouraging them to elaborate upon their ideas. Videotapes of literature discussions are particularly useful in giving teachers a sense of the dynamic nature of instruction. KEEP staff members also conduct demonstration lessons and arrange for teachers to visit one another's classrooms to view lessons or learn about new forms of classroom organization.

Administrators may also help by making books and articles on literature-based instruction available to teachers and by providing time for teachers to read and discuss these materials. Useful references for classroom organization include Routman (1991), who provides detailed, practical information on all aspects of managing the classroom reading program, and the April 1991 issue of *The Reading Teacher*, which contains articles describing approaches across the grades. Helpful articles on literature discussions include Zarrillo (1991), which emphasizes a balance between the aesthetic and efferent questions, and Eeds and Peterson (1991), which addresses the dynamics of talk.

A principal can support literature-based instruction by instituting a time for daily, schoolwide sustained silent reading. Some schools hold an annual book fair so that students can purchase books. Other schools involve students and parents in incentive programs such as Books and Beyond that promote the habit of reading. Further information about Books and Beyond is available through the federally funded National Diffusion Network.

GUIDELINE #5: PROVIDE SYSTEMATIC INSTRUCTION IN SKILLS TAUGHT IN A MEANINGFUL CONTEXT

The constructivist and whole language perspectives highlight the importance of involving students in authentic literacy activities that engage students in the full processes of reading and writing. For example, students might read a chapter in a novel, write down their responses, and then share their responses with peers and the teacher in a literature circle. Reading and responding to literature and sharing one's responses with others are all activities that can have value in students' lives outside, as well as within, the classroom.

But involving students in authentic literacy activities and the full processes of reading and writing does not complete the job of reading instruction. While students should have opportunities to make their own discoveries about reading and writing, many students also benefit from systematic instruction in strategies and skills. Systematic skill instruction, in the context of meaningful literacy activities, is not viewed as inconsistent with the whole language philosophy (Mills, O'Keefe, & Stephens, 1992; Spiegel, 1992; Weaver, 1990).

Delpit (1986, 1988) argues that skill instruction can make explicit to students understandings that it might take them a long time to infer on their own. In some cases, students will learn more quickly if they are simply shown how to handle a particular problem, rather than being left to struggle on their own. Delpit suggests that withholding instruction in specific strategies and skills, including standard English grammar, may handicap students of diverse backgrounds who are less familiar than mainstream students with the codes of the language of power. Delpit does not endorse a return to skill-and-drill and rote learning, but favors approaches oriented toward developing higher-level thinking, supported by systematic instruction that will enable students of diverse backgrounds to read and write with the same proficiency as their mainstream peers.

Constructivist and whole language approaches to the teaching of strategies and skills differ significantly from earlier transmission approaches. Constructivist approaches begin with students' involvement in a meaningful, motivating activity. In transmission approaches, the starting point for instruction is the skills themselves. In the absence of a meaningful context for skill instruction, students sometimes do not understand the purpose of the skill and how it can be applied during real reading and writing. In constructivist approaches, teachers begin with an authentic literacy activity, then teach students the skills they need to complete the activity successfully (Au, 1993). In this way, students understand the purpose of skills and how they fit with real reading.

In kindergarten and first grade classrooms in the KEEP program, teachers teach children how to identify words by using meaning, visual/ graphophonic, and structural cues in the context of reading and discussing big books with predictable language patterns. Much learning of word identification skills occurs during the writers' workshop, when children use invented spelling to draft stories on topics of their own choosing. Students learn skills such as recognizing the sequence of events and constructing the theme for a story by reading and discussing literature, and they carry these skills over to their own writing.

Some skill instruction in KEEP classes takes place during lessons at the start of the readers' or writers' workshop. These lessons address skills that teachers judge most students in the class have not yet grasped. For example, if a first grade teacher observes that students need help with the concept of problem and solution, she might read a story aloud and work with the class on the skill in the context of understanding that story. Frequently, certain skills are needed by just a few children in the class. In this case the teacher will organize small group lessons just for these children. The group is disbanded after the students have gained an understanding of the skill, and another group may be formed. Teachers may also provide a mini-lesson in the context of a literature discussion circle. Suppose that students have noticed an interesting word but do not understand its meaning. The teacher might take the opportunity to provide students with a mini-lesson on strategies for deriving word meanings.

Administrators can help teachers provide students with effective, systematic skill instruction. A first step might be to have teachers discuss the skills they believe students should be taught at particular grade levels. A logical next step is to have teachers consider how these skills might be taught in meaningful contexts such as those provided by thematic units, literature-based instruction, science projects, and so on. Teachers can be encouraged to try their ideas and then meet at a later date to describe the approaches they have tried.

GUIDELINE #6: USE PORTFOLIO AND OTHER ALTERNATIVE FORMS OF LITERACY ASSESSMENT AND AVOID OVERRELIANCE ON STANDARDIZED TESTING

Alternative forms of assessment, and portfolios in particular, are being explored in many classrooms, schools, and districts across the United States. Although it can take years for explorations in alternative assessment to reach fruition, improved forms of assessment are viewed as critical to the movement toward constructivist and whole language approaches to literacy instruction. If assessment drives instruction, it is argued, then assessment must be changed to support the kinds of instruction that will be most beneficial to students' literacy learning.

Portfolios and other innovative forms of assessment are seen as an important counterbalance to the extensive use of multiple choice, norm-referenced standardized tests. The negative effects of standardized testing have been well documented (Shepard, 1991). One of the most damaging effects is that standardized tests generally do not evaluate the kinds of reading and writing emphasized in constructivist and whole language approaches to literacy learning. For example, the tests usually evaluate comprehension through the use of short passages followed by multiple choice items. In contrast, in the classroom students read authentic works of literature and show their comprehension by writing and discussing their responses. Standardized tests with multiple choice formats cannot adequately evaluate students' critical thinking and interpretation, which may lead to unique, diverse, individual responses.

In schools and districts that rely on standardized tests as the sole measure of student achievement, the mismatch between the tests and constructivist, whole language, and literature-based curricula puts teachers in a bind. Teachers who have moved into literature-based instruction feel that they must narrow the curriculum to teach to the test. Valuable instructional time is lost not only in having students take the test, but in preparing students to deal with the test's content and format. A final irony is that the test results are likely to reflect but a fraction of students' literacy learning, and in some cases the assumptions of the test may even cause students to be punished for reading in a thoughtful manner. For example, KEEP staff members discovered that students who had been taught to reflect on their reading were reluctant to rush through test passages and mark answers quickly.

Part of the logic of portfolio assessment is that portfolios can reflect the range of students' accomplishments in literacy throughout the school year, not just on a single occasion (Valencia, 1990). The work shown in a portfolio can be based on tasks, such as reading and interpreting a novel or writing a research report, far more complex and valuable than those in multiple choice standardized tests. Documents in a portfolio can show the process of reading, writing, and thinking that students followed in arriving at a final product. Portfolios may also contain evidence for affective outcomes, such as students' ownership of literacy, as well as for cognitive outcomes. For example, students may respond to a survey with questions about whether they like to read, how often they read, and the kinds of books they prefer. Or teachers may include anecdotal notes on students' behaviors, such as going to the library at recess, that show students' interest in reading and ownership of literacy.

Portfolios do not lead to wasted instructional time, because the content of the portfolio is work that students have been doing in the course of literature-based instruction, content-area study, and other ongoing classroom literacy activities. Portfolios help teachers to improve instruction in a way that standardized tests cannot, because the analysis of students' portfolios reveals to teachers the skills and strategies with which students need help. For example, third graders' portfolios in the KEEP program include summaries of the literature they have read. An examination of summaries in one classroom revealed that some students were retelling the entire story instead of centering their summaries on key points and events. The teacher learned that she needed to conduct a mini-lesson to teach students the difference between a summary and a lengthy retelling.

KEEP uses a portfolio assessment that centers on the use of grade-level benchmarks for each of the six aspects of literacy in the curriculum (Au, 1994). The use of these benchmarks makes it possible to rate students as above, at, or below grade level on the basis of evidence in their portfolios. For students performing below grade level, teachers gain ideas for further instruction from the benchmarks and the contents of students' portfolios. Portfolios usually contain students' written responses to literature, drafts and published pieces on self-selected topics, research reports, running records (miscue analyses of students' oral reading), logs showing the titles of books students have read at home, and surveys that contain students' written or oral responses to questions about their ownership of literacy. In addition, teachers often keep a class portfolio, including observational checklists, status-of-the-class forms completed during writers' workshops, and other evidence about the class as a whole.

The grade-level benchmarks permit aggregation of KEEP's portfolio assessment data. Graphs can be prepared showing the number of students in each classroom who are above, at, or below grade level in each of the six aspects of literacy. For program evaluation purposes, graphs can also be prepared to show the results for grade levels within a school, and for grade levels across the 10 schools in the KEEP program. Comparing results from one year to the next allows KEEP staff members to make determinations about the program's effectiveness and to identify areas of instruction in need of improvement.

Administrators can support the use of alternative forms of literacy assessment by providing teachers with information, inservice opportunities, and time to work together. They may gather and provide teachers with information about the procedures for portfolios developed in other settings. Two edited volumes provide a wealth of background information and practical advice: *Authentic Reading Assessment: Practices and Possibilities* (Valencia, Hiebert, & Afflerbach, 1994) and *Assessment and Evaluation in Whole Language Programs* (Harp, 1991). *Educational Leadership*, the journal of the Association for Supervision and Curriculum Development, is an excellent source of brief articles on alternative assessment.

GUIDELINE #7: INVOLVE PARENTS AND OTHER FAMILY MEMBERS IN CHILDREN'S LEARNING TO READ

Schools need to have a plan for educating parents about current approaches to reading and language arts instruction, including whole language, literature-based instruction, the process approach to writing, and portfolio assessment. Because most parents did not experience these approaches in their own schooling, they are likely to be puzzled by the kinds of instruction their children are receiving. For example, they may wonder why their child's homework involves reading a book rather than completing a phonics worksheet. Or they may question the value of invented spelling and wonder if their child is ever going to learn proper spelling.

Administrators can help by encouraging grade-level or schoolwide parent education efforts. Presentations and activities for parents may be organized for evenings when the school has scheduled an open house. Different teachers can be responsible for giving parts of the presentation or for leading activities that draw on their expertise in reading and writing instruction. Slides or videotapes showing the different experiences in which students are involved, such as literature circles or the writers' workshop, can help parents to visualize the new forms of instruction.

Once they understand the school's philosophy, parents can often do much to support the overall goals of the elementary reading program. To ensure that interested parents have the opportunity to become involved in their children's learning to read, multiple ways of communicating with parents need to be worked out. Beginning in kindergarten, children can borrow books to read at home on their own, or to be read to them by a family member. The school newsletter can include information about the reading program and suggestions for ways in which parents can help. Many parents are willing to support their children's voluntary reading and may also be interested in suggestions to foster writing. Schools following a process approach to writing may give parents information about the importance of drawing and letting children try out their own invented spellings. Parents of older students may give their children some quiet time to read on their own and encourage the keeping of a diary, note-taking, or story writing. Parents may arrange regular visits to the library so their children always have access to interesting books.

Parents (and other family members, such as grandparents) can be invited to serve as volunteers in the classroom. For example, parents can read to children or listen to individual children read aloud. Or parents can accompany students to the library to look up information needed for research projects. Parents can help with other school reading activities, such as setting up a book fair where children can purchase or trade books.

Principals can encourage teachers to provide parents with complete explanations of their children's progress, using student portfolios as the focus for parent conferences. In some schools these conferences include the student as well. By going over the contents of the student's portfolio with parents, the teacher can give them an overview of accomplishments since the beginning of the school year. Parents can learn a great deal by seeing samples of their children's writing and the kinds of materials they are currently reading. Some schools go a step further and hold "back to school" days when parents come to school and participate with their children in typical literacy activities (see also Chapter 11).

GUIDELINE #8: CREATE AN ATMOSPHERE FOR CHANGE BY VIEWING PEOPLE, NOT COMMERCIAL PROGRAMS OR CURRICULUM GUIDES, AS THE KEY TO A SUCCESSFUL READING PROGRAM

The key to a successful elementary school reading program is a shared vision of what the program should accomplish for students, along with a sense of its important elements. This shared vision can rarely be transmitted in a top-down way but generally develops as all involved with the program meet to air their views.

Time for staff to meet for discussions is the key factor. No program, however wonderful in design, can be successful if staff members have not contributed to shaping it and do not feel ownership of it. One way of stimulating discussion would be to share an article such as this one with staff members and then to meet for discussion. Questions for discussion should be open-ended. For example:

With which ideas did you agree? Why?
With which ideas did you disagree? Why?
What changes do you want to try first? Why?

The idea is for staff at the school level to become involved in thinking the issues through for themselves. As mentioned earlier, there is no simple formula for success, and abstract ideas need to be made concrete through an infusion of knowledge about the students to be served, the community, the school setting, and the staff members themselves.

Finally, once an effective program is in place, there must be room for improvement and individual initiative. The process of discussion should continue so that the program can be constantly updated on the basis of new experiences at the school and in the classroom, new research knowledge, and new insights.

Without doubt, the task of developing a successful elementary school reading program is extremely challenging. Yet new theories of learning and literacy and new instructional approaches, combined with an understanding of the human dynamics of the change process, offer administrators and supervisors the best chance ever of collaborating with teachers in a manner that will bring students of all backgrounds to high levels of literacy.

REFERENCES

Allington, R. L. (1991). Children who find learning to read difficult: School responses to diversity. In E. H. Hiebert (Ed.), *Literacy for a diverse society: Perspectives, practices, and policies* (pp. 237–252). New York: Teachers College Press.

Anderson, R. C., & Pearson, P. D. (1984). A schema-theoretic view of basic processes in reading comprehension. In P. D. Pearson (Ed.), *Handbook of reading research* (pp. 255–291). New York: Longman.

Au, K. H. (1979). Using the experience-text-relationship *method* with minority children. *The Reading Teacher, 32*(6), 677–679.

Au, K. H. (1993). *Literacy instruction in multicultural settings.* Fort Worth, TX: Harcourt Brace Jovanovich.

Au, K. H. (1994). Portfolio assessment: Experiences at the Kamehameha Elementary Education Program. In S. W. Valencia, E. H. Hiebert, & P. P. Afflerbach (Eds.), *Authentic reading assessment: Practices and possibilities* (pp. 103–126). Newark, DE: International Reading Association.

Au, K. H., & Kawakami, A. J. (1984). Vygotskian perspectives on discussion processes in small group reading lessons. In P. L. Peterson, L. C. Wilkinson, & M. Hallinan (Eds.), *The social context of instruction: Group organization and group processes* (pp. 209–225). New York: Academic Press.

Au, K. H., Scheu, J. A., & Kawakami, A. J. (1990). Assessment of students' ownership of literacy. *The Reading Teacher, 44*(2), 154–156.

Au, K. H., Scheu, J. A., Kawakami, A. J., & Herman, P. A. (1990). Assessment and accountability in a whole literacy curriculum. *The Reading Teacher, 43*(8), 574–578.

Barr, R. (1984). Beginning reading instruction: From debate to reformation. In P. D. Pearson (Ed.), *Handbook of reading research* (pp. 545–581). New York: Longman.

Bird, L. B. (Ed.). (1989). *Becoming a whole language school: The Fair Oaks story.* Katonah, NY: Richard C. Owen.

Blackburn, E. (1984). Common ground: Developing relationships between reading and writing. *Language Arts, 61,* 367–375.

Cairney, T., & Langbien, S. (1989). Building communities of readers and writers. *The Reading Teacher, 42*(8), 560–567.

Calkins, L. M. (1991). *Living between the lines.* Portsmouth, NH: Heinemann.

Clay, M. M. (1985). *The early detection of reading difficulties* (3rd ed.). Auckland, New Zealand: Heinemann.

Collins, A., Brown, J. S., & Larkin, J. M. (1980). Inference in text understanding. In R. J. Spiro, B. C. Bruce, & W. F. Brewer (Eds.), *Theoretical issues in reading comprehension.* Hillsdale, NJ: Erlbaum.

Delpit, L. D. (1986). Skills and other dilemmas of a progressive Black educator. *Harvard Educational Review, 56*(4), 379–385.

Delpit, L. D. (1988). The silenced dialogue: Power and pedagogy in educating other people's children. *Harvard Educational Review, 58,* 280–298.

Eeds, M., & Peterson, R. (1991). Teacher as curator: Learning to talk about literature. *The Reading Teacher, 45*(2), 118–126.

Flood, J., & Lapp, D. (1991). Reading comprehension instruction. In J. Flood, J. M. Jensen, D. Lapp, & J. R. Squire (Eds.), *Handbook of research on teaching the English language arts* (pp. 732–742). New York: Macmillan.

Goodlad, J. (1983). *A place called school.* New York: Harper.

Goodman, K. (1986). *What's whole in whole language?* Portsmouth, NH: Heinemann.

Graves, D. (1983). *Writing: Teachers and children at work.* Exeter, NH: Heinemann.

Harp, B. (Ed.) (1991). *Assessment and evaluation in whole language programs.* Norwood, MA: Christopher-Gordon.

Harwayne, S. (1992). *Lasting impressions: Weaving literature into the writing workshop.* Portsmouth, NH: Heinemann.

Heald-Taylor, G. (1989). *The administrator's guide to whole language.* Katonah, NY: Richard C. Owen.

Heath, S. B. (1983). *Ways with words: Language, life, and work in communities and classrooms*. Cambridge: Cambridge University Press.

Holdaway, D. (1979). *The foundations of literacy*. Sydney, Australia: Ashton Scholastic (distributed in the United States by Heinemann).

Huck, C. S. (1990). The power of children's literature in the classroom. In K. G. Short & K. M. Pierce (Eds.), *Talking about books: Creating literate communities* (pp. 3–15). Portsmouth, NH: Heinemann.

McMahon, S. I. (1992). Book club: A case study of a group of fifth graders as they participate in a literature-based reading program. *Reading Research Quarterly, 27*(4), 292–294.

Mills, H., O'Keefe, T., & Stephens, D. (1992). *Looking closely: Exploring the role of phonics in one whole language classroom*. Urbana, IL: National Council of Teachers of English.

Ogle, D. M. (1986). K-W-L: A teaching model that develops active reading of expository text. *Reading Teacher, 39*(6), 564–570.

Pearson, P. D. (1985). Changing the face of reading comprehension instruction. *The Reading Teacher, 38*(8), 724–738.

Probst, R. E. (1991). Response to literature. In J. Flood, J. M. Jensen, D. Lapp, & J. R. Squire (Eds.), *Handbook of research on teaching the English language arts* (pp. 655–663). New York: Macmillan.

Purves, A. C. (1985). That sunny dome: Those caves of ice. In C. R. Cooper (Ed.), *Researching response to literature and the teaching of literature: Points of departure* (pp. 54–69). Norwood, NJ: Ablex.

Rosenblatt, L. (1978). *The reader, the text, the poem: The transactional theory of the literary work*. Carbondale, IL: Southern Illinois University Press.

Routman, R. (1988). *Transitions: From literature to literacy*. Portsmouth, NH: Heinemann.

Routman, R. (1991). *Invitations: Changing as teachers and learners K–12*. Portsmouth, NH: Heinemann.

Shannon, P. (1989). *Broken promises: Reading instruction in twentieth century America*. New York: Bergin & Garvey.

Shepard, L. A. (1991). Negative policies for dealing with diversity: When does assessment and diagnosis turn into sorting and segregating? In E. H. Hiebert (Ed.), *Literacy for a diverse society: Perspectives, practices, and policies* (pp. 279–298). New York: Teachers College Press.

Short, K. G., & Pierce, K. M. (1990). *Talking about books: Creating literate communities*. Portsmouth, NH: Heinemann.

Smith, F. J. (1988). *Understanding reading* (4th ed.). Hillsdale, NJ: Lawrence Erlbaum.

Spiegel, D. L. (1992). Blending whole language and systematic direct instruction. *The Reading Teacher, 46*(1), 38–44.

Teale, W. H. (1987). *Emergent literacy: Reading and writing development in early childhood*. In J. E. Readence & R. S. Baldwin (Eds.), *Research in literacy: Merging perspectives* (pp. 45–74). Rochester, NY: National Reading Conference.

Valencia, S. (1990). A portfolio approach to classroom reading assessment: The whys, whats, and hows. *The Reading Teacher, 43*(4), 338–340.

Valencia, S. W., Hiebert, E. H., & Afflerbach, P. P. (Eds.). (1994). *Authentic reading assessment: Practices and possibilities.* Newark, DE: International Reading Association.

Vygotsky, L. S. (1987). Thinking and speech. In R. W. Rieber & A. S. Carton (Eds.), *The collected works of L. S. Vygotsky, Volume 1. Problems of general psychology* (pp. 37–285). New York: Plenum.

Weaver, C. (1990). *Understanding whole language: Principles and practices.* Portsmouth, NH: Heinemann.

Wixson, K. K. Peters, C. W., Weber, E. M., & Roeber, E. D. (1987). New directions in statewide reading assessment. *The Reading Teacher, 40*(8), 749–754.

Zarrillo, J. (1991). Theory becomes practice: Aesthetic teaching with literature. *The New Advocate, 4*(4), 221–234.

5 Middle School and Junior High Reading Programs

MARK W. CONLEY
Michigan State University

In theory, middle schools differ from junior high schools in fundamental ways. Middle schools are supposed to be more like elementary schools. In many middle schools, teachers work in teams, with a focus on the individual and on personal development. Junior high schools, on the other hand, are supposed to look more like secondary schools. They are often departmentalized, with a focus on academics and college preparation (Lipsitz, 1984).

In practice, confusion persists about the nature of middle and junior high schools. Few schools entirely adopt a middle school or junior high emphasis. Criticized for a lack of academic rigor, middle schools are pressured to become junior high schools. Criticized for not attending to the needs of the adolescent as an individual, junior high schools are pushed to become middle schools. Though current trends favor the movement toward middle schools, junior high schools are still much in evidence.

The confusion about middle schools and junior highs is also evident in the reading curriculum. Like the schools themselves, approaches to middle and junior high reading have been drawn from both the elementary and secondary levels. Little is known about reading programs in the context of the goals of middle and junior high schools. Like the schools, middle and junior high reading programs struggle to establish and maintain an identity and meet the various needs of early adolescent learners.

The purposes of this chapter are to

1. Distinguish between the goals of middle and junior high schools
2. Describe the reading needs of the early adolescent
3. Examine various programs that are commonly found in middle schools and junior highs
4. Provide guidelines for developing middle and junior high school reading programs

THE GOALS OF MIDDLE AND JUNIOR HIGH SCHOOLS

Before middle schools, there were junior high schools. Junior high schools were first organized at the turn of the century (Peeler, 1974). First thought of as "little high schools," junior highs were supposed to prepare students for the vocational and academic subjects they would experience at the secondary level.

Then and now, junior highs typically cover grades seven, eight, and nine, with a curriculum that parallels the high school. Emphasis is usually on mastery of subject matter, though attempts have been made to extend the curriculum to encourage exploration and personal development. Peeler's (1974) goals for the junior high are a good example of a broader perspective on what junior highs should do. According to Peeler, junior highs should stress the needs of the early adolescent, especially the need for a smooth transition from the elementary to the secondary school. In addition, junior highs should offer opportunities for students to discover their interests and capabilities, providing vocational education and programs that will reduce the number of dropouts. Ultimately, suggests Peeler, junior highs should assist students in realizing their fullest potential to offer service to the society in which they live.

Unfortunately, though Peeler's goals promise to broaden the focus of the junior high to students' personal and social adjustment, most reform efforts lead back to an exclusive focus on academics. Personal exploration in the junior high usually involves entertaining different vocational and academic choices. Personal development often means making decisions about educational opportunities but not about extracurricular activities (Wiles & Biondi, 1981).

Middle schools, typically covering grades five through eight, emerged in the late 1950s and early 1960s, in part as a reaction against junior highs. Critics argued for a reorganization of schools in the middle levels, based on the junior high's neglect of the physical, intellectual, and emotional needs of the early adolescent (Peeler, 1974).

Several other factors contributed to the development of middle schools (Wiles & Biondi, 1981). Concerns over the quality of schooling in the United States created an obsession for academic achievement in the middle and upper grades. Calls came for a four-year high school (grades nine through twelve), viewed as a college preparatory school. Grades five and six were combined with grades seven and eight so that teachers could introduce more specialized content and instruction at earlier levels.

Racial desegregation and increased enrollments also contributed to middle school development by creating incentives for reorganization. Segregation and overcrowding at the elementary level were often relieved by moving grades five and six to the middle school. The factor that continues to influence middle school development is the "bandwagon effect." Favorable reports on middle schools convince many administrators that middle schools are "the thing to do."

A recurring problem of middle schools is that reorganization often occurs without a clear conception of what middle schools should accomplish. The National Association of Secondary School Principals (NASSP, 1985) recently described the goals of the effective middle school. Rather than rigidly emphasizing academics, these goals focus on teaching students to become lifelong learners, with attention to developing students' knowledge, skills, and motivation. Specifically, the NASSP recommends that middle schools should

1. Articulate and disseminate core values that address personal responsibility, the importance of learning, and respect for diversity in the school and community
2. Develop a climate in the school that supports excellence and achievement
3. Support students' personal development, offering frequent opportunities for responsible social behavior as well as promoting a positive self-concept

4. Implement a curriculum that effectively balances skill development with content coverage, offering lifelong skills for the future along with an understanding of different content areas
5. Challenge each student at his or her ability level
6. Use a variety of instructional approaches (e.g., lectures, simulations, discussion, demonstrations, and labs), combined with high expectations and guidance

These goals illustrate how middle schools try to deal with many different aspects of a student's life, from personal and academic development to helping students understand their place in the community. Note how many of these goals resemble those meant to reform the junior high. Effective middle schools take these goals seriously. In a recent survey of exemplary middle schools, a large percentage stated a commitment to students' personal development and development of skills for continued learning and exploration. These goals are often addressed through use of interdisciplinary teams, a home-base period, and a teacher advisor for each student, as well as flexible scheduling (George & Oldaker, 1986).

In contrast to these promising signs, several problems persist with the middle school curriculum. The middle school's commitment to student development sometimes translates into an overemphasis on facts at the expense of abstract thought. This stems from the belief that middle school students are not ready for more sophisticated types of thinking. In addition, while there is a concern for reading instruction in some form, there is uncertainty about what kind, how it should occur, and who should be served (Lipsitz, 1984).

The goals of the middle school and junior high have become more clearly differentiated over the years: Junior highs stress academics and preparation for secondary school, while middle schools emphasize the development of the student as an individual. Despite this clarity in goals, middle schools and junior highs continually strive to translate them into actual practice, striking a balance between academics and meeting students' needs. An important part of this balancing act is a concern for identifying and addressing the reading needs of the early adolescent.

THE NEEDS OF THE EARLY ADOLESCENT READER

Despite differences in emphasis, middle schools and junior highs set high goals for the early adolescent reader. These goals, in turn, create specific requirements for students, or expectations for what students need to do in order to succeed. Duffy and Roehler (1986) describe students' needs in terms of three areas of the curriculum: content, process, and attitudes. At the middle school and junior high level, the content that students are expected to read can be very complex. The simple stories students are exposed to in the early grades are replaced by more sophisticated stories, poetry, and folklore. Simple expository texts are exchanged for specialized texts in science, mathematics, and social studies. Students at this level need to be able to deal successfully with more complicated types of content.

The shift to more complicated content also creates a need for students to know more about the process of comprehension. Simply stated, comprehension is the ability of the reader to use prior knowledge to gain meaning from text. Prior knowledge that facilitates comprehension can either be topical knowledge (knowledge that relates to the topic of a particular lesson) or knowledge of a particular reading skill (e.g., forming interpretations). Students need both the appropriate prior knowledge to complete the tasks required at this level and the ability to apply their knowledge at the right place and at the right time. The same knowledge, particularly knowledge about reading, needs to be applied differently as students deal with various types of text across the curriculum.

At the elementary level, instruction on attitudes about reading centers on helping students build positive feelings about reading and themselves. For the early adolescent, the emphasis on attitudes becomes more functional in nature: getting students to see themselves as readers who can use reading as a tool for understanding. Students at this level need to perceive themselves as enthusiastic, successful readers who can use reading to understand better not only their school subjects but also the world around them.

The goals created by the curriculum — what students are expected to accomplish — must be considered alongside the needs of the students themselves — what they are actually capable of doing. Early and Sawyer (1984) have described the features of three different types of early adolescent readers: problem, average, and superior readers. All vary in the extent to which they are capable of meeting the challenges posed by the curriculum at this level.

Problem readers experience difficulty in virtually every curriculum area. These students are still struggling to master basic learning-to-read skills. They tend to use phonics as their only approach to reading. Because they have not learned to make sense of what they read, their attitudes about print are generally poor. In addition, because of their inability to process information and their poor attitudes, they view the content of what they read as inaccessible and uninteresting.

As a group, average readers have mastered phonics and are often accurate and fluent in their oral reading. Mistakes they do make orally generally do not interfere with their understanding. Average readers have also, for the most part, acquired basic comprehension skills, yet they have not necessarily integrated skills adequately to be flexible and strategic in their comprehension. Some of these students can be slow in their reading, that is, they need more time than others to comprehend. Others may read too fast, only to sacrifice their comprehension (Singer & Donlan, 1980).

The main characteristic of this group is that they don't read much. Many in this group can read proficiently but won't read. Like problem readers, they need good reasons for reading. They especially need to see connections between themselves and the content they are learning.

Superior readers have a great deal of background from experience with reading, yet they still need to refine their approach. They may be especially proficient at factual learning and even be capable of forming sophisticated interpretations. These students need to enhance their ability to apply what they know. This includes using their imagination for self-motivation and creative thinking and developing both speed and flexibility while reading.

The challenges posed by the middle school and junior high curriculum and the strengths and weaknesses of the early adolescent have created a diversity of needs in the early adolescent reader. The response in schools has been a diverse range of reading programs. While these programs can be tailored to the needs of the early adolescent, they are also subject to middle school and junior high constraints.

READING PROGRAMS FOR THE MIDDLE SCHOOL AND JUNIOR HIGH

Many different types of programs are available to help the early adolescent reader (Early & Sawyer, 1984). Beyond the elementary level, reading is most often taught as a separate course. As of 1982, remedial courses were the most prevalent, followed by corrective and developmental courses and courses with labels like "Recreational Reading," "Everyday Reading Skills," and "Independent Reading" (Greenlaw & Moore, 1982).

Remedial programs are intended for problem readers, the students who have acquired few if any basic skills. These programs are characterized by intensive, one-on-one or small-group instruction outside the regular classroom. The emphasis is almost always on learning-to-read skills, such as phonics and basic comprehension, that these students have yet to master. Teachers in these programs are specialists who have been clinically trained (Early & Sawyer, 1984).

Corrective programs are for students who have mastered most basic skills but need selective instruction in areas they have not mastered. Corrective programs are usually administered in a reading or English class by a reading or English teacher. Students work on specific skill weaknesses in corrective programs.

In general, reading instruction in remedial and corrective classes focuses on the identical basic reading skills taught at the elementary level. All too often, this instruction consists of workbooks, skill-builders and boxes or machines that offer a carefully controlled environment for learning about reading. Not only do students become cynical about this type of instruction, these experiences fail to prepare students for the variety of content and sophisticated concepts they will encounter in their content-area classes (Nelson & Herber, 1982).

Developmental programs help average students refine and extend their existing skills. For the average reader, this means learning how to apply the comprehension and study skills they already know. Developmental programs are also used for superior readers. For them, the emphasis is on creating interest and challenge through reading. Elective courses, such as courses in personal reading and studying, are frequently reserved for better readers as part of a developmental program (Early & Sawyer, 1984).

In contrast to the learning-to-read skills characteristic of remedial programs, developmental programs emphasize "reading-to-learn" skills, or the use of reading for functional or personal reasons (Singer & Donlan, 1980). Developmental programs take place in many types of settings, from specialized classes outside the regular classroom to instruction in all content areas. Teachers in the developmental program may be reading or English teachers, or teachers from any curricular area.

Content reading is a term applied to some developmental programs. This involves helping all students comprehend and apply the materials they are required to read in their school subjects. Reading skills in content-reading programs are taught functionally; that is, skills are taught as they are needed, particularly when students need assistance in comprehending materials they are required to read. Content-reading programs are typically administered in the regular classroom by the content-area teacher, sometimes with the support of a reading teacher or specialist (Herber, 1978).

A feature of many content-reading programs is the use of guided reading. Figure 5.1 illustrates a comprehension guide used to help students understand the relationship between fractions and decimals. Notice how the guide focuses on helping students understand the content of the lesson (part I) while emphasizing the function of the information students are learning (part II). This can be especially important in mathematics.

Figure 5.1 Comprehension Guide: Fractions and Decimals

Content Objective: To understand that fractions can be written as decimals and decimals can be written as fractions.

Part I: Below are pairs of fractions and decimals. Check the pairs that are equal. Be ready to tell why they are equal.

		FRACTION	DECIMAL
_____	1.	$\dfrac{3}{10}$	.30
_____	2.	$\dfrac{27}{100}$	.27
_____	3.	$\dfrac{3}{4}$	.75
_____	4.	$2\dfrac{4}{5}$	2.80
_____	5.	$\dfrac{3}{8}$	.375
_____	6.	$\dfrac{3}{500}$	.006

Part II: Check the statements below that can be used to support the ideas presented in part I. Think about what we have learned in this and other lessons so far.

_____ 1. Some fractions are easier to rewrite as decimals than others.

_____ 2. Knowing about fractions and decimals could save you money.

Another type of guided reading strategy heightens students' awareness of question-and-answer relationships (QARs) (Raphael, 1984). During QAR instruction, students are taught three different ways that questions and answers may be related when they read a text: (1) "right there" — words used to create the question and words used for the answer are in the same sentence, (2) "think and search" — the answer is in the text, but words used to create the question and those used for the answer are not in the same sentence, and (3) "on my own" — the answer lies outside the text. Teachers can introduce students to these concepts and create specific activities for students to complete. (For example, they can generate and then label different types of questions and related answers.) This training offers students opportunities to practice and then independently apply their understanding of QARs.

Reasoning can be stressed with a guide like the one in Figure 5.2, a prediction guide used in social studies. Notice how the guide gets students to think about their own perspectives first, before they consider the U.S. Constitution. This builds background and motivation for what could otherwise be a very difficult and abstract topic. Once students have completed the first part and read about the Constitution, they should be well prepared to think about how constitutional issues continue to affect their own lives.

A structured overview, a guided reading strategy used to teach vocabulary, appears in Figure 5.3. This type of strategy goes by many names, including "semantic map" and "graphic organizer" (Conley, in press). Its main purpose is to organize discussion and provide students with a familiar framework within which to understand the meaning of new words and concepts. This overview has been successfully used to teach words that offer insight into different worlds represented in "The Secret Life of Walter Mitty" (Thurber, 1965). Words and concepts taught within this overview become the key to appreciating characters and themes in this story and in other types of literature read throughout the year.

Figure 5.2   Prediction Guide: The U.S. Constitution

Content Objective: To know that the U.S. Constitution balances the rights of the many with the rights of the few.

Part I: Place a check in the blank if you think the statement is true. Be ready with one example from your own experience to support each decision.

_____ 1. Without freedom, you have nothing.

_____ 2. The majority should *always* rule.

_____ 3. The individual is the most important part of any society.

_____ 4. It is important to compromise whenever possible.

_____ 5. Though all people are created equal, not everyone has the same opportunities.

Part II: Now that you have studied the U.S. Constitution, circle the number of the statements you can support, based on what you have learned about the U.S. Constitution. Be ready with evidence from what you have read to support your decisions.

Figure 5.3   Vocabulary Development: "Walter Mitty"

Content Objective: To understand how some people use fantasies to escape their troubles in the real world.

WALTER MITTY

REAL WORLD ◄————————————————————————► FANTASY WORLD

henpecked husband	famous anesthesiologist
drives his wife to town	flies hydroplane
washed-up old man	famous defendant
mocked by people with "insolent skill" and "derisive whistling"	"intimate airways" of Mitty's mind

An unresolved question in content reading concerns whether or not students gain a greater understanding of the reading process through use of these and other types of approaches. Guided reading typically occurs in the context of whole-class and small-group discussions. If teachers use guided reading to encourage memorization rather than reasoning, then students will leave with little if any knowledge about content or process. In addition, students' attitudes about what they are reading will not be particularly affected. If, on the other hand, teachers use guided reading to show students how to integrate new information with what they already know, students' knowledge of content and process can be enhanced, along with their perception of the usefulness of what they are learning (Conley, 1986; Roehler & Duffy, in press).

Developmental programs typically face at least two problems: a lack of clearly defined purposes and a tendency to reserve more worthwhile (and motivating) reading experiences for better readers. In some schools, electives in developmental reading programs may be plentiful yet lack a coherent focus, either in relation to one another or in terms of how the courses will eventually benefit students. Speed reading is an example of a frequently offered course that can give students the wrong impression about proficient reading, namely, that reading faster means reading better. Instead, students should become aware of the need to be flexible in light of different materials and purposes while reading.

Reserving some of the better offerings in developmental programs (such as courses in study skills) for superior readers ignores the needs of problem and average readers. While problem and average readers need some type of instruction in basic skills, they also need to learn how to deal with the increasing demands of the curriculum at the middle school and junior high levels. Offering developmental reading to better readers overlooks the benefits that problem and average readers might receive from enrichment in reading.

A major issue for remedial, corrective, and developmental programs for early adolescents concerns how to involve students and teachers. It has been popular to recommend that every early adolescent be provided with specialized reading instruction (Cooper & Petrosky, 1976). It has also been suggested that every teacher should be a teacher of reading (Karlin, 1984). Many middle schools and junior highs recognize the need to offer services in reading to their students, but the cost of extra reading classes for every student can be prohibitive (Early & Sawyer, 1984). Because of limitations in resources, many schools are faced with the unfortunate choice between hiring a reading teacher to meet reading needs or hiring a content-area teacher to keep class sizes at reasonable levels.

Middle schools, with their tendency to emphasize teachers working in interdisciplinary teams, are often in the best position to deal with these issues. Shared responsibilities at the middle school should help teachers focus on reading as a way to integrate learning experiences (Aulls, 1978). Content reading is a natural choice for middle schools to use in helping students learn from text as well as develop and refine the processes and attitudes they need for success at this level. A problem with this approach, however, is that content-area teachers don't have the time or the expertise necessary to meet all of the reading needs of students in their classrooms. It is not always clear how remedial issues are addressed in middle schools or how a remedial specialist can contribute to middle school teams. Some teachers resist becoming involved in reading at the middle school level because they are uncertain about the relationship between reading and their content area (Ratekin, Simpson, Alvermann, & Dishner, 1985).

The response of the junior high to reading needs and limited resources has been either to set up separate reading classes or to incorporate reading into English departments (Early & Sawyer, 1984). This is consistent with the tendency of the junior high to departmentalize subjects (Lipsitz, 1984). These solutions contribute to at least two other problems in meeting the needs of the early adolescent reader. First, reading or English teachers can become overly burdened, while other teachers get the impression that reading is not their responsibility. Second, the reading skills taught in separate classes have not been shown to transfer to the successful reading of content-area textbooks (Nelson & Herber, 1982). By setting up separate classes or making reading the responsibility of the English department, junior highs run the risk of isolating reading and failing to help students with the increasing demands of the curriculum. Given the organization and the constraints of many middle and junior high schools, the challenge remains of how to build an effective reading program for the early adolescent.

BUILDING EFFECTIVE MIDDLE SCHOOL AND
JUNIOR HIGH READING PROGRAMS

This section provides five guidelines for developing successful reading programs for students in the middle school and junior high.

1. *Involve reading specialists, reading coordinators, content-area teachers, building principals, and district-level administrators in the planning.*
Planning and involvement by these key participants are crucial to building an effective middle school or junior high reading program (Nelson, 1981). Some schools and districts opt for using reading committees with representatives from each of these areas. Their job is to initiate, improve, extend, or evaluate reading programs (Early & Sawyer, 1984).

Each participant in the planning process serves an important function. Reading specialists gather information about the needs unique to students and staff in their own building. Reading coordinators provide consistent support for those in different buildings, and they facilitate communication among administrators and other planning staff. It is especially desirable to involve content-area teachers representing all subjects, in order to avoid the misconception that reading is isolated from the rest of the curriculum. Pay special attention to ways of developing interdisciplinary teams responsible for decisions about remedial and content-area reading. Though it is unreasonable to expect the content-area teacher to conduct remediation, she or he needs to participate in developing a relationship between the remedial and content-area curriculum.

Without administrative support, chances for building a reading program can be severely limited. In one school district, a content-reading program developed outside the regular framework for staff development. This effort began with content-area teachers and reading coordinators who participated in the program based on the strength of their own commitment. Building-level administrators, believing in the objectives of the program, began to reward the participants with release time. As the program became popular, more and more teachers volunteered to participate. District-level administrators eventually killed the program, however, when they learned that an unofficial staff development program was using up district resources. Planning that took into account the need for administrative awareness as well as ownership over the program could have avoided this problem (Whitford, 1987).

2. *Base your program on clear goals for the role reading should play in what and how students learn in your building.*

Arriving at these goals requires both a research and a classroom perspective. For middle schools, developing a research base may involve gathering information about how reading contributes to the personal development of the early adolescent. Junior high programs might focus on how reading is used to help students become independent learners, especially in their academic subjects.

Any examination of research on middle school and junior high reading programs should be balanced by a study of the unique needs and constraints of classrooms in your school or district. Doing this requires a needs assessment and then a careful consideration of existing needs in relation to types of programs and available resources. This examination should help middle schools and junior highs alike, not only to design and clarify program goals but also to avoid the pitfalls of overly stressing academics or students' personal and social development.

3. *Use reading materials and instruction, even for remedial and corrective programs, that emphasize success and independence with students' own content-area textbooks.*

Reading kits and workbooks divorced from the rest of the curriculum do not encourage this kind of success. Instead, students need to learn specific reading strategies *while* they are learning content in their other classes. These strategies should help students unlock meaning not only for the immediate lesson but also in other situations that require independent reading. Vacca (1977) offers several recommendations for helping students to master content while they simultaneously learn to use reading as a functional, thinking process in the content-area classroom. Vacca (1977) states that reading instruction should

- Encourage students to relate their experiences to their reading
- Help students consider what they already know about what they are going to learn
- Set clear purposes for reading
- Offer students opportunities to discuss their reading
- Pose problems and encourage different interpretations
- Involve questions that require thinking rather than recall

Techniques that are consistent with these recommendations focus on comprehension, reasoning, and vocabulary development and emphasize independence. Study guides, like the one in Figure 5.1, can be used to facilitate independent comprehension on a personal level. For example, knowing how fractions and decimals are sometimes used interchangeably to mislead can help students become wary consumers.

4. *Integrate guided reading strategies with whole-class and small-group discussions.*
In classroom discussions, teachers and students share ideas that help them construct meaning and think about the content. Teachers, however, need to know how to conduct discussions that are responsive to students' needs during instruction (Conley, 1987). Otherwise, study guides or other approaches to guided reading become no better than a teacher's manual that replaces rather than supports effective classroom decisions.

To avoid this problem, teachers must be sensitive to the need to phase in greater sophistication and student responsibility during discussions (Pearson & Gallagher, 1983). Early in a lesson, teachers must be able to recognize when students have misconceptions that could interfere with the concepts they are required to learn. Teachers must be capable of providing alternative explanations and model processes necessary for students to grasp the content. In addition, they must be able to verify that students are understanding the content and processes important in the lesson. Finally, students need opportunities to practice and apply new concepts. Using whole-class and small-group discussions as part of this phasing-in of student responsibility is one way for teachers to guide students toward greater independence.

5. *Plan reading programs so that they are implemented over long periods of time.*
This approach is essential, first because of the organization of the junior high and second because of the natural reluctance of content-area teachers to participate in reading programs. Junior high faculties that thrive on departmentalization are naturally resistant if content reading is presented without a concern for the uniqueness of each subject area. Planning should focus on eventually breaking down the departmentalization and isolation of reading, gradually implementing programs intended to assist readers throughout the school. Teachers who participate in any program should be volunteers. Many middle school and junior high reading programs that fail do so because programs have been thrust on content-area teachers who are not ready for them. When this occurs, remedial and corrective programs can become dumping grounds for problem students or students who experience difficulty interacting with others in the regular classroom.

The complexity involved in implementing content-reading strategies in the classroom is yet another argument for taking a long-term approach to developing reading programs in the middle school or junior high. In one school district, a content-reading program was built over a three-year period. In the first year, content-area teachers learned how to implement content-reading approaches like those described in this chapter. In the second year, teachers refined their understanding by reviewing concepts, focusing on classroom implementation, and designing curriculum units. In the third year, teachers were given the opportunity to help other teachers learn about content reading. At the end of the third year, content-area teachers had acquired considerable expertise in adapting content reading to the specific needs of their students (Conley, 1986).

Approaches to reading program development should be both long-term and continuous. Middle schools and junior highs are faced with changing expectations about the best ways to meet the needs of students at that level (Hargreaves, 1986). An ongoing analysis of the reading needs of the early adolescent reader in relation to the organization and the resources of the middle school and junior high can contribute substantially toward meeting those expectations.

CONCLUSION

While the current structure of middle schools and junior highs is due mostly to changes in population or just the desire for change, goals have emerged that make middle schools and junior highs truly distinct. In particular, the middle school emphasizes the whole student while the junior high focuses on preparation for success in later academic subjects. Within each view, reading holds a special place. Designed appropriately, remedial and corrective programs offer students a chance both to build and to refine skills in ways that directly influence their success in the content-area classroom. Content-area teachers can apply strategies that simultaneously teach students content and the attitudes and processes necessary for lifelong learning. Reading programs that are both sensitive to the needs of the early adolescent and responsive to the changing organization of middle schools and junior highs stand the best chance of fostering achievement.

REFERENCES

Aulls, M. (1978). *Developmental and remedial reading in the middle grades*. Boston: Allyn and Bacon.

Conley, M. (1986). The influence of training in three teachers' comprehension questions during content area lessons. *Elementary School Journal, 87*(1), 17–28.

Conley, M. (1987). Teacher decisionmaking. In D. Alvermann, D. Moore, & M.

Conley (Eds.), *Research within reach: Secondary school reading* (pp. 142–152). Newark, DE: International Reading Association.

Conley, M. (in press). *Content reading instruction: A communication approach.* New York: Random House.

Cooper, C., & Petrosky, A. (1976). A psycholinguistic view of the fluent reading process. *Journal of Reading, 20,* 184–207.

Duffy, G., & Roehler, L. (1986). *Improving classroom reading instruction: A decision-making approach.* New York: Random House.

Early, M., & Sawyer, D. (1984). *Reading to learn in grades 5 to 12.* New York: Harcourt Brace Jovanovich.

George, P., & Oldaker, L. (1986). A national survey of middle school effectiveness. *Educational Leadership, 43*(4), 79–85.

Greenlaw, M., & Moore, D. (1982). What kinds of reading courses are taught in junior and senior high school? *Journal of Reading, 25,* 534–536.

Hargreaves, A. (1986). *Two cultures of schooling: The case of the middle schools.* New York: Falmer Press.

Herber, H. (1978). *Teaching reading in content areas.* Englewood Cliffs, NJ: Prentice-Hall.

Karlin, R. (1984). *Teaching reading in the high school.* Philadelphia: Harper & Row.

Lipsitz, J. (1984). *Successful schools for young adolescents.* New Brunswick, NJ: Transaction Books.

National Association of Secondary School Principals. (1985). *An agenda for excellence at the middle level.* Reston, VA: National Association of Secondary School Principals.

Nelson, J. (1981). *A staff development program for teaching reading in content areas.* Binghamton, NY: A Network of Secondary School Demonstration Centers for Teaching Reading in Content Areas.

Nelson, J., & Herber, H. (1982). Organization and management of programs. In A. Berger & H. A. Robinson (Eds.), *Secondary school reading: What research reveals for classroom practice* (pp. 143–158). Urbana, IL: ERIC Clearinghouse on Reading and Communication Skills and the National Conference on Research in English.

Pearson, P., & Gallagher, M. (1983). The instruction of reading comprehension. *Contemporary Educational Psychology, 8,* 317–344.

Peeler, T. (1974). The middle school: A historical frame of reference. In G. Duffy (Ed.), *Reading in the middle school* (pp. 7–15). Newark, DE: International Reading Association.

Raphael, T. (1984). Teaching learners about sources of information for answering comprehension questions. *Journal of Reading, 27,* 303–311.

Ratekin, N., Simpson, M., Alvermann, D., & Dishner, E. (1985). Why teachers resist content reading instruction. *Journal of Reading, 28,* 432–437.

Roehler, L., & Duffy, G. (in press). The content area teacher's instructional role: A cognitive mediational view. In J. Flood & D. Lapp (Eds.), *Instructional theory and practice for content area reading and learning.* Newark, DE: International Reading Association.

Singer, H., & Donlan, D. (1980). *Reading and learning from text*. Boston: Little, Brown.

Thurber, J. (1965). The secret life of Walter Mitty. In R. Pooley, A. Grommon, V. Lowers, & O. Niles (Eds.), *Accent: USA* (pp. 242–247). Glenview, IL: Scott, Foresman.

Vacca, R. (1977). Reading comprehension in the middle school. *Middle School Journal*, 8(3), 12–13.

Whitford, B. (1987). Effects of organizational context on program implementation. In W. T. Pink & G. W. Noblit (Eds.), *Schooling in social context: Qualitative studies* (pp. 83–104). Norwood, NJ: Ablex.

Wiles, J., & Biondi, J. (1981). *The essential middle school*. Columbus, OH: Charles E. Merrill.

6 High School Literacy Programs

RICHARD T. VACCA
LEE WILLIAMS
Kent State University

There is major construction on a rural but busy road just outside of Kent, Ohio, that has caused traffic to come to a complete standstill during the morning and evening rush hours. Construction crews brought in huge machinery and demolished the roadbed and the concrete bridge over a fast-moving creek. The roadway, including the narrow, curving bridge, was being straightened. Although straightening the approach road and the bridge made a great deal of sense, we couldn't help but wonder why the road and bridge had been built with such a dangerous curve in the first place. About 20 years ago, the bridge had been wooden, but the concrete bridge replaced the wooden bridge in exactly the same place. Why had a bridge been built there in the first place? A local historian provided an answer to our questions.

"When the roads around here were still dirt roads," he told us, "that was a popular place to drive livestock across the creek. The current was slow there and it was relatively shallow. When roads were finally paved, they followed the original dirt roads so as not to disturb houses and property lines."

New methods of transportation made crossing creeks at spots where the current was slow obsolete, but tradition and pragmatics put a bridge in a place that was actually more, rather than less, dangerous for automobiles. When the roadway was finally reengineered, it entailed an expensive and disruptive rerouting of traffic, with months of construction expense, and tried the patience of motorists as well.

Old habits that are no longer productive, that no longer make sense in terms of changed needs, often continue to drive secondary school reading programs as well. As with a reengineered roadway, changing the way schools respond to students' literacy learning seem disruptive and expensive. Herber and Nelson (1982) report that secondary reading programs often exist because of pragmatics and tradition, not because of the real needs of students. Yet some secondary reading programs are indeed changing in the same kinds of fundamental, direction-changing manner as the rebuilt bridge. In order to understand the nature of such change, it is necessary to examine the history of secondary reading programs and the manner in which research in psycholinguistics, sociolinguistics, cognitive psychology, composition, and literary theory have contributed to our understanding of how students learn as well as what it means to become literate.

HIGH SCHOOL READING AND WRITING PROGRAMS AS THEY WERE

Secondary school reading and writing programs 30 years ago were not so different from most high school programs today. Thinking back to our own high school days, we can remember secondary schools pretty much as they still exist. Instruction was departmentalized by discipline. Fifty-minute-long class periods in a subject were signaled by the ringing of the bell, the 3-minute run through the hallway, the slamming of locker doors, and quick conversations with friends on the way to the next 50-minute class period in another subject area. The reading and composition program were probably outlined in the curriculum plan that was sitting on a dust-covered shelf in the office, and were probably designed to serve a few students in special programs.

In most cases, the high school reading curriculum was characterized by the following three components:

1. *Developmental:* For students near, at, or above grade level in reading, where instruction took place in regular classroom settings.
2. *Corrective:* For students below grade level who were capable of reading effectively if provided with instructional assistance from the classroom teacher within the regular classroom setting, or from the reading teacher in the regular classroom setting.
3. *Remedial:* For students who needed concentrated assistance from a reading specialist in a laboratory setting.

Remedial work in reading and writing focused around a medical metaphor — students who had a language illness, who were deficient in reading and writing, went to the laboratory for intervention and treatment. By looking at the students' symptoms (slow reading? poor comprehension? error-laden writing?) the specialist could diagnose the problem, prescribe a treatment (usually worksheets or drill on isolated reading or writing skills), and effect a cure (Pemberton, 1992). The secondary writing program consisted mostly of compositions assigned in English class without much instruction; these were often returned to their writers bleeding with red ink where punctuation was missed, spelling was incorrect, or words were used that didn't fit the teacher's expectations for school writing.

In the 1960s and 1970s, content-area reading — the idea that reading could not be approached separately from the content material of the subjects requiring reading — was touted as the way to reach all students who needed instructional support in using reading to learn. The phrase "every teacher a teacher of reading" was well-known. It was believed that content-area teachers could best help students master the vocabulary, comprehension strategies, and study skills necessary to master that particular discipline. However, most content-area teachers misunderstood what it meant to be "a teacher of reading," believing that the skills for reading were best taught by reading teachers. Content-area teachers did not feel prepared to undertake the kinds of teaching that would enable students to be proficient readers in their disciplines.

Another literacy idea that was frequently incorporated into the planned curriculum of a district's program in the 1960s and 1970s was the idea of writing across the curriculum. Writing to learn in every subject, not just English, was proposed as a way to increase understanding in content areas. Yet for the most part, teachers believed it was their job to teach students *what* to know, not *how* to know. It was the job of the elementary school, so the reasoning went, to teach students how to read, and the job of the English teacher to teach them how to write. High school teachers then, as now, were resistant to the notion of teaching reading strategies and assigning writing to learn. Deep-seated beliefs of secondary teachers and the practices of secondary schools contributed to teachers' reluctance.

Even if content-area reading and writing were a part of the stated curriculum of the school, the institutional practices that supported high school teachers worked at cross-purposes to instruction that focused on how to read to learn. In high schools, the number of students that each teacher sees in a day, the organization of subject matter specialties into departments, and the segregation of reading and writing to English classes all contribute to secondary teachers' belief that their job is to teach content only. So while literacy activities may have existed in the planned curriculum, they were realized in practice in only a very few classrooms. Most of us do not have knowledge of reading programs from our own secondary schools that focused on literacy within the content-area subjects themselves.

What were the students' actual experiences with the reading and writing curriculum? For the most part, high school reading was an assignment in a content-area textbook, consisting of questions to be answered or a quiz to be taken to "prove" that the reading had been accomplished, and a class lecture or recitation the next day to make sure that the students had "grasped" the essential concepts in the reading. Students learned to read narrowly in order to answer questions, or not to read at all, since the important concepts would be covered during class. School reading for many students became purposeless and passive. As Bintz (1993) notes, students usually become "resistant readers," separating the strategies they use for out-of-school reading from strategies they use for school reading. Writing was judged as much by the number of errors the teacher found as it was by the meaning it conveyed. Such focus on the products of literacy, rather than the process of literacy, was common in high schools in the past. Unfortunately, it still is.

CHANGING PARADIGMS OF TEACHING AND LEARNING

Implicit in the assumptions of those high school teachers who resisted integrating reading to learn with learning content is a model of teaching and knowing that has been called the *transmission model* (Pahl & Monson, 1992). The transmission model is associated with a paradigm of instruction that can be considered subject-centered; that is, it organizes itself according to a worldview that considers the subject as the most essential aspect of learning (see Chapter 12).

The idea that ways of understanding the world (worldviews) in a discipline can be described as paradigms was introduced in 1942 by S. C. Pepper. It was popularized by Thomas Kuhn's (1970) description of the ordering of the discipline of science in his book *The Structure of Scientific Revolutions*. During the past century or so in American education, the dominant worldviews in education have fluctuated between a subject-centered emphasis, associated with the transmission or accommodation model of education, and a student-centered emphasis, associated with discovery and activity-oriented learning, modifying the content and presentation of the lesson so that the student will be able to understand the teacher's message.

The student-centered paradigm is more common in elementary classrooms, where hands-on activities may be designed to accommodate concrete learners who need direct experience to learn, or lesson sequences may be slowed to accommodate slower learners. However, even in an *accommodation model*, the emphasis is still on knowing as factual, on reading as finding the meaning that resides in the text.

A third paradigm in education is one that explains learning not as subject- or child-centered, but rather as meaning-centered. How learners make meaning and teachers interact with subject matter or with texts in a manner that changes both the known and the knowing is not an accommodation model or transmission model of teaching, but rather a *transactional model*. Grounded in theory and research from various disciplines (including linguistics, cognitive psychology, and child development), the educational paradigm that focuses on meaning as the core of learning is known as *whole language*.

Whole language "happened," so to speak, when teachers looking at the dangerous curve in the roadway saw that the bridge was in the wrong place. Learning isn't about transmitting truth to students, but about creating meaning. High school reading programs that focus on literacy as a way to know and make sense of the world in specific contexts or communities move the bridge so that it aligns with the road. Such reading programs must often involve a fundamental change in teachers' beliefs about what it means to learn, to teach, and to be literate.

The tenets of whole language — that students are active participants in creating their own learning by creating bridges (with teacher help) from what they already know (their prior knowledge) to what they are learning; that language is learned in social contexts, where it is used to make meaning; that affect (or subjective response) contributes to how we know the world, as does cognitive response; that literacy is not a skill that a student has, but a set of responses and strategies functioning to make meaning — are instrumental for constructing a reading program in secondary schools that makes use of what we know about literacy and learning instead of retaining a program that follows the old path because it feels comfortable and easy (Vacca & Vacca, 1993).

WHOLE LANGUAGE IN HIGH SCHOOL PROGRAMS

Barbara King-Shaver (1991), a high school English and reading teacher who has changed her classroom and teaching from traditional transmission of knowledge to whole language, notes that whole language for most people brings to mind a nonbasal reading program in the elementary school. However, she reminds us that whole language is not about materials and methods, but rather is a set of beliefs based on theory and research about how language is learned and used and how it might best be taught. Since language is the essential element for learning at the secondary and college levels as well as the elementary level, whole language has important implications for teachers and learners in every grade.

The fields of psycholinguisitics, sociology, anthropology, cognitive psychology, child development, composition, and literary theory have all contributed to our understanding of what it means to learn language and to be literate. Some of the essential beliefs of whole language teachers at the secondary level are:

1. *Connectedness is essential to learning and knowing.* Richard Prawat (1992) notes that constructivists have heightened our awareness that connection is an integral aspect of knowledge acquisition and use. Research supports cognitive structures consisting of associations (connections) among elements of knowledge. The primary difference between novice and expert practitioners, it seems, is the ability to see the big ideas in a field and how all the elements fit together.

2. *Context is essential to learning.* There is a special type of connectedness between knowledge and context. Using knowledge contributes to understanding; the situation becomes an essential element of knowing about a skill or concept (Brown, Collins, & Duguid, 1989). Brown et al. acknowledge that most real-world knowledge occurs naturally through a process of enculturation rather than through the learning of isolated skills.

3. *Learning is social.* Learners need to participate in a culture that provides a context for authentic activity, giving them a way of interpreting reality that is consistent with the cultural norms of the group (or the discipline).

4. *Learning is best accomplished when the environment for learning is supportive and encouraging of risk-taking.* Approximations toward proficiency are expected and encouraged in whole language classrooms. However, teachers as well as students need the time and encouragement to be experimental and self-reflective on their way to expert status. Interacting with the unknown takes both cognitive and physical energy, and a sense that missteps won't be punished with red ink.

5. *Knowledge is transactional.* The work of Lev Vygotsky (1978) in child development and Louise Rosenblatt (1982) in reading response theory and the research by cognitive scientists have explained that the influence of the interactions between teacher and student, as well as reader and text, cannot be separated in principle or reality. Meaning is what we construct for ourselves out of our experiences.

GOOD TEACHING AND GOOD LEARNING: THE CORNERSTONES OF SECONDARY LITERACY PROGRAMS

In the past, organizing secondary reading programs was like building a road over the creek where it was shallow. New research and understanding of reading and learning call for a reading program that helps all students transact with concepts and textbooks in order to read and write to learn. But moving the road so that classrooms reflect the whole language paradigm is not easy. In whole language classrooms, the roles of the teacher and the students are very different from their expected roles in traditional classrooms. Teachers can no longer assign reading, tell students unproblematic facts, and test them on their recall.

The job of teachers today is to be responsive to students' search for meaning, to decide what ideas have disciplinary (related to the content area) as well as pedagogical value. There is no rubber-stamped, always-appropriate recipe for successful teaching, but there are several guidelines for reading instruction in every classroom. These guidelines foster the students' ability to construct meaning and emphasize the contextual, social nature of learning in the classroom as a community of readers and learners.

What we know about language and learning forms the basis for reading instruction in any classroom, whether the learners are proficient or not. In fact, as early as 1979, Otto noted that although little research on secondary remedial reading existed, it pointed out the benefits of a whole language approach. Two main characteristics identified such classrooms. One, the teacher immersed students in an environment that encouraged meaning-making and response with both reading and writing; and two, sharing and collaboration make the classroom a learning community.

The high school literacy teacher's most important role is to encourage an active response to reading, creating a classroom community where readers and learners support each other in the making of meaning with text. Teachers in response-based classrooms are instrumental in encouraging students to make connections, modeling for them appropriate strategies for comprehension and helping students to examine their own processes for making meaning. By examining how they come to know something, students take responsibility for their own meaning.

This kind of classroom looks very different from traditional classrooms based on the transmission model of learning. Teachers are no longer center stage, telling and testing. Response journals and learning logs, trade books in the content areas, collaborative inquiry projects, and shared reading can be found in all content areas that are based on whole language principles. Students are active meaning-makers, responsible for constructing their own learning with teacher guidance. Classroom talk among peers or with the teacher provides support and guidance to students as they strategically attempt to create meaning about important concepts in content areas.

VISIBLE AND INVISIBLE LITERACY PROGRAMS

When the paradigm that organizes classroom instruction is whole language and reading and writing to learn occurs in all classrooms as described above, the secondary school reading program is largely invisible. Like the steel beams that undergird our newly straightened bridge, reading instruction is an invisible but absolutely essential component of all instruction. In effective secondary reading programs, all students are recognized as having reading instruction needs, and instruction is integrated with the reasoning strategies that ground each discipline. Unlike traditional reading instruction, which offers highly visible reading programs to a relative few students who are deemed deficient, reading and writing taught in the content areas are not readily seen.

In traditional secondary school reading programs, students who do not make smooth transitions from learning to read to reading to learn are considered to need more instruction in learning to read, the same type of instruction they had in elementary school. Teachers often assume that students have not mastered the basic decoding skills or basic comprehension strategies (Noden & Vacca, 1994).

Secondary reading is complex. Students who read well at the elementary level often exhibit a loss in "the skill and the will" (Paris, Lipson, & Wixson, 1983). Students who exhibit resistance or avoidance of school reading often read avidly out of school, employing note-taking strategies to remember information, rereading favorite books or articles, and sharing insights about their reading with friends and family members (Bintz, 1993). Yet teachers often see these same students as nonreaders or dysfunctional readers who don't know how to read effectively. Secondary readers exhibit resistance to school reading that, while it may not hurt their grades in classrooms where the teacher tells and tests, is counterproductive in the long run because it hurts their ability to read and learn with content-area textbooks. These readers may need reading instruction, but it certainly isn't more of the skill-and-drill testing that forms the backbone of traditional secondary reading programs.

All too often, the visible reading program in the secondary school is the only reading program. It often consists of a reading or writing lab, a place for deficient students to be fixed, where problems can be diagnosed and corrected apart from any learning context. Expensive and arcane equipment, tachistoscopes, controlled readers, computer tutorials, and isolated skill-and-drill workbooks form the centerpieces of these labs, often to the pride of the administration and the staff. These programs, giving students instruction that they don't need in isolated, basic skills, mask the need for an integrated, invisible reading and writing to learn program in all classrooms.

But when the visible literacy program is NOT the entire program, but rather exists to support and serve the invisible program, then it has an appropriate and important place in the secondary reading program as a whole. A wonderful example of a visible aspect of the literacy program that functions as an adjunct to the invisible program is the middle school and high school writing center. Once rare occurrences, these centers are finding a place in more and more school districts, providing a place where students can write to learn how to write, and where they can get assistance in various stages of the writing process in a friendly, low-risk environment (Wright, 1993).

In traditional classrooms, writing is most often a display of knowledge in which the teacher judges its worth based on the number of errors. However, Spandel and Stiggins (1990) found that student writing improves when teachers stop focusing on errors and correction and respond instead to the what and the how of students' attempts at meaning. When a literacy program incorporates writing to learn, the writing center provides an integral service to students, teachers, and even parents.

Writing centers, if they are truly effective, not only work with students who have writing assignments in progress, but become the center for school-based writing activity. James Upton (1990) describes his school's writing center, which publishes the student literary magazine, has a book swap area, is a clearinghouse for writing contests, assists teachers with writing to learn assignments, supports collaboration among teachers, has parent/student study skills nights, and invites parents to sessions explaining how to work on college entrance essays.

WORKING TO CHANGE SECONDARY LITERACY PROGRAMS

When reading and writing to learn are fully integrated into content-area courses, teachers are no longer disseminators of information and skills. The majority of the research on how teachers begin to implement whole language has been conducted in elementary classrooms, where whole language is often embraced districtwide for younger readers. But secondary teachers do have success with whole language programs, and the reading specialist can play an important role in the transitions teachers make.

The factors associated with implementing reading programs and with staff development procedures are addressed in detail in other chapters in this book. But it is important for the person who wants to develop a new reading program at the secondary level to be aware of some of the specific dynamics of change that occur in middle and junior and senior high schools.

First, the organizational structure of secondary schools works at cross-purposes to changing reading programs across the board. Yet with the proper support, individual teachers who think critically and reflectively about their instruction and instructional alternatives can make important transformations in the way they understand and practice teaching (Vacca & Vacca, 1993).

Second, a key element in the success and substance of any new program is the support and positive attitude of a caring principal (Danehower, 1993). Administrative support is essential in encouraging participation in workshops and inservices; allocating time, resources, and materials that are crucial to a program's success; and taking an active approach in the solving of implementation problems that may occur.

Finally, successful implementation of any curriculum change takes time. During the transition phase, teachers who are unaccustomed to feeling uncomfortable with their role in the classroom, and who are unused to not knowing where the classroom interactions are heading, may want to return to a more comfortable "tell and test" mode of teaching. But just as the classroom must become a learning community for the students, so must the whole language school become a learning community for teachers.

The separateness and time constraints that often characterize secondary schools must be replaced by a schoolwide system of support for teachers who are experimenting with new ways of teaching. Sharing insights, reflections, suggestions, failures, and successes is a hallmark of successful programs.

THE YEAR 2000: WHAT LIES AHEAD?

It's not easy to be optimistic about the secondary schools of the future, given all the bad press about secondary schools today. But the time seems right for changes in the way we approach teaching and learning at all grade levels. Whole language and constructivist teaching have a head start in the elementary schools, but caring teachers in the secondary schools are reflecting on their teaching practices and their students and deciding that a transformation is in order.

Our students will not need megabytes of discrete information (computers will probably store all the bytes they'll need and provide rapid access to it as well), but they will need to be curious, to define and explore which issues are the important ones, and find a common ground. The best news, though, is that the kinds of classrooms that reflect best practice, the response-based, collaborative, and transactional classrooms that help our students construct meaning and manipulate it in the context of each discipline, will send them out into the 21st century not only equipped for the workplace, but personally and culturally empowered.

Teachers in these kinds of classrooms are empowered, too, making their own decisions on what to teach their students, how to teach them, and why to teach them. The new literacy for the next century is not about techniques, or methods, or content. Rather, secondary school literacy in the future is less about what is on the page and more about what is beyond the page, and about how we come to understand our opinions and make meaning in a complex society. The next century requires us to straighten out our roadways.

REFERENCES

Bintz, W. P. (1993). Resistant readers in secondary education: Some insights and implications. *Journal of Reading, 36*(8), 604–615.

Brown, J., Collins, A., & Duguid, P. (1989). Situated cognition and the culture of learning. *Educational Researcher, 18*(1), 32–42.

Danehower, V. (1993). Understanding the change process. *Schools in the Middle, 2*(4), 45–46.

Herber, H. L., & Nelson, J. (1982). Organization and management of programs. In A. Berger & H. R. Robinson (Eds.), *Secondary school reading: What research reveals for practice.* Urbana, IL: ERIC Clearinghouse on Reading and Communication Skills and National Conference on Research in English.

King-Shaver, B. (1991). Whole language: Implications for secondary classrooms. *English Leadership, 13*(1), 4–5.

Kuhn, T. (1970). *The structure of scientific revolutions.* Chicago: University of Chicago Press.

Noden, H., & Vacca, R. T. (1994). *Whole language in middle and secondary classrooms.* New York: HarperCollins.

Otto, J. (1979). A critical review of approaches to remedial reading for adolescents. *Journal of Reading, 23*(3), 244–250.

Pahl, M., & Monson, R. (1992). In search of whole language: Transforming curriculum and instruction. *Journal of Reading, 35*(7), 518–534.

Paris, S., Lipson, G., & Wixson, K. (1983). Becoming a strategic reader. *Contemporary Educational Psychology, 8*(3), 293–316.

Pemberton, M. (1992). The prison, the hospital, the madhouse: Redefining metaphors for the writing center. *Writing Lab Newsletter, 17*(1), 11–16.

Pepper, S. C. (1942). *World hypotheses: A study in evidence.* Berkeley, CA: University of California Press.

Prawat, R. (1992). Teachers' beliefs about teaching and learning: A constructivist perspective. *American Journal of Education, 100*(3), 354–395.

Rosenblatt, L. (1982). The literacy transaction: Evocation and response. *Theory into Practice, 21,* 268–277.

Spandel, V., & Stiggins, R. J. (1990). *Creating writers.* New York: Longman.

Upton, J. (1990). Expanding services of the high school writing center. *Writing Lab Newsletter, 15*(1), 6–7.

Vacca, R. T., & Vacca, J. L. (1993). *Content area reading* (4th ed.). New York: HarperCollins.

Vygotsky, L. (1978). *Mind in society.* Cambridge: Harvard University Press.

Wright, A. (1993). Establishing a high school writing lab. *Writing Lab Newsletter, 17*(5), 4–6.

Part III

PROGRAM IMPLEMENTATION AND EVALUATION

As discussed in Part II, a multiplicity of factors contribute to sound, effective reading program development. The collaborative efforts of administrators and teachers to (1) select and use appropriate materials, (2) evaluate teachers' instructional practices, (3) participate in staff development, (4) assess students' progress with instruction, and (5) reach out to the community to represent the strides that need to be taken during program implementation. This part of the book provides guidelines for these five critical areas.

Chapter 7 helps administrators and teachers to understand the criteria and processes needed to select basals and trade books that are well suited to students' needs. Under the assumption that teachers are making decisions to create child-centered classrooms, Chapter 8 provides guidelines on how to observe and give feedback to teachers in the context of the total teaching/learning environment. Chapter 9 sets forth ideas and provides guidelines for negotiating changes in staff development so that it involves both administrators and teachers. Chapter 10 discusses changes in large-scale and local assessment practices, and how these changes are impacting on instructional reform. Chapter 11, the last chapter in this part, offers models for reaching out to urban and suburban parents about their children's literacy instruction.

This part of the book helps educational leaders to fine-tune previous programmatic efforts in order to provide the best possible instructional programs.

7 A New Look at the Materials Selection Process

JOAN T. FEELEY
CAROLE S. RHODES
William Paterson College of New Jersey

A growing network of teachers who were experimenting with teaching writing as process and reading through literature rather than through basal materials ended up becoming the materials selection committee in a suburban K-6 district in New Jersey. Having already engaged in developing a writing curriculum, they were crafting an expanded, integrated reading/writing curriculum that would allow teachers to choose either trade books or a combination of trade books and basals for their literacy program when they were asked to seek a replacement for the district's outmoded, decade-old basal.

Rather than avoid the task (since most of them would not be using the basal), the Reading-Writing Committee assumed the responsibility of selecting a basal so that they could get other teachers involved in staff development and a search for a basal that would best fit in with their emerging literature-based, holistic curriculum. Under the leadership of the principal of one of the district's two elementary schools (who also served as Language Arts Coordinator), the 15- to 20-member committee met regularly to orchestrate the staff development and adoption process.

Over the course of a year and a half, monthly workshops on language, literacy, literature, and learning given to the entire staff by outside experts and network members were interspersed with presentations by publishers' representatives. Everyone was gaining a broader view and, consequently, was able to look at basal materials with an informed view of how literacy develops. Finally, the choice was narrowed to two of the newer literature-based basals; next the committee had to look closely to see which one best met the adoption criteria that had evolved through the staff development/screening process.

The criteria for selecting a basal were listed on a checklist, with the areas to be considered showing how successful the committee had been in their staff development efforts. Five broad concerns were addressed, with questions to be answered for each. A sampling follows:

Philosophy of the Basal

- Did it integrate reading/writing/thinking?
- Did it encourage reading for enjoyment?
- Was it based on current research?

Content of the Student Text

- Was there a variety of real, unabridged literature by recognized authors and illustrators?
- Were selections grouped by authentic themes?
- Were predicting and thinking encouraged?

Workbook

- Were activities related to text selections?
- Were instructions and examples clear enough to foster student independence?
- Were subskills taught in meaningful context?

Teacher Manuals

- Did they encourage teachers to use pre-, post-, and during-reading strategies?

- Did activities require higher levels of thinking?
- Was skill development context-based?

Supplementary Materials

- Were there big book and trade book lists to accompany selections?
- Were the assessment tools more than subskill tests?
- Was there useful software?

Next followed a yearlong pilot test of the two basals, with both being tried out in two classes on the primary, mid-elementary, and upper grade levels. The six teachers involved in the pilot test met monthly with the Reading-Writing Committee (some were members) and with grade-level peers to encourage wide participation. The Committee used the basal materials and input from the pilot teachers to apply the criteria that had been developed.

The Language Arts Coordinator/Principal who was leading the whole search tried to attend all meetings and remain impartial. She made it clear from the beginning that no matter which basal was chosen, teachers would have the option of using components of the basal plus trade books or trade books alone. There was a strong message from the superintendent, who attended selected meetings, that he supported the choice of materials as long as the eventually agreed upon literacy curriculum was being followed. He also made clear his lack of enthusiasm for disposable workbooks. "If you choose the basal and feel that you absolutely need the workbook in the first year, go ahead and order it. But I would hope in the future that you will be able to use the workbook money to purchase trade books to implement our new literature-based curriculum," he announced. "Furthermore," he added, "it makes much more sense to have kids responding to reading in notebooks that can be reviewed than on throwaway worksheets."

After the yearlong pilot test, many meetings, and the completion of the checklists by the pilot teachers and committee members, the final decision was made by the Reading-Writing Committee. The district now has a new basal series for those teachers who want to use it with trade books, but they are encouraged to purchase only those components that they feel they really need.

*   *   *

One principal, new to an urban K-5 school with a diverse student population, found a common situation: while the primary teachers had abandoned basals and were teaching reading and writing together through big books, poems, songs, and Language Experience Approach (LEA) charts, the teachers in grades three to five, with one exception, were still hanging on to one of the older basals. The principal, who had been a staff developer for writing and literature-based reading in his former district, decided to meet regularly with the middle grade teachers to see if he could begin to bridge the gap between the two levels.

The meetings were held monthly (he provided lunch) and were conducted in a workshop fashion, with teachers coming prepared to discuss articles that had been circulated. The one teacher already using only trade books with her fourth-graders often demonstrated how she set up reading pairs or groups and encouraged response through discussions and logs.

Early on, the principal suggested that they set goals for their literacy program. All agreed that they wanted to develop students who were real readers, who read both at home and in school, and who could talk and write about their books. They further agreed that most of their students were not real readers who could discuss authors and genres, perhaps because they were reading only basals and school texts and doing the limited-response activities that were suggested in the teachers' manuals.

Soon the principal became aware of two major problems: The teachers did not know authors and titles of childrens' books and did not know how to work with literature in the classroom. The former concern was met by having the librarian and resource center teacher bring in books to share and circulate at each session; the latter was handled by the principal modeling with a book they read together. The teachers met in literature circles, kept response logs, and shared mini-lessons on story webs, character profiles, and "sketch to stretch" postreading art activities. They even began to draft a handbook of strategies to implement literature in the classroom. Eventually, the principal established a part-time staff position for the one teacher who had been successfully using literature so that she could visit classrooms to help others get started.

At the end of the school year, the principal had the teachers vote on what materials they would like to order for the next year. He offered them three choices: (1) stay with the basals; (2) go with *Bridges*, Scholastic's literature program for teachers who want to use trade books with a structured approach; or (3) use their emerging handbook for strategies and graded goals and buy all trade books (literature-based approach). All 21 teachers opted for the third choice. The principal then located a vendor who carried a large inventory of children's paperbacks with reinforced covers and arranged for the teachers to browse through the book warehouse to select books they would like to read with their students. By June they had dozens of sets of children's books to use to develop their real readers.

*   *   *

A suburban Long Island school district hired Sue, a consultant, to help with staff development. Sue's job was to foster and facilitate teachers' use of trade books in the primary grades, and to help the teachers as they moved toward whole language classrooms. During their first few weeks together, Sue and the teachers read and talked about trade books. They explored ways in which they could incorporate "real books" into their curriculum.

During the next few weeks, the group explored the reading/writing connection, the writing process, and literature-based instruction. Six of the primary grade teachers collaborated and created thematic units which they decided to implement across their grades. They found trade books that could be used in various grades. The teachers talked about interdisciplinary teaching, and they explored ways to integrate the language arts with math, science, social studies, art, and music. The participants were enthusiastic as they planned the project, one that would involve children in grades one through three. Members of the group elaborated on each other's ideas with excitement, passion, and creativity. They discussed the books to use. The group explored ways to acquire more books and ways to keep abreast of new titles for classroom use.

A subsequent group meeting began informally, as had the earlier sessions. Trade books were brought in and strewn upon the table. The teachers discussed some of the trade books they had recently discovered. Andrea, a second grade teacher, brought in samples of an ad campaign her students had created. After a short while, the discussion changed direction.

Meryl, another teacher, brought up the fact that they had just been given one week to decide which basal reading series their school district would adopt. Bonnie wondered why they had to order a basal series if they really didn't want to use one. She discussed this with her school principal, who told her that "even though we are a whole language district, the administration wants teachers to use basal readers. We must be sure the children are getting the skills in an orderly way." Another teacher took out a "Basal Adoption Checklist" that she had been given by the reading coordinator of the district. The 20-item checklist included 6 about the comprehensiveness and clarity of the teacher's manual. The remaining items were designed to ascertain whether each series included enough tests, phonics practice, and skill-and-drill. No items on the checklist investigated whether the basals included "real stories," nor did any items on the checklist inquire whether any of the reading series connected reading and writing. No items dealt with interdisciplinary themes.

Several problems became evident. There was a lack of congruence between the stated philosophy of the district and the model and means for the selection and use of materials. Teachers were given a mandate regarding the types of reading materials they could use. Exacerbating this situation were the insistence on the use of a checklist that was incompatible with the teachers' beliefs and the short time they were given to select the basal series.

The teachers begrudgingly went through the process, trying to ignore the checklist they were given. With Sue's help, they began to develop their own criteria. A few days before the final selections were to be made, the district reading coordinator met with the group to review criteria. She talked about whole language, literature-based instruction and skills. She reviewed the checklist with the group. The group continued the review process, focusing on the original checklist. They selected a series that most closely matched the skills-oriented checklist they had been given. Literature would be interspersed when time permitted.

*   *   *

As we can see from the above vignettes, materials selection grows out of a district's and school's perception of how children learn to read. Those that view teaching/learning to read as the delivery of carefully sequenced lessons with many reinforcing practice activities look to basals to form the mainstay of their program (the Long Island district). Others such as the urban school that see reading instruction as influential in developing real readers who read both for information and recreation prefer to use only trade books. And then there are districts such as the suburban New Jersey example that permit teachers to use either basals or trade books or a combination thereof. This latter approach seems to be borne out by the latest National Assessment of Educational Progress (NAEP) findings, in which teachers report that 50 percent of the nation's fourth graders receive a heavy emphasis on literature-based reading (*Executive Summary of the NAEP 1992 Reading Report Card for the Nation and the States*, 1993). Since we know that about 90 percent of the schools use basals, the combination approach seems to be the way that many are going.

So, for most, selecting materials still comes down to picking a basal and deciding on what components are really needed, which we will address next. Selecting literature to use with basals or alone will be discussed later.

COMPARING BASALS

Aware of the criticisms about basals expressed in the 1980s — for example, inconsequential, contrived text in the pupil editions (PEs); compendious, prescriptive teachers' manuals (TMs) that belittled teachers' intelligence; and myriads of skill activities in workbooks and practice pads—Hudak-Huelbig et al. (1991) conducted a content analysis of sample stories from the first and fourth grade PEs, TMs, and skills materials found in seven popular basals. Since only the 1989 editions were available, the results would not hold for current editions (which may certainly have been affected by studies like this one), but the process was valuable. It became clear that "all basals are not the same" (Wepner & Feeley, 1993).

Pupil Editions

Since the most important part of any basal is the content of the books the students read, Hudak-Huelbig et al. (1991) looked closely at the sources for the selections. Were they taken from good children's literature? If so, were they excerpted or adapted to fit readability formulas or skill work to be taught through the piece? Or were they created specifically for the basal? On average, more than half of the stories were not literature but simple text created by technicians. Of those PEs with literature (one had all of its selection created), large percentages of the stories, in some cases a third, of the stories were adapted or excerpted. Not one whole piece of literature was found in any book. There was much more original source literature in the fourth grade book. Over 80% came from outside sources. Still, there were no full-length pieces, just excerpts and suggestions in the TMs for other related titles.

Teachers' Manuals

The TMs were very large and cumbersome. For the first grade PEs (books used after the primers), the TMs ran from 368 to 553 pages. For the fourth grade PEs, the manuals went from a low of 672 pages to a whopping 1,035 pages! In language, they tended to be didactic, often putting words into the teachers' mouths: "Now say to the children, 'What do you think this story will be about?' Next, ask them to discuss the picture on p. –.'"

Skill Activities

Hudak-Huelbig et al. (1991) also looked at the amount of skill work students had to do for each selection. They counted the number of pages students read from the PEs (defined as coherent reading) and the number of skill pages that went with them. Generally, first graders could end up doing more than one skill sheet for every page of coherent reading. Fourth graders could end up doing one skill sheet for every one to two pages of coherent reading. In addition, Hudak-Huelbig et al. (1991) counted the number of skills the basals addressed for these two levels. For the first grade, the numbers went from a low of 30 to a high of 98; for the fourth grade, they went from 37 to 130. Clearly, basals can be more or less skill-dominated, and this factor should be considered during the selection process.

Newer Basals

To see if the publishers of the new literature-based basals of the 1990s have addressed these concerns, Gieniec and Westerholt (1994) replicated the work of Hudak-Huelbig et al. (1991), using the last book designed for first grade and the fourth grade book from four basals with copyright dates from 1992 to 1995. Besides perusing the PEs, TMs, and scope and sequence charts, they sampled the activities for the first and last stories in both the first and fourth grade student texts.

Regarding the content of the PEs, Gieniec and Westerholt (1994) found that most of the pieces (84% to 100%) for both levels are reprinted, without being excerpted or adapted from original sources. They are presented under logical themes and represent a variety of genres; often author profiles and pictures accompany their work. Also, there appears to be much more poetry than in past editions. There is virtually no text created specially for the basal in these samples. This appears to be a big and very welcome change from past editions.

Although still weighty, the TMs have also changed. There seems to be a concerted effort by the publishers to make them appear to be less cumbersome. For example, on the fourth grade level, the TMs for one pupil text are usually divided into two volumes. Interestingly, when the teacher-researchers tried to count pages to compare the 1990 versions with the earlier ones, they found the pagination hard to follow because the publishers often use the page numbers from the pupil texts and add un-paged inserts. By doing a hand count of the sample stories, they concluded that there were approximately two pages in the TM for every page in the student text. They also found that the format and language of the TMs have changed. For the most part, after some prereading suggestions, the notes to the teacher appear as marginal glosses around a replica of the pupil page; they are not worded like a script that appears to be putting words into the teacher's mouth.

There is still a heavy emphasis on skills in the current basals. According to the scope and sequence charts, the first grade level covers from 85 to 141 skills; the fourth grade level introduces or reinforces from 95 to 141. Gieniec and Westerholt (1994) found a new cluster of skills emerging called "strategic reading," emphasizing strategies such as ways to figure out unknown words and the study technique known as K-W-L (What do I KNOW? What do I WANT to know? What have I LEARNED?) This trend shows a concern for developing metacomprehension strategies that were loosely addressed in the earlier basals. Still, if teachers did all the suggested skill pages, first graders would be doing approximately one skill page for every PE text page read, and fourth graders would be doing about three pages of skills for every seven pages of coherent reading. These findings are better than the 1989 skills versus coherent reading figures, but they still show that students can be asked to do a great deal of skill work around a basal story.

Two bright spots in the new basals are a greater emphasis on writing and a greater focus on literature appreciation. Most of the new basals have "journals" or separate workbooklike booklets in which students write or draw responses to selections read. These offer prompts and many "frames" or blank spaces with a few lines for children to use. As our teacher-researchers noted, "It would be just as easy and far less expensive to have kids respond in blank notebooks." As for literary appreciation, it is good to see suggestions for genre and author studies and plenty of lists of related trade books, fully referenced for teachers to purchase through the basal publisher or other paperback purveyors.

Assessment Materials

While Hudak-Huelbig et al. (1991) did not look at the assessment components for the basals they analyzed, Gieniec and Westerholt (1994) did examine assessment materials that were sent by some of the basal publishers. These were indeed different from the "management systems" these teacher-researchers remember from their older basals. The new assessment activities mirror the reading and writing activities that the children did in the unit or theme being assessed. For example, if the theme of a unit was folktales, students would read a new, full-length folktale and respond to it in many ways. They might draw or write about a favorite character, answer questions about elements of a folktale, and write about their favorite folktale.

While the new literature-based basals appear "to be wearing new clothes" (Greenlaw, 1990), it's still fair to say that they are not all the same. Some provide spelling booklets to enable them to say that they offer "integrated language arts." For some teachers, this just means more workbook pages. While some basals have more emphasis on writing and literature, others offer more decoding and phonics. All offer a wide variety of components, and purchasing without careful scrutiny can be costly.

GUIDELINES FOR SELECTING BASALS

To help schools select basal materials, we offer the following guidelines:

1. Develop a philosophy and your own literacy curriculum instead of using a scope and sequence chart written by some publisher who may not know your students and district. Reutzel and Cooter (1992) describe a "nonnegotiable" set of skills that schools can use as a backbone for an integrated, literature-based curriculum. Once done, and once you decide that a basal can help you to deliver this curriculum, commence a search to find the one that will best fit your needs.
2. Select a committee of teachers, administrators, and parents to help you in your search. Many schools leave parents out, but they can be very helpful volunteers in the gathering and organizing process. They can also give a special kind of feedback and bring community support to the work of the committee.
3. Look beyond the fancy packaging and confetti and examine the materials carefully. You can do some of the analyses that our teacher-researchers did, such as:

   - Check the content of the pupil text to see if the selections are mainly whole, original text by known authors.
   - Examine the teachers' manual for its suggestions, language, and general usefulness. It is best to go through a few stories to see if you approve of the general approach. Is the lesson structure flexible, representing the latest research? Does it fit into your philosophy?
   - Count the number of skill sheets the manual suggests be done for a few stories; scrutinize the skill work to see if it is related to the story, easy for children to do on their own, and, above all, worth doing. Frank Smith (1985) says that children learn to read by reading and write by writing; therefore, we want them to spend their time mainly on real reading and writing, not on filling out endless skill sheets.
   - Compare the scope and sequence chart with your own "nonnegotiable" list of skills that you have developed for your literacy curriculum.

- Look closely at the assessment components. Do the assessment measures match the teaching materials and structure? For example, after reading a science fiction unit in which they responded in journals and shared responses, are students asked to read a new piece of science fiction and respond to it as they did in their unit study? This response may better assess their concept of the genre.

4. Select components judiciously. You may want to order only the pupil editions and one teachers' manual per grade. While some teachers may want the skill books and journals, others may prefer to have children do skill work and response activities in notebooks. Check on the prices for trade books, since many of these can be purchased less expensively through purveyors that specialize in paperbacks such as Scholastic and Trumpet Books. Cost-effectiveness is always a consideration.
5. Field-test two of your top choices for at least half a year to see which one works best for you and your students. The teachers who pilot the series should meet regularly with the search committee to provide information for both formative evaluation (along the way) and summative evaluation (the final decision).

SELECTING TRADE BOOKS

Administrators and supervisors can provide invaluable support in the implementation, selection, and acquisition process of using trade books in classrooms. Inherent in this role is a recognition of the value of literature-based instruction and a dedication to facilitating its use. Administrators and supervisors can help in this process by encouraging teachers and librarians to work together, by providing resources that help inform teachers and librarians about new trade books, and by providing the monetary support vital to the use of trade books in classrooms.

Children do not necessarily discover great books on their own. Neither do most teachers. There are many resources for teachers and librarians to use in their quest to find good books for children. The selection of books is, to a large measure, contingent upon an awareness of books available. While lists and reviews are helpful, they should serve as guides, not mandates. Those involved in the selection process must read books before recommending them to children. In order to select the most appropriate books for use in classrooms, educators should consider readers' age, interests, and abilities; types of books; curriculum connections; and social and cultural diversity.

The Readers

The selection process should begin with an awareness of the readers. There are no "universally great books" for all children. True, some books tend to be favorites, but it would be rash to conclude that all children would enjoy the same book. Interests vary among children. Children struggling with the plight of inner-city survival may not relate to the same books as those from suburban or rural areas; children interested in science fiction may not enjoy books that are set in Victorian times. After reading the same book, sixth graders in different settings discussed their experiences:

> I don't understand why everyone is so hot on this book. I think people like it just because it's sad and they think that the drama makes it so good. Personally, I think it's kind of boring and unrealistic. What does this have to do with my life or the fact that there are homeless people everywhere I go? What does this mean to me? I want to read about things that are real, that's what I like. I want to read about "now," not some magical island where everything is great, that's just not where I'm at.

> This book was great. It really got to me. Even though I'm a guy, it really hit home, I mean, it's okay for me to like a book that sad. I didn't get all weepy or anything, I just liked the book.

> The book was magical, it was beautiful. I felt like I was in another land along with the characters. It was nice to go someplace where things were so peaceful.

> It was okay. I mean I read it and it wasn't a chore and for me that means it was okay. I usually don't like these kinds of books, but I think the writing was good and it kept my interest. I'd rather read other kinds of books though, more adventure, more excitement, but this was okay.

In selecting books for students' independent reading, it is important to be aware of the varying and varied stages of development within and among readers. Marie Radford, a librarian and curriculum materials specialist at William Paterson College, highlights the need for a "good match" between the interests and abilities of a child and available quality literature. In order to do that, the teacher needs to have an intimate knowledge of both the reader and the literature. Educators can learn about readers' interests and abilities through formal as well as informal means. Many read-

Figure 7.1   Questions to Assist in Selecting Trade Books: Readers

Who are the readers?

What are their interests? (Do they enjoy sports, fantasy, or history? What are their favorite movies or television shows? What type of video games do they favor?)

What reading background do they bring? (Are they readers who willingly read? Do they see reading as a pleasurable activity?)

What books do they like? (Do they favor realism, fantasy, or adventure? Do they read series books?)

What books do they dislike? (Do they shun books with sad endings? Do they shy away from books dealing with social issues?)

What can they read independently?

What can they handle emotionally?

ing interest inventories gather generalized information about specific areas such as gender preferences and subject preferences. Teacher-developed inventories can explore student preferences more closely (for example, see Atwell, 1987; Norton, 1992). Through these inventories, teachers may glean information on students' favorite sports, hobbies, movies, or television shows. Observations as well as conversations can afford great opportunities to gather data about preferences among children and information as to readers' interests, backgrounds, and likes and dislikes. It is also important to know what subject matter they can handle emotionally. Such information can prove invaluable as we try to guide and encourage childrens' reading experiences and cultivate them as lifelong readers. Figure 7.1 lists questions about readers that teachers can think about as they select trade books for their classrooms.

The themes and issues that are important to adolescents may be different from those that adult readers and reviewers identify. What engages children, what they view as important to their lives, and what they want from books are not necessarily congruent with the views of adults who often make decisions about texts. This highlights the need for publishers, reviewers, librarians, and teachers to elicit the opinions of their target audience. It may well be that adult-imposed and implied perceptions of what adolescents want to read is not harmonious with what adolescents really want to read.

The Books

The selection of books should provide balance in terms of reading level, genre, interests, and social and cultural diversity. Teachers, as those closest to the children, must play a strong role in the selection of trade

Figure 7.2   Questions to Assist in Selecting Trade Books: The Books Themselves

What books are within the students' ability?
What books are currently being read? (Do they read only certain types of books, do they read only series books or comic books?)
What authors have they enjoyed?
What books connect with their lives?
What authors' works are worth pursuing? (Are books readily available? Can we gain information about the authors?)
Would the books engage the reader?
Do the books represent high literary quality? (Evaluate the author's use of plot structure, characterization, setting, theme, style, language. Is the story engaging?)
Have the books been reviewed or recommended by authorities, kids, etc.?
Do the books reflect and accurately represent social and cultural diversity?

books for classroom use. Criteria for selection must include attention to not only what the children can read and enjoy reading, but also how well the book's author develops plot, characterization, setting, theme, and language. Figure 7.2 provides teachers with questions to keep in mind as they look for books to capture the interests of their students.

Each year, thousands of books for children are published; tens of thousands more are in print. Book reviews in journals such as *The Journal of Children's Literature, The Horn Book, The School Library Journal,* and *The New Advocate* provide educators with information about new books as well as previously published titles.

Awards such as the Newbery and the Caldecott Medals are given yearly and provide educators with information about important new books. The Newbery Award is based on literary quality, the Caldecott on quality of illustration. The medal and honor winners are selected by committees that read all of the books published during the year. The Coretta Scott King Award is presented annually to both an African-American author and an African-American illustrator for outstanding contributions to children's literature. Organizations such as the International Reading Association (IRA) and the National Council of Teachers of English (NCTE) have established committees that annually develop lists of notable books. IRA's Teacher's Choices is a national project involving teachers in the selection of books for use across the curriculum. The Teacher's Choices lists are published annually in *The Reading Teacher.* (A more complete list of book selection aids can be found in the Appendix at the end of this chapter.)

A caveat: lists are generated and reviews are written mostly by adults.

Adults are making assumptions about what children purportedly will enjoy. Books are sent by publishers to adult reviewers of children's books. Ironically, children, the consumers of these books, are rarely afforded opportunities to speak about what they want to read. Those involved in the selection of trade books for classroom use need to listen to children. They need to provide educative environments where students feel free to express their opinions about books and where those who make choices about books for classroom use recognize that not all students relate to the same types of books.

Inherent in a literature-based philosophy is the inclusion of literature that reflects diversity. Children need to see themselves and the world around them reflected in the books they read. While in recent years educators have highlighted the need for inclusion of multicultural literature in the school program (for example, see Harris, 1993; Sims Bishop, 1994), literature that reflects social diversity must also be included. Real characters, those with mental, emotional, or physical disabilities or limitations, should appear in the books youngsters read. Books that confront topics such as homelessness, war, death, and other social issues help youngsters deal with the realities of life.

Reading experiences provide a secondary world in which youngsters vicariously face new worlds and interpret new experiences. These secondary worlds enable them to embark on new journeys, to create new adventures, and to escape from their own existence.

The Curriculum

Curricular issues in the selection and use of trade books involve two aspects. The first deals with the integration of trade books across the curriculum. The second is concerned with the way books are to be used. Figure 7.3 poses questions for teachers to think about as they explore the integration and use of books in classrooms.

Textbooks have been the primary content-area instructional materials in schools. Trade books, however, can provide valuable information while capturing the imagination, excitement, and interest of readers. The following vignette clearly shows the impact of literature-based instruction.

The fifth grade class was studying the Revolutionary War. The primary source of information was the textbook. Although the teacher was dynamic and knowledgeable, she lamented the fact that her students were not particularly enthusiastic about the subject matter. She decided to offer an optional assignment and encouraged some of the students to read *My Brother Sam Is Dead* (Collier and Collier,

Figure 7.3   Questions to Assist in Selecting Trade Books: The Curriculum

How can books be incorporated into the curriculum?
Are the books accessible?
What aspects of the curriculum will be enhanced through the use of trade books?
Is the content of the books accurate?
Will the books capture students' interest?
Do the books stimulate divergent responses? (Will the books foster sharing of ideas, experiences, and thoughts?)
Do the books present varied perspectives?
What can readers learn through reading of the book? (Is there specific subject matter information? Can the reader learn more about the world through the reading?)

1974), a story set in Revolutionary times and dealing with a family as it struggles with conflicting loyalties. Initially, only two youngsters opted to read the book. Greg, one of them, read it in two days and came into school excited. He proclaimed to all who would listen, "I was there, I was in the war." He eagerly detailed *his* experiences in the war. His enthusiasm was infectious. Others opted to read the book and their reactions were similar. Their knowledge of the Revolutionary War increased, as did their interest in historical fiction.

Trade books dealing with social studies as well as science help students become more critical readers as they compare and contrast ways in which information is presented and explore differing points of view. Literature can provide the springboard for unifying or integrating curriculum. Trade books are an important component in thematic units. The use of trade books, particularly in middle and secondary schools, can help students make connections, and lessen the fragmentation of content-area instruction.

The ways books are used can have a profound effect on the development of lifelong readers. Early research on response to literature dealt with the degree to which individual readers were able to approximate what were considered "correct" reactions to a text. The background and experience of the reader were viewed as factors that might hamper and interfere with the reader's quest for correct interpretation (Richards, 1929). Proper literary criticism involved the mastery of meaning as it had purportedly been set forth by the author of the text. This view was dogmatic; it implied that interpretation of a work by a reader was externally induced by the text, and the reader was viewed merely as a receptacle to understand the author's meaning and purpose.

Rosenblatt (1938) challenged this view, saying that it neglected the element of the reader's psyche. In *Literature as Exploration*, Rosenblatt described the literary experience as one in which a "live circuit [is] set up between the reader and text: the reader infuses intellectual and emotional meanings into the pattern of verbal symbols" (p. 25). Thus, according to Rosenblatt, the reader's past experiences, knowledge, and wisdom have great bearing on meaning suggested by the text. Meaning is internally induced and generated by readers as they interact with the words on the page. The transaction between the reader and the text results in the "poem"—the personal meaning created by the reader (Rosenblatt, 1938).

Through books, youngsters compare, contrast, and consider their own values and ideas with those of their parents, teachers, and peers. It is vital that school contexts foster and facilitate this process. Educators need to be aware of and address the varying and varied stages of development within and among the individuals in their classes. The curriculum should afford ample opportunities for students to explore, hypothesize, and investigate thoughts and ideas evoked during their interaction with text. Teachers must provide educational environments that are conducive to this process. By continually testing or monitoring how many books they have read or how many details the youngsters can recall, teachers interfere with this crucial developmental stage, which is so vital to cognitive and emotional growth. Classrooms should be places that encourage divergent responses, integration of ideas, reflection, and sheer enjoyment of literature. Classrooms should provide opportunities for readers to respond to books in a natural way, just as they would respond to other media.

Teachers, indeed schools, need to examine the educative environments they create and foster in order to ensure that these environments are harmonious with the needs of the youngsters. Students should not be required to "take away" specific, preordained information from texts.

Books offer many contexts for experimentation. So, too, can classrooms. Teachers need to offer varied contexts for readers to contemplate, consider, and offer response. School experiences can threaten or invigorate; they can challenge and stimulate growth or they can provide obstacles that retard growth. Schools can and must help these youngsters forge the road to adulthood by providing many routes.

CONCLUDING REMARKS

Today's literacy programs use many different types of materials, but usually the mainstay will be a large library of trade books (single and multiple copies) and/or components of a major basal system. This chapter has attempted to offer schools guidelines and questions to help them in their materials selection process.

APPENDIX: BOOK SELECTION AIDS

Periodicals about Children's Literature

Booklist. American Library Association, published biweekly. Reviews of children's and adult books. Periodic bibliographies on specific subjects.

CBC Features. Children's Book Council, published semiannually. A newsletter about current issues and events, free and inexpensive materials, topical bibliographies and essays by authors.

Children's Literature in Education. Agathon Press, published quarterly. Essays on children's books, including critical reviews.

The Horn Book Magazine. Published bimonthly. Reviews and starred reviews for outstanding books, comprehensive reviews of recommended books, articles by authors.

The Horn Book Guide. This extensive guide contains a review of all hardcover trade children's and young adult books. It is issued semiannually.

The Journal of Children's Literature. Published twice annually by the Children's Literature Assembly of the National Council of Teachers of English. Covers a wide range of topics from a variety of perspectives; provides in-depth reviews.

The New Advocate. Christopher Gordon, publisher. Addresses current issues and topics of interest in the children's book world.

School Library Journal. Reviews of children's books; often includes comparisons of several books on similar topics.

Projects that Field-Test Books

International Reading Association:
Teacher's Choices Lists (annotations published each November in *The Reading Teacher*)
Children's Choices Lists (annotations published each October in *The Reading Teacher*)
Young Adult's Choices Lists (annotations published in the fall in *The Journal of Reading*)

REFERENCES

Atwell, N. (1987). *In the middle: Writing, reading, and learning with adolescents*. Portsmouth, NH: Heinemann.

Collier, J. L., & Collier, C. (1974). *My brother Sam is dead*. New York: Macmillan.

Gieniec, C., & Westerholt, S. (1994). *Have the basals really changed?* Unpublished report, William Paterson College, Wayne, NJ.

Greenlaw, M. J. (1990). The basal's new clothes. *Learning, 18*(8), 33–36.

Harris, V. (Ed.). (1993). *Teaching multicultural literature in grades K–8*. Norwood, MA: Christopher-Gordon.

Hudak-Huelbig, E., Keyes, M. L., McClure, A., & Stellingwerf, E. (1991). *You can't judge a basal by its cover: A comparison of seven basal reader series*. Unpublished report, William Paterson College, Wayne, NJ.

National Association of Educational Progress (NAEP). (1993). *Executive summary of the NAEP 1992 reading report card for the nation and the states*. Washington, DC: Office of Educational Research and Improvement, U.S. Department of Education.

Norton, D. (1992). *The impact of literature based reading*. New York: Merrill.

Reutzel, D. R., & Cooter, R. B. (1992). *Teaching children to read: From basals to books*. Columbus, OH: Merrill.

Richards, I. A. (1929). *Practical criticism: A study of literary judgment*. New York: Harcourt, Brace and World.

Rosenblatt, L. (1938). *Literature as exploration*. New York: Noble and Noble (reprinted in 1976); New York: Modern Language Association (1983).

Sims Bishop, R. (1994). A reply to Shannon the canon. *Journal of Children's Literature, 20*, 6–9.

Smith, F. (1985). *Reading without nonsense*. New York: Teachers College Press.

Wepner, S. B., & Feeley, J. T. (1993). *Moving forward with literature: Basals, books and beyond*. Columbus, OH: Merrill.

8 Observing the Reading Teacher: Teacher Evaluation in the Child-Centered Classroom

BILL HARP
University of Massachusetts, Lowell

This chapter is based on the following set of assumptions about bringing children to literacy:

1. *Teachers make a very clear decision regarding what drives the curriculum.* In some classrooms the curriculum is driven by the texts. The texts determine what will be taught, how it will be taught, and in what order it will be taught. In some classrooms the curriculum is driven by tests. The tests may be basal tests, teacher- or district-made tests, or norm-referenced tests, but in all cases success on the tests is the driving

force behind the curriculum. In some classrooms the needs of the child, the learner, drive the curriculum. The teacher looks carefully at each learner, determines strengths, and identifies the next learning goals. This chapter is based on the assumption that the teacher discussed here is teaching in a child-centered classroom.

2. *Teachers of reading are also teachers of writing.* Reading and writing are inverse processes that are best taught together.

3. *The reading/writing teacher is a knowledgeable teacher whose instruction is informed by a very solid knowledge base.* This knowledge base is ever growing and changing, because the reading/writing teacher is a continual researcher/learner.

4. *The reading/writing teacher's instruction is guided by a very well-defined philosophical base.* The teacher's philosophy is the filter through which all instructional decisions are made.

The movement toward child-centered instruction has brought with it a series of reexaminations. First, this grass-roots movement invited teachers to rethink their philosophies about teaching and learning, the role of the learner, the relationships between coming to literacy and learning oral language, and key ways in which classroom practice was to be changed. After we operationally defined *child-centered* we were faced with rethinking classroom practice. After we redesigned classroom practice, we were challenged to rethink assessment and evaluation of children's learning. This work continues.

Yet there is another natural, evolutionary rethinking that must follow. That is rethinking how we evaluate the work of the teacher of reading. If we were to apply the basic precepts of child-centered instruction to the evaluation of the work of the reading teacher, there would be dramatic change. This change must come from first considering the precepts that should guide us and then from considering specifically what information the administrator should seek in observing the work of the teacher.

GUIDELINES FOR THINKING ABOUT TEACHER OBSERVATION

One of the first sources of guidance in thinking about evaluating the work of the reading teacher is to look to the nature of child-centered instruction. Harp (1992a,b) has outlined the characteristics of child-centered instruction:

- Children are exposed to literature that confirms what they know about how language works.
- Teachers think about readers developmentally. The same text can

be used with all children, but the expectations for response from the children will vary. Emergent readers may benefit from shared reading of the text with the voice support of the teacher. Other children will be able to engage in guided reading activities with limited support from the teacher and peers. Still others will be able to read the text independently.

- Teachers empower children to make choices about what they learn and how they demonstrate that learning. Learning activities children choose are meaningful and functional to them.
- Teachers create learning activities that are language-rich, success-oriented, and carried out in a noncompetitive environment. The *process* is of equal or greater importance than the *product*.
- Teachers create environments in which children use print in a variety of forms for a variety of authentic purposes.

In the characteristics listed above, choice, activity, and authenticity are key elements. The notions of choice, activity, and authenticity should guide the observation and evaluation of the teacher of reading. (For further information on how administrators can become more knowledgeable about the philosophy and implementation of child-centered instruction, see Chapter 12.)

Choice

A basic tenet of child-centered instruction is that learners must exercise choice as a part of having ownership for their learning. If we believe that, it then follows that reading teachers must be permitted to exercise choice in the evaluation process. Ownership for one's own growth as a teacher means reflective practice. Reflective practice leads to the teacher identifying his or her next learning steps — the next piece of personal growth to take. The evaluation process for the reading teacher must offer that teacher opportunities for choice in identifying his or her next learning steps as a teacher.

Choice is critical to the evaluation process in another dimension as well. We have recognized that if learners are to take ownership of their learning, they must be empowered to evaluate their own learning, based on work samples they help choose, and against criteria they help establish. The evaluation process for the reading teacher must offer teachers opportunities to evaluate their own work, to offer samples of their work, and to help identify the criteria against which their work will be evaluated.

Yet another aspect of choice comes into play in the evaluation of the reading teacher. Teachers are becoming more and more skillful at looking at their learners as readers and writers, "kid watching," as Goodman (1978) called it. In the process, teachers are beginning to ask their own research questions. The teacher as researcher is fast becoming accepted practice. As researchers, reading teachers ask questions, seek answers, and are potential contributors to educational theory and practice. Their classrooms become teaching and learning laboratories. The questions the reading teacher identifies for research reflect another aspect of choice in the professional life of the teacher. The evaluation process for the reading teacher should examine the choices that the teacher makes as a researcher. Research orientation has been used to distinguish teachers from those following "traditional practice" (Bright, 1989).

Activity

The new child-centered learning paradigm holds that the learner is an active participant in the learning process. The role of the teacher is to create, in collaboration with the learner, the environment that encourages active reading, researching, experimenting, writing, thinking, speaking, investigating; this is learning. In evaluating the work of the teacher, attention must be focused on the nature of the activities he or she creates for learners. The first concern is for collaboration with the learner. Are the activities created for children done in collaboration with the learner? Are students and the reading teacher partners in the creation of learning activities?

A second consideration is that of the nature of activities. Are the activities designed by, for, and with learners ones that allow the learners to behave as real readers, real writers, and real learners? Real readers often select their own reading materials to satisfy their own purposes. They write to known audiences for their own purposes, and they learn by determining what they know, what they want to know, and how they will find out. The issues centered around the activities the teacher creates are tied to issues of authenticity.

Authenticity

Just as we expect the teacher to orchestrate authentic learning activities for children, we should expect authenticity in the criteria by which the work of the reading teacher is evaluated. *Authentic* in this context means real. Authenticity in the evaluation of the reading teacher means we examine the learning environment to draw conclusions about the nature of teaching and learning. We look at the nature of the environment, the activities of the learners, and the work of the teacher there.

GUIDELINES FOR LOOKING AT THE
TEACHING/LEARNING ENVIRONMENT

Brian Cambourne (1988) has helped us understand that the conditions that foster learning oral language and the conditions that facilitate coming to fluency in reading and writing are the same. The conditions that exist to facilitate oral language learning must exist to promote fluency in literacy. He has identified seven such conditions. Consider these conditions as the potential criteria by which we would observe and begin to evaluate the teaching/learning environment created by the reading teacher.

1. *Immersion.* As learners of oral language, we were constantly immersed in language. Many parents talk to children who are in the womb. We assign intentionality to the gurgles of newborns. Just as these very young children are immersed in oral language, so must emergent readers and writers be immersed in texts of all kinds. Evidence of the existence of this condition would be a classroom in which print is used for a variety of purposes: informing, persuading, directing, controlling. The classroom library would be well stocked, including the publications of class authors.

2. *Demonstration.* Each time the oral language learner was immersed in language, the use of language was demonstrated. Literacy learners need many demonstrations of how texts are constructed and used. It seems that it is easy for teachers to demonstrate reading. Children need to be read to many times during the day, not just for fifteen minutes after lunch. However, teachers seem to have difficulty demonstrating writing. This is probably because we have received so few demonstrations of writing ourselves. By demonstration of writing, we mean actually showing children how you think through the process of writing a piece — and then demonstrating that writing.

Cambourne makes the critical point that unless children are engaged with immersion and demonstration, little learning will occur. Engagement implies that the learner is convinced that he or she is a potential doer or performer of the demonstrations, that learning these things will be beneficial, and that these new learnings can be tried out without fear of harm if the performance is not "correct."

3. *Expectation.* Parents of young children fully expect that their toddlers will make tremendous leaps toward oral language fluency, and will accomplish the task within a few years. Rarely do parents (barring unfortunate circumstances) worry about their children coming to fluency in oral language. Why, then, do some parents respond so negatively when young children spell a word the best they can at the time or make a mistake when reading orally? Teachers of reading must have high expecta-

tions that children will learn to read and write, and at the same timehelp parents (and others) value the importance of successive approximations.

4. *Responsibility.* Parents are often grateful that they do not have to teach their children to speak. In fact, in coming to fluency in oral language, children take responsibility for their own learning. They appreciate the need for clear, useful communication and modify their language to maximize its use. Children can also be responsible for learning to read and write. We need to help children decide what their next learning steps are to be and how they will take them.

5. *Use.* As oral language users we practiced our control over language in very real ways—to get things done and to get our needs met. In the reading/writing classroom children need many daily opportunities to practice reading and writing in ways that are real, communicative, and authentic. Probably no one reading this text has, as an adult, drawn three rectangles on a piece of paper and then practiced addressing envelopes in the rectangles. Why? Because this is a truly inauthentic exercise. We address envelopes for the purpose of mailing something. Children need non-artificial ways to use reading and writing.

6. *Approximation.* Most families can identify certain words or phrases that a youngster approximated that were deemed so charming they have become part of that family's vocabulary. When the 2½-year-old approached with a plate at a 45-degree angle and said, "Mommy, cookies all gonded, all gonded," Mommy didn't reply with, "Now, honey, that isn't the way we would say that." Mommy responded to the communication and probably enjoyed the child's approximation of standard speech. Why is it that parents who were so charmed by approximations in oral language are so disturbed by their children's approximations in reading and writing? Mistakes are a natural, developmental part of all learning. Knowledgeable teachers of reading see the mistakes as road signs that lead to better understanding of the developing reader and writer. Such teachers are very careful about how they respond to approximations.

7. *Response.* Cambourne asserts that learners must receive feedback on their attempts at reading and writing that is relevant, appropriate, timely, readily available, nonthreatening, and with no strings attached. We must help children understand that mistakes are a natural part of learning, that mistakes help them define what they need to learn next. The responses parents and teachers make to the child's efforts in literacy are critical factors in success.

Initial classroom observations should consider the degree to which the seven conditions described here are in place. The next consideration should be the activities of the learners.

OBSERVING THE WORK OF CHILDREN

When principals visit classrooms to evaluate the work of reading teachers, they should look for evidence of the things reading teachers value the most in teaching. Ideally, these will include the following.

Children Should Be Reading, Reading, Reading

One of the hallmarks of a reading/writing classroom is that children are frequently and enjoyably reading a variety of texts for a variety of purposes.

Authentic Texts.   The children should be eagerly and freely reading texts that are authentic, that is, texts that confirm what they know about how language works rather than the dumbed-down texts that children have previously been given. Very young children come to school knowing that print communicates, and that knowledge should be confirmed by every encounter they have with print.

Books of Choice.   Children should be reading books of their choice. Certainly, there will be times when the teacher is engaging a group of children with a common text through guided reading or shared reading. But there should be ample evidence of children reading good books of their choice. And such reading should be happening throughout the day, across the curriculum.

Discussion of the Reading Process.   The principal should see evidence of the teacher engaging children in discussion of the reading process. Bringing to consciousness what children know about a topic before they read, engaging them in predicting, confirming those predictions, and then integrating what they have just read with what they already know (Goodman & Burke, 1980) should all be evident. Asking children about how their reading is going and what they do when they have difficulty and helping them to monitor their own comprehension (metacomprehension) should all be evident as well (Harp & Brewer, 1991). The observer should see these discussions happening one on one with individual children, with small guided reading groups, and with larger groups doing shared reading.

Children Should Be Writing, Writing, Writing

We know that just as reading is one of the best ways to learn to read, so writing is one of the best ways for children to learn to write. The classroom should be a text-rich environment, and much of that writing should come from the children.

Topics of Choice. For the most part, the things children are writing should be on topics they have chosen rather than topics assigned by the teacher (Graves, 1983). Real writers write on topics of their choice and about subjects they know. So should it be with children.

Invitations. Some of the best evidence that children in a classroom are emerging as real writers is their behavior toward classroom visitors. Typically, authors in reading/writing classrooms invite visitors into their literary worlds with, "Do you want to see what I am writing?" or "I just published a book. Do you wanna see it?" Such invitations into children's literary worlds are clear evidence that they see themselves as writers and take pride in their craft.

Discussions of the Writing Process. Principals should examine the interaction between the teacher and students as they are writing. Is there evidence of prewriting activities in which children are invited to think, observe, experience, talk, research, and brainstorm in the process of selecting a topic? Are children engaged in thinking about purpose, audience, and form before they write? Is there evidence that rough drafts are tentative and exploratory, recursive, with the possibility that some rough drafts will not be brought to publication? Is there evidence that children engage in getting responses to their writing that lead to revision? Are provisions made for editing in which writers get help from a variety of sources (classmates, teacher, editing committees, and so on)? Is there evidence that final drafts make their way to the intended audience, and that the classroom library houses the work of resident authors?

All of the above should be evident as the teacher engages individuals and small groups of children in conversation about their writing, how it is going, and where a particular piece is in the writing process at the moment.

Children Are Empowered to Make Choices

While there should be ample evidence that the school district curriculum goals are being met, there should also be evidence of children making choices about what they are learning and how they are going about the task. For example, as the teacher introduces a thematic unit, the children should be asked what they know about the theme and what they would like to learn. This way the current interests of the children are accommodated as well as the district curriculum goals. Children set their own learning goals. Themes can be very simple or very complex and can last for varying lengths of time. Some teachers use themes for enrichment activities accompanying textbook studies; others organize reading and writing programs around themes. In any event, the use of a great deal of children's literature should be evident.

OBSERVING THE WORK OF THE TEACHER

In the recent past, and in some teaching situations still today, the criteria by which the teacher of reading is evaluated are very different from those posed in this chapter. We have come a long way from judging the work of the teacher based on the following:

Arranges adequate ventilation and lighting
Maintains a quiet, serious classroom
Teaches to an objective
Dresses in appropriate professional manner
Demands attention of learners while in charge of class
Prepares interesting bulletin boards

The criteria suggested here are dramatically different, and are based on the view of the teacher as creator of the learning environment, not the director of it. The teacher is viewed as professionally knowledgeable, making instructional decisions based on the observed strengths and needs of the learner.

The Teacher Is a Set Director

In child-centered classrooms the teacher spends more time on creating an environment in which children are free to communicate, explore, experiment and take risks than in direct instruction. When the principal walks into this classroom he or she should have the feeling that the room belongs to the children rather than the teacher.

The Teacher Is Relatively Invisible.   The teacher may at first be difficult to find when the principal enters the room. He or she is likely to be kneeling at eye level with a child, discussing a writing piece. The teacher may well be on the floor working an experiment with a group of children, or doing guided reading activities. In short, the teacher is more likely to have melded into the group of children than to be positioned in front of them lecturing. This is not to say that whole-class instruction is inappropriate; it just isn't the norm.

Attention Is Focused on Activities of Children.   The attention of the principal should be drawn to the activities of the children if the classroom is student-centered and teacher-guided rather than teacher-directed. There is a significant difference between reading a story to children and telling them to write about it as opposed to reading a story to children and asking, "What would you like to do with this story now?" The second way of handling children's responses puts them in charge of their learning and leads to a far greater variety of responses than the teacher would likely ever think of on his or her own.

Children Behave as Real Readers and Real Writers.   The teacher has created an environment that invites children to use reading and writing for authentic purposes: to communicate, to persuade, to inform, to entertain. When children have read a piece, they respond the way real readers respond to literature. They don't get out the papier-mâché and create a three-dimensional representation of a character; instead, they tell someone about the book, they read another book by the same author, they recommend the book to a friend, they research something that piqued their curiosity, or they do nothing. They respond to the literature the way real readers respond.

Children Behave as Real Learners.   The teacher has created a learning environment that invites children to explore, to experiment, to investigate—to take responsibility for their own learning. Real learners assess what they already know, determine what they need to learn, and plan strategies for learning. The principal observing the work of a reading/ writing teacher should see evidence that the teacher has handed over much of the responsibility for learning to the children. Thematic and other units should begin, for example, with a discussion of what the children already know about the topic (maybe charting the information) and planning for how they will learn what they want to learn.

There should also be evidence that the teacher understands that his or her function is to create an environment that will take the child further along the learning path than the child could achieve by him or herself— Vygotsky's (1978) notion of the Zone of Proximal Development. Reading/ writing teachers understand that there is a distance between what learners can accomplish on their own and what they can reach through the help of a teacher and others. In creating a classroom environment, the reading teacher plans for cooperative/collaborative learning links from children to children and from children to teacher.

The Teacher Is Focused on Strategies

The child-centered teacher recognizes the importance of teaching basic skills when needed, but the focus of attention is on the degree to which children are mastering strategies in a classroom that is process-oriented rather than product-oriented in literacy.

Knows Which Strategies Children Use.   The teacher can engage the principal in conversation about the fact, for example, that Roberto is now making predictions when he reads, and that he has a strategy for rereading when he cannot confirm those predictions. The teacher can tell which children are learning to sample from the myriad of cues on the printed page in order to make predictions. He or she can offer evidence that children are integrating what they read with what they already know. Those children who have strategies for dealing with unfamiliar words can be identified.

Relies on Authentic Literacy Experiences.   Rather than making extensive use of workbooks or worksheets, the reading/writing teacher will teach and reinforce knowledge of "basic skills" as children are making real use of language to communicate. For example, the teacher might point out and discuss certain text features while introducing an enlarged text story. Review of the "short \ a \ sound" might be made as the title to a story is being discussed or as a child inquires about how to spell "attic." The teacher is well aware of the basic skills that have been learned and that need to be reinforced, but those needs are met in real communicative contexts, not in artificial drill and practice lessons.

Is a Learner/Researcher.   Evidence should exist in both classroom practice and professional development activities that the teacher is a learner/researcher. Teachers must operate from a solid knowledge base that is soundly rooted in language development, linguistics, psycholinguistics, sociolinguistics, anthropology, and education. Reading/writing teachers are professionals who carefully critique their own work, collaborate with other professionals, conduct research in their own classrooms, and take responsibility for their successes and failures. They expect to be granted professional freedom to perform in the best ways they know, and they expect to be held accountable. All of this should be taken into account in the observation/evaluation process.

The Teacher Is Attuned to Developmental Processes

Discussions of "grade level" have given way to discussions of the uses of processes and strategies. Reading/writing teachers are asking, "How can I engage this child with this text at this time?" Instead of looking at artificial grade boundaries placed over curriculum, teachers are looking at children coming to literacy in developmental ways.

How Children Are Using the Cueing Systems.   The teacher will be able to engage in conversation about children, for example, who in the fall were relying primarily on graphophonic cues with little attention to creating meaning. The teacher will now be able to describe how those children are making increasingly more miscues that have semantic and syntactic acceptability. The reading/writing teacher is an observer of children. He or she will be able to describe ways in which children are making increasingly more sophisticated use of the cueing systems in reading. Such a teacher is adept at miscue analysis.

How Children Are Using the Writing Process.   The teacher will be able to share writing portfolios with the principal and document ways in which each child's writing is advancing. It will be possible to document that instead of grading writing pieces, the process of writing is evaluated. The editing group or editing committee is the primary responder, and children write several ever-improving drafts.

The teacher can describe where each child is along a developmental continuum from emerging reader and writer to developing reader and writer to maturing reader and writer.

SUGGESTED SEQUENCE OF ACTIVITIES

The following is a set of activities in which the reading/writing teacher and supervisor might engage in the evaluation process. The list is presented here only as one possibility, not as a definitive list. The activities engaged in by the teacher and supervisor should be agreed upon in advance and designed to best meet the needs of the teacher. Sample evaluation forms for Steps 3 through 5 are depicted in Figure 8.1.

1. The reading/writing teacher is asked to write a self-assessment of strengths as a teacher, and to identify desired next learning goals as a teacher.

Figure 8.1   Sample Observation/Evaluation Forms

Step 3: Environmental Scan	
Condition	Evidence That the Condition Exists
Immersion	
Demonstration	
Expectation	
Responsibility	
Use	
Approximation	
Response	

Step 4: Observing the Work of Children	
Condition	Evidence That the Condition Exists
Children Are Reading, Reading, Reading	
Authentic Texts	
Books of Choice	
Discussion of reading process	
Children Are Writing, Writing, Writing	
Topics of Choice	
Invitations	
Discussion of writing process	
Children Are Empowered to Make Choices	

Step 5: Observing the Work of the Teacher	
Condition	Evidence That the Condition Exists
Teacher Is Set Director	
Relatively invisible	
Observer's attention is focused on activities of these children	
Children behave as real readers and real writers	
Children behave as real learners	
Teacher Is Focused on Strategies	
Knows which strategies children use	
Basic skills taught in context of authentic literacy events	
Teacher is learner/researcher	
Teacher Is Able to Discuss Developmental Processes	
Knows how children are using cueing systems	
Knows how children are using writing process	

2. The reading/writing teacher assembles a portfolio to document strengths and from which to make conclusions about next learning goals as a teacher. The teacher is asked to include:

- classroom research conducted,
- collaborations between teacher and learners in creating learning activities,

- documentation that learning activities encourage learners to behave as real readers, real writers, and real learners, and
- evidence that reading and writing are viewed as processes.

3. The reading/writing teacher joins the principal or supervisor in doing an environmental scan of the classroom, documenting evidence of the existence of Cambourne's (1988) conditions for literacy learning.
4. The teacher joins colleagues, parents, and administrators in listing the knowledge, skills, and attitudes they value in emergent readers, developing readers, and fluent readers. A list is also made for emergent writers, developing writers, and fluent writers. The list of values generated through these activities should enrich or replace the observation criteria under "Observing the Work of Children" in this chapter. Once identified, classroom observations should document that these activities take place.
5. Classroom observation of the reading/writing teacher should complete the process. The criteria offered under "Observing the Work of the Teacher" in this chapter should be modified, in consultation with the teacher, and used here.

SUMMARY

This chapter has offered a dynamic view of the observation/evaluation process with the reading/writing teacher. It began with a consideration of the guidelines for teacher observation. Highlighted here was the importance of the teacher having choice about the dimensions of the evaluation, the importance of self-evaluation on the part of the teacher, the value of collaborative decisionmaking between teacher and learners, and the need for creating authentic learning activities for students.

Cambourne's seven conditions for literacy learning were proposed as the basis for an environmental scan of the classroom. This was followed by criteria through which the activities of the children and the activities of the teacher could be used to make evaluative decisions about the work of the reading/writing teacher. These criteria should be modified by the members of the learning community coming together to determine what they *value* in readers and writers.

REFERENCES

Bright, R. (1989). Teacher as researcher: Traditional and whole language approaches. *Canadian Journal of English Language Arts, 12*(3), 48–55.

Cambourne, B. (1988). *The whole story: Natural learning and the acquisition of literacy in the classroom*. Auckland, New Zealand: Ashton Scholastic Limited.

Goodman, Y. (1978). Kid watching: An alternative to testing. *National Elementary School Principal, 51*, 41–45.

Goodman, Y. & Burke, C. (1980). *Reading strategies: Focus on comprehension*. Katonah, NY: Richard C. Owen Publishers.

Graves, D. (1983). *Writing: Teachers and children at work*. Portsmouth, NH: Heinemann Educational Books.

Harp, B. (1992a). What should principals see teachers doing when evaluating whole language teachers? *Teachers Networking: The Whole Language Newsletter, 11*(1), 12–13.

Harp, B. (1992b). What should principals see children doing when evaluating whole language teachers? *Teachers Networking: The Whole Language Newsletter, 11*(2), 12.

Harp, B., & Brewer, J. A. (1991). *Reading and writing: Teaching for the connections*. San Diego: Harcourt Brace Jovanovich.

Vygotsky, L. S. (1978). *Mind in society: The development of higher psychological processes* (M. Cole, V. John-Steiner, S. Scribner, & E. Souberman, eds.). Cambridge, MA: Harvard University Press.

9 Staff Development

JOANNE L. VACCA
HOLLY GENZEN
Kent State University

Staff development in this transitional era, in which teachers are engaging in research and administrators are seeking to collaborate, necessitates change. In fact, as we experiment with changes in our respective roles and learn about current trends in staff development, our very willingness to change becomes critical to the success of the staff development process. Building on this premise, this chapter begins with a look at some shifts in the roles of administrators and supervisors in relation to professional development.

THE ROLE OF THE ADMINISTRATOR

The primary role of administrators is one of allowing and assisting teachers to talk about teaching and to create and use knowledge about

146

their own teaching. Gone are the days when the principal or curriculum director hand-picks a topic and inservice speaker to "enlighten" a group of teachers, to infuse change in the system with little input from teachers (Ohlhausen, Meyerson, & Sexton, 1992).

Although the danger still exists of using staff development for administrative mandates, today's staff development planning stage involves input from administrators, teachers, supervisors, and others involved in the literacy program.

The administrator must be an active and informed participant in the staff development team. Current research often speaks of the teacher as researcher, but recent literature also refers to the administrator as researcher (Beck, 1990). Administrators should be able to meaningfully discuss educational research and theory with other team members and to model teaching practice based on this research and theory (George, Moley, & Ogle, 1992). The administrator/supervisor should be committed to the program and be eager to collect data, do observations, experiment with new strategies, and reflect with the rest of the staff on what is happening in the classroom. The administrator must sustain change through his/her continuing presence in workshops, immediate response to teachers' concerns, and spirit of celebration over successes (Courtland, 1992).

Administrators/supervisors can be supportive of professional development in many ways. One resource that is in short supply for teachers is time. Teachers need time during the school day to meet and talk about their students, their schools, and their visions of education (Murphy, 1993). Careful arrangement of planning times may facilitate the formation of study groups (see Chapter 12) or planning groups among the faculty. Part of weekly staff meetings can be set aside for sharing questions, observations, and concerns about a staff project (Clyde et al., 1993). Articles relevant to classroom practice, such as the action research projects described in *Teachers Are Researchers* (Patterson et al., 1993), can be read by all faculty members and discussed.

A systemwide commitment to change should be demonstrated by, for example, support for release time, reimbursement for conferences, and establishment of local workshops. Teaching materials to support literacy, a video library of model lessons, and a print library for teacher study on literacy issues also illustrate the administration's commitment to change. Growth-oriented evaluations, where teachers can choose to set personal or team goals for the year and work on these goals without fear of punishment if goals are not met, provide a new level of understanding for teachers' professional development (Duke, 1993).

Just as students must be partners in the construction of their own knowledge, so teachers must have a voice in both the process and in the content of staff development (Pahl & Monson, 1992). Teacher input must be "sought, valued, and considered" (Henk & Moore, 1992, p. 48) during the process of implementing curriculum initiatives. When participation in staff development programs is voluntary, teachers are empowered to make choices about their own professional development (Courtland, 1993).

At the local site, the staff may brainstorm educational concerns and agree to investigate a shared problem. Teachers may, for example, share a concern about ways to mainstream special education students into regular classroom writing workshops. The staff development for the first part of the year may be used to plan how to implement and evaluate different strategies for mainstreaming students. The latter part of the year would be used for the staff to implement the program and come together to reflect upon, revise, and support the effort in progress.

Staff development is most successful when its focus stems from problems identified from the immediate setting, and its planning involves teachers and administrators (Sucher 1990). Maeroff (1993) emphasizes the great benefits inherent in a group development approach. In staff development as usual, the single teacher goes off as a loner, often coming back to derisive or disinterested colleagues, or the whole faculty attends an inservice with cynicism. Teams (especially if the principal or coordinator is a member) can be credible, well-received agents in the school when they assume ownership of new ideas and learn strategies for implementing them, and garner support among their colleagues in the school community.

STRATEGIES TO SUPPORT CHANGE

Change is difficult. The traditional cookbook-style inservice format generally does not bring about meaningful change (Pahl & Monson, 1992). Teachers teach as they do for very individual reasons: personal theory, past practice, comfort. Many reform efforts have failed because they have tried to change behavior without changing a teacher's belief system (Pahl & Monson, 1992).

Change is individual. Teachers are as diverse in their learning as are their students. Those persons responsible for staff development must respect and work with this diversity.

Courtland (1992, p. 36) describes a "creative tension" between these teacher differences and the goals of the program, which are knowledge, skill, and teacher reflection. In order for a staff development program to be successful, teachers need to desire change (George, Moley, & Ogle, 1992), and see the benefit of change for their students (Kakela, 1993).

It is important for staff developers to realize that change is a continuous process and that there is a greater guarantee of success if there is follow-through over a long period of time. Often the struggles that come with change are the result of the change process itself rather than of the particular innovation that is being presented (Ohlhausen, Meyerson, & Sexton, 1992).

To manage effective change, ongoing support is a must. Courtland (1992) describes a "constellation of factors" that contribute to successful change. Some of the stars in this constellation are time, continued support at the school and system levels, teacher ownership, and collaboration between individuals and institutions. Staff development must include opportunities for training, experimentation, and collegial exchange (Pahl & Monson, 1992). Suggestions for support strategies include:

- Regularly scheduled meetings with a predictable pattern
- Discussion of research theory and literature with other teachers
- Modeling a strategy with peers
- Microteaching lessons in follow-up sessions (lesson demonstrations)
- Peer coaching (coworkers give feedback to one another as they use strategies with their classes)
- Guided practice (facilitator leads participants in trying out strategies)
- Structured feedback sessions (facilitator elicits participant response after strategy is tried)
- Peer support teams (coworkers share the ups and downs that accompany change)
- Mentor and lead teacher models
- On-site and off-site consultants
- Telephone hotlines
- Visiting functional sites either in one's own or another building (Courtland, 1992; George, Moley, & Ogle, 1992; Henk & Moore, 1992)

Portfolios

There is a growing movement in education today to use portfolios for assessment, for evaluating the progress of learners in the classroom, and for deciding about the hiring of prospective teachers. Teachers can use this tool to assess their own progress in implementing a program, particularly as it applies to staff development.

Administrators/supervisors of reading programs encourage educators to view their students as active readers and writers. What better way to understand the process of writing and of portfolio development than for educators to be involved in the development of their own portfolios? Graves (1992) states, "We need more policy-makers, administrators, and teachers who know portfolios *from the inside* [emphasis in the original]. Their decisions about portfolio use must include the reality of living and growing with the process of keeping one" (p. 5).

The person responsible for staff development may choose to gather the teachers together to discuss the expectations for personal portfolio development. Dates can be set for periodic sharing and for the final portfolios to be presented (although it is assumed that once a portfolio is begun, it will be continued throughout a teacher's career).

The group may discuss pieces to include in a portfolio. Items that could be part of this portfolio are "journal entries, letters to colleagues, anecdotal writing, formal writing, written plans for classroom lessons, levels-of-use checklists, and script tapes" (George, Moley, & Ogle, 1992, p. 54).

The group would meet periodically to share the material from their portfolios and the experiences they have had in selecting this material. This experience gives educators firsthand experience with a strategy they may be using with their students and also encourages teachers to look at their own continuing development.

University–School Collaboration

University–school collaboration can also be an excellent support system (Courtland, 1992; Harris & Harris, 1992). There is a wonderful link between the "ivory tower" and the "real world" when professors and educators work together to address educational questions.

One model of university–school collaboration is found in the link between preservice and inservice teachers. Close working relationships among the student teacher, the cooperating teacher in the field, and the supervising teacher from the university can foster reflection on the interaction between course instruction and field site application. Teacher leaders from the participating schools can serve the role of university faculty associates, assuming the supervisory role and closing the gap between the university and the school (Ambrose, Vacca, & Vacca, 1992).

The careers of teachers involved in collaborative preservice/inservice programs can be enhanced through the increased collegiality shared with other cooperating teachers, personal reflection on their own teaching strategies, the empowerment that comes with preparing a preservice teacher for the profession, and an increased interest in current research and literature (Weaver, Weaver, & Franko, 1992). One of the most stimulating, career-enhancing developments in professional education in the 1990s is the movement toward the teacher as researcher.

TEACHER AS RESEARCHER: ACTION RESEARCH

Often tied to the university–school collaboration model is *action research*, the practice of teachers in the classroom investigating questions that they have generated about teaching and learning. This type of investigation begins with the questions, What do I think? How will I know? Teacher-researchers gather evidence in their classrooms to test their hypotheses and then evaluate their results (Gove & Kennedy-Calloway, 1992).

What better person to raise questions about practice, test assumptions, and evaluate results on student learning than the classroom teacher? For example, Colleen, a fifth grade teacher, is frustrated that her students do not do more independent reading. She wonders if they will be motivated to read more books if they are asked to share their book thoughts in letters to friends. She decides to investigate this question through her own action research in the classroom.

Colleen chooses to initiate a program of dialogue journal writing in which her students write letters to a partner in the class, describing their thoughts about the books they read. She decides to introduce this new method through mini-lessons and modeling, and allocates time for writing letters during writing workshop. She also decides what evidence she will need to determine what effect the journal writing has on student reading.

She then begins her program. Colleen sees herself as a professional, a researcher, and a learner. She has come to "see all events, behaviors, institutions, and intentions as open to teacher research and, therefore, changeable" (Patterson & Shannon, 1993, p. 9).

At the end of the quarter, Colleen evaluates what has happened. She reads the students' dialogue journals, reviews the charts where the students have recorded the books they have read, reflects on her own professional journal, and asks the students how they felt about dialogue journals and independent reading.

Colleen decides that most of her students enjoyed the dialogue journals and that the number of books read increased significantly. Colleen will probably make letter-writing part of her writing workshop from now on.

Action research closes the gap between theory and practice, creates a problem-solving mindset in teachers, improves instructional practice, improves the professional status of teachers, empowers teachers, and provides the potential for an improved educational process for children (Olson, 1990). What steps are involved in the action research process?

Steps 1 and 2: Identify a problem and form specific research questions around it. As Beck (1990) indicates, virtually any aspect of the school or the classroom can be investigated with an action research model.

Colleen believes that a major problem in her class is a lack of motivation among the children for selecting books to read independently. She wonders, "Will writing letters about books in dialogue journals to peer partners encourage reading in my room?"

Many questions about classroom practice and student learning come to mind throughout the teacher's day. These may appear as repeated concerns in a teacher's professional journal, often with a feeling of tension (Hubbard & Power, 1993). The focus must be specific rather than too general in scope.

Step 3: Determine the method and procedure for investigating the question. Possible methods may be the use of checklists, student observations, review of journal entries or other student written work, student self-evaluation, teacher-kept notes, and tapes. Although the methodology used need not be sophisticated, it should be systematic, in order to be able to report one's work to others (Patterson & Shannon, 1993).

Step 4: Carry out the research and collect data. Although teacher time and energy are limited resources, it is important that teachers remain up to date in their data gathering. It is also important to record observations as soon as possible in order to provide quality primary data for later reflection (Isakson & Boody, 1993).

Step 5: Look at the data frequently and draw conclusions at a predetermined time. Colleen decides from her record sheets, observations, and the information gathered from her professional journal and from the dialogue journals that writing letters to peer partners was a strong motivator for reading in her classroom. She notes that 85 percent of her children have read more books this quarter than last. She marks the enthusiasm that the children have shown in book selection, and hears their self-evaluation as they tell her how much they enjoy sharing books with friends.

Step 6: Make decisions from the results of the research. Classroom practice may change as a result of the study, the ultimate goal of teacher research. This type of action is altogether different from the instinctive reaction professionals often make in the short term when confronted with a problem (Patterson & Shannon, 1993).

Two additional steps may be added to this action research plan. Teachers should be encouraged to share the results of their work with other professionals through publication, newsletters, staff meetings, or simply professional conversation. In addition, teachers will find that *the investigation into one research question will raise more questions.* Research is an ongoing process, having no end. "Teacher researchers know that when it comes to research, the joy is in the doing, not in the done" (Hubbard & Power, 1993, p. 24).

Three trends seem to have emerged from this action research, according to teachers who have participated in this design: (1) there is great involvement in teaching; (2) collegiality among members of the research team is enhanced; and (3) focused, data-based feedback is generated. Figure 9.1 depicts the sequence of steps in action research.

A word of caution is probably in order at this point. Although the foregoing discussion about the action research process suggests an inherent practicality in implementation, it is important to keep in mind the pressures weighing on teachers. Although there are big demands for teachers' time, today's public schoolteacher is "better educated, has more experience

Figure 9.1   Action Research Sequence

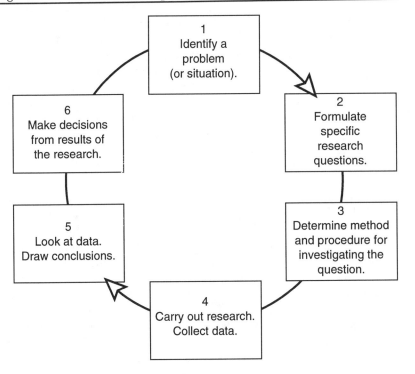

and works harder and is putting in longer hours than ever before" ("Teachers Have More Experience," 1987, p. 2). The average teacher spends more than 10 hours per week on school-related activities without financial compensation, and a majority of teachers hold one or more advanced degrees. Thus, as reading supervisors prepare to implement staff development for today's teachers, sensitivity to the pressures on teachers, as well as careful and systematic planning, is a must.

PLANNING

In order to make staff development successful, administrators/supervisors need information, through data collection, before making any decisions. Next, they need to work with participants in setting goals. A study by Rycik (1986) confirmed the importance of including teachers in every phase of the staff development program. Teachers who were knowledgeable about reading instruction preferred supervisors who provided them with the freedom to put their knowledge into practice, rather than insisting that they conform to a preexisting program. Furthermore, Rycik concluded, teachers would be amenable to a collaborative relationship in which they would have a say in targeting goals for improvement.

Probably the most efficient and effective way for the reading supervisor/staff developer to engage in planning is to follow a model that is both systematic and participatory. In other words, it should be orderly and flexible and depend on input from those most directly involved. Above all, the cyclical design is conducive to collaboration among teachers, administrators, coordinators, and committees. A plan such as this virtually guarantees the reading supervisor that staff development will be well designed and tailored to meet participants' needs.

Another way to assist a committee in planning is to focus on three major types of questions in designing the staff development program: What? Why? How? What is the current situation? What needs to be improved? What is the baseline? What exists right now? Why do we want improvement in a particular area? Why are teachers and administrators doing what they are doing in the classroom, in the building? How can we begin to make some changes in the status quo? How should we initiate the staff development, and how do we proceed?

As a rule, planning proceeds in phases, beginning with a proposal to initiate change in the school's reading program. This phase of planning should rely on information and ideas from several sources, especially the group for whom staff development is intended. Needs assessment enables the reading supervisor and planning committee to identify needs, attitudes, interests, and potential resources. Two types of assessment surveys to collect information from the teaching staff are shown below: one for intermediate grade teachers in Figure 9.2, and one for primary grade teachers in Figure 9.3.

At this juncture in the planning process, basic goals and objectives can be set by the committee. The next phase — actual implementation of content and process — is soon under way.

Figure 9.2   Survey of Competency Needs for Intermediate Grade Teachers

Directions: Indicate whether or not you would like assistance in each area of competency related to reading comprehension in the intermediate grades:

	NEEDS		
COMPETENCY	I feel confident in this area.	I would like a little more help here.	I would like lots of help here.
1. Building background activities to develop a frame of reference			
2. Showing students how to generate their own questions			
3. Involving students in process of predicting and verifying			
4. Getting students involved in group discussions			
5. Sensitizing readers to sources of information where answers to questions can be found			
6. Using literature in response groups and in journal writing			

Figure 9.3   Survey of Needs and Concerns for Primary Grade Teachers

Directions: Please number in order of importance (1=most important; 5=least important) the areas in which you feel you need additional help in order to teach reading in the primary grades. Then, answer each question as completely as possible.

_____ Using shared reading with beginners (for example, big books, songs, charts, poems)

_____ Using conversation to encourage individual or group language experience stories

_____ Linking singing, dancing, and other rhythmic activities to reading and writing instruction

_____ Creating a dress-up area for dramatic activities

_____ Using evaluation procedures that are developmentally appropriate for the children

_____ Using the language children bring to school as a base for language activities

1. What is your area of greatest concern about teaching reading?

2. What is your area of least concern?

IMPLEMENTATION

The implementation of staff development involves delivery of the program. It should occur over a series of planned activities, lasting anywhere from a month to a year or two. To work effectively with teachers, the reading supervisor/staff developer needs to be open to new ideas and demonstrate identified strategies and techniques for improving instruction. Interpersonal skills, as well as one's basic delivery and knowledge base, are important whether conducting a workshop or assisting in an action research project. Following are some personal characteristics that are associated with effective presenters at staff development sessions (Vacca & Vacca, 1993):

Demonstrates enthusiasm and interest in the topic
Stimulates excitement
Relates in open, honest, and friendly manner

Answers questions patiently
Doesn't talk down to participants
Displays sense of humor

As reading supervisors take on the role of staff developer, they need to be confident and collaborate with teachers on ways to work with each other. They need a tolerance for ambiguity and a realization that participants are involved in a learning effort, with no one having the "right" answer.

One of the most practical ways to implement a staff development project is to follow a four-stage model based on the process of change (Lewin, 1948). Essentially, adults go through a change process beginning with unfreezing or readiness, then moving forward and gaining experience, then refreezing, and, finally, incorporating changes into the environment. Figure 9.4 shows how this four-stage model was applied in a suburban Ohio school district (middle and high school buildings) over the course of one academic year. The project's overall goal was to develop teachers' knowledge of the writing process and their ability to plan and implement writing instruction. Ten workshops, each two hours long, were held during the first half of the year; five workshop sessions and six all-day coaching sessions were held during the second half. Figure 9.5 reviews the operational chronology developed by the planning committee.

Implementing staff development with this four-stage model allows

Figure 9.4   Four-Stage Staff Development Implementation Model

Stage 1: Stimulation and Motivation

Create relaxed setting to discuss problems and felt needs; lessen feelings of discomfort and/or hostility; establish a feeling of open-mindedness toward what is to follow; engage in writing and responding to one another as writers.

Stage 2: Simulations and Explanations

Introduce participating teachers to new approaches, concepts, strategies for instruction; demonstrate strategies; increase willingness and ability to incorporate new knowledge into writing instruction; model process strategies by engaging teachers in writing activity.

Stage 3: Planning and Organization

Provide time for lesson planning; create writing activities to be used in classroom situations.

Stage 4: Coaching

Coach and support the efforts of teachers who are now applying new ideas in their classrooms.

Figure 9.5   Staff Development for Process Writing: Operational Chronology

Stage 1: Workshop Sessions

September	Introduction and overview; writer's workshop Issues in middle school and secondary writing instruction; process vs. product; writer's workshop
Early October	Writing as development Writer's blocks Writer's workshop

Stage 2: Workshop Sessions

Mid-October	Helping students find topics for writing Stages of writing Prewriting strategies Coaching in classrooms
November	Strategies for writing and rewriting Receiving, responding, evaluating Coaching in classrooms
December	Conducting conferences, revising, editing Valuing finished products: publishing and sharing writing Coaching

Stage 3: Workshop Sessions

January	Create an environment Develop writing activity lessons Coaching
February	Develop writing activity lessons Coaching

Stage 4: Coaching for Application

March	Coaching for application
April	Coaching for application

reading supervisors and staff developers to introduce a range of action-oriented instructional options to participating teachers. The key to effective delivery is involvement through hands-on activities such as role-playing, demonstration teaching, observations, interviewing, and problem-solving groups. As the teachers sense the process of reading by playing the role of reader and experiencing new strategies and materials, the leader explains the how and why of selecting techniques to use in a workshop series. The leader will need to sustain the rapport that was established in the beginning and will need to vary the choice of activities, remembering that no single technique will be effective in all situations.

Frequent and informal evaluation by participants can help keep the staff development program on track. Simple rating scales to provide information on the perceived value and usefulness of a workshop session should help the leader decide on modification in planned implementation. Feedback at the end of each coaching session might be a two-way street, with both staff developer and teachers exchanging suggestions for improvement. This, in turn, would result in follow-up at the next whole-group workshop session. Evaluation in this context, then, becomes an integral and responsive part of the staff development implementation.

CONCLUSION

One of the greatest shifts in thinking in the educational world has been that of moving from learning as transmission, the "banking concept of education" (Freire, 1990, p. 58), to learning as *transaction*, where the student is the center and the teacher facilitates the active construction of meaning. Staff development must make this shift, too. Teachers must be empowered to construct meaning of what is happening in the classroom, to investigate different approaches and current theories. Staff developers, supervisors, and administrators are the facilitators in this process. To the extent that we are each willing to reexamine our roles and reflect on the value of current trends such as action research, the more likely we are to achieve success in staff development.

REFERENCES

Ambrose, R., Vacca, J., & Vacca, R. (1992). A university collaboration in teacher education: Components of an inquiry orientation. In A. M. Frager & J. Miller (Eds.), *Using inquiry in reading education* (pp. 49–55). Pittsburgh, KS: College Reading Association Monograph Series.

Beck, J. (1990). Preparing principals for an action research agenda in the schools. In M. W. Olson (Ed.), *Opening the door to classroom research* (pp. 97–111). Newark, DE: International Reading Association.

Clyde, J., Condon, M., Daniel, K., & Sommer, M. (1993). Learning through whole language: Exploring book selection and use with preschoolers. In L. Patterson, C. Santa, K. Short, & K. Smith (Eds.), *Teachers are researchers:*

Reflection and action (pp. 42–50). Newark, DE: International Reading Association.

Courtland, M. C. (1992). Teacher change in the implementation of new approaches to literacy instruction. In J. Vacca (Ed.), *Bringing about change in schools* (pp. 30–36). Newark, DE: International Reading Association.

Courtland, M. C. (1993). *Towards a holistic model of staff development for language arts teachers.* Unpublished manuscript, Lakehead University, Thunder Bay, Ontario, Canada.

Duke, D. (1993). Removing barriers to professional growth. *Phi Delta Kappan,* 74(9), 702–704, 710–712.

Freire, P. (1990). *Pedagogy of the oppressed.* New York: Continuum.

George, J., Moley, P., & Ogle, D. (1992). CCD: A model comprehension program for changing thinking and instruction. In J. Vacca (Ed.), *Bringing about change in schools* (pp. 49–55). Newark, DE: International Reading Association.

Gove, M., & Kennedy-Calloway, C. (1992). Action research: Empowering teachers to work with at-risk students. In J. Vacca (Ed.), *Bringing about change in schools* (pp. 14–22). Newark: DE: International Reading Association.

Graves, D. (1992). Portfolios: Keep a good idea growing. In D. Graves & B. Sunstein (Eds.), *Portfolio portraits* (pp. 1–12). Portsmouth, NH: Heinemann.

Harris, R., & Harris, M. (1992). Preparing teachers for literacy education: University/school collaboration. In J. Vacca (Ed.), *Bringing about change in schools* (pp. 56–63). Newark, DE: International Reading Association.

Henk, W., & Moore, J. (1992). Facilitating change in school literacy: From state initiatives to district implementation. In J. Vacca (Ed.), *Bringing about change in schools* (pp. 44–48). Newark, DE: International Reading Association.

Hubbard, R., & Power, B. (1993). Finding and framing a research question. In L. Patterson, C. Santa, K. Short, & K. Smith (Eds.), *Teachers are researchers: Reflection and action* (pp. 19–25). Newark, DE: International Reading Association.

Isakson, M., & Boody, R. (1993). Hard questions about teacher research. In L. Patterson, C. Santa, K. Short, & K. Smith (Eds.), *Teachers are researchers: Reflection and action* (pp. 26–34). Newark, DE: International Reading Association.

Kakela, J. (1993). The vocational interactive reading project: Working with content area specialists. *Journal of Reading, 36*(5), 390–396.

Lewin, K. (1948). *Resolving social conflicts.* New York: Harper & Row.

Maeroff, G. (1993). Building teams to rebuild schools. *Phi Delta Kappan, 74*(7), 512–519.

Murphy, J. (1993). What's in? What's out? American education in the nineties. *Phi Delta Kappan, 74*(8), 641–646.

Ohlhausen, M., Meyerson, M., & Sexton, T. (1992). Viewing innovations through the Efficacy-Based Change Model: A whole language application. In J.

Vacca (Ed.), *Bringing about change in schools* (pp. 24–29). Newark, DE: International Reading Association.

Olson, M. (Ed.). (1990). *Opening the door to classroom research*. Newark, DE: International Reading Association.

Pahl, M., & Monson, R. (1992). In search of whole language: Transforming curriculum and instruction. In J. Vacca (Ed.), *Bringing about change in schools* (pp. 6–12). Newark, DE: International Reading Association.

Patterson, L., Santa, C., Short, K., & Smith, K. (Eds.). (1993). *Teachers are researchers: Reflection and action*. Newark, DE: International Reading Association.

Patterson, L., & Shannon, P. (1993). Reflection, inquiry, action. In L. Patterson, C. Santa, K. Short, & K. Smith (Eds.), *Teachers are researchers: Reflection and action* (pp. 7–11). Newark, DE: International Reading Association.

Rycik, J. (1986). *Teachers' perceptions of supervision of reading instruction*. Unpublished manuscript, Kent State University, Kent, OH.

Sucher, F. (1990). Involving school administrators in classroom research. In M. Olson (Ed.), *Opening the door to classroom research* (pp. 112–125). Newark, DE: International Reading Association.

Teachers have more experience and education than ever before, NEA finds. (1987, July 2). *Education Daily*, pp. 1–2.

Vacca, R., & Vacca, J. (1993). *Content area reading (4th ed)*. New York: HarperCollins.

Weaver, C., Weaver, S., & Franko, S. (1992). Teacher education and staff development: A win-win combination. *Phi Delta Kappan, 73*(8), 652–654.

10 Assessment of Reading Programs

BARBARA A. KAPINUS
Council of Chief State School Officers

The scene is a roomful of teachers working to develop tasks for a large-scale assessment. As the teachers talk at their tables, the discussion includes questions about what will work, what is important for students to know or do, how challenging activities should be, how to allow for creativity while providing direction and focus, how to provide for regional and cultural differences, and how to design classroom activities and environments that promote the learning and achievement that they hope the assessment will tap. When they leave the workshop, these teachers will take new insights back to their classrooms. Not only their classroom assessment, but also their instruction will change.

*   *   *

This link between assessment and instruction has always been strong, but has not always been beneficial. Witness how the use of standardized tests has led to silly practice activities in many classrooms. The good news is that assessment is improving, and with that improvement it has the potential to promote good teaching and high achievement.

Educational assessment has one ultimate purpose: to support effective teaching and learning. It accomplishes this by documenting the individual accomplishments of students and looking at how groups of students are performing, in order to determine student progress and the success of instructional approaches and programs, school organization, and state and local policy. There are currently some important trends in reading assessment that affect both individual assessment and large-scale assessment for accountability. This chapter outlines those trends that administrators and supervisors should know and offers guidelines for establishing an assessment system in schools and districts.

We address classroom and large-scale assessment separately, since the purposes of each, while ultimately the same as stated above, are at some points different. Classroom assessment directly informs instruction and can be useful to students, parents, and teachers, all of whom can be involved in some parts of the process. Large-scale assessment, on the other hand, has to inform policymakers and the general public, who are not as interested in specific instructional implications of the results, but rather in whether the curriculum and school programs are effective. It is usually tied to public accountability and must be rigorously, publicly defensible to a degree far greater than classroom assessment. As a consequence of these different orientations, there are different constraints, at least at present, on the types of activities that can be used in each type of assessment, although there is an increasing merge of the two. A system of related assessment tools — such as tasks done on demand as part of a test, projects, and portfolios — appears to be the best way, at present, to meet all the demands and concerns related to assessment.

LARGE-SCALE ASSESSMENT TRENDS

Large-scale reading assessment has been changing dramatically in the last 10 years. Newer assessments are characterized by the following:

- a focus on outcomes or goals.
- increased authenticity or congruence with real-world and sound instructional activities.

- increased complexity of assessment tasks and procedures.
- increased involvement of teachers in all stages of assessment, including development, scoring, and reporting.

Each of these characteristics reflects an improvement in assessment but has both advantages and disadvantages for schools and teachers. These mixed effects are sometimes due to the developments being new and not yet fine-tuned. It is important to weigh all the consequences and implications of these characteristics of new assessments when designing an assessment system for a school or district, choosing or developing district and school assessments, or participating in some of the larger assessments at state and national levels.

Focus on Outcomes or Goals

Newer large-scale reading assessments focus on the goals of education rather than the enabling skills necessary to reach those goals. These goals tend to be broad and complex. For example, one goal from the state of Maryland is, "Students will construct, extend, and examine meaning when reading for literary experience, to be informed, and to perform a task." Focusing on complex goals lead to complex, challenging assessment tasks such as this:

Using the information from the two passages you just read, write an article for your school newspaper on environmental concerns. Relate the scientific and historical aspects of environmental issues to current environmental issues that are global, national, or local. You will draft your article today and tomorrow you will share your draft with a peer and prepare a revised draft.

One of the problems with focusing on outcomes is that assessments using rich tasks that reflect the more general goals of schooling provide information about those goals but have limited utility for individual diagnosis. This is not a new development. There has long been a caveat, usually ignored, against drawing conclusions about individual students' specific instructional needs based on the results of large-scale assessments such as norm-referenced tests. However, teachers and parents are sometimes dissatisfied with the amount of individual student information provided by newer assessments, especially in the light of the increased amount of student time such assessments require. This leads to pressure to report individual scores and overrely on those scores as sources of information about individual reading achievement.

Another aspect of focusing on goals is that students' achievement is measured relative to standards for performance. In some states, and on the National Assessment of Educational Progress (NAEP) in Reading, the standards are set purposely high to indicate high expectations for all students. These high standards represent a commitment to providing the best, most challenging education to *all* students. They also have sparked intense discussions on how to allow for cultural differences and yet hold high expectations for diverse populations of students. In some ways, a standard for all can be seen as both more fair and more enfranchising for students who in traditional assessments would not be expected to perform well because of their exceptional status or diverse backgrounds. However, high standards need to be accompanied by a deep conviction that all students can achieve those standards and a commitment to supplying the necessary resources and learning opportunities to support that achievement.

Increased Complexity of Assessment Tasks and Procedures

Large-scale assessments are not only beginning to include complex tasks like the one described above, but are also using complex arrays of activities, interviews, projects, and portfolios. The last, portfolios, is particularly challenging to implement on a large scale. In spite of the difficulties, some states and districts are beginning to build large-scale assessment programs that incorporate the use of portfolios. In the classroom, portfolio assessment is characterized by:

- samples of student work from regular and special activities and other evidence such as observations and interviews that indicate progress over time.
- negotiation between the teacher and the student to determine what goes into the portfolio and what it indicates about achievement.
- a focus on improvement over time rather than achievement at one point in time.

Large-scale assessment programs tend to modify portfolio approaches in order to make them manageable, comparable, and reliable. At present, when portfolios are used on a large scale, students are assessed based on samples from the portfolio rather than the entire portfolio. For example, the state of Vermont asks teachers to provide samples of students' work from their portfolios. Schools, districts, and states can ask teachers and students to provide evidence from larger classroom portfolios of growth and achievement related to common goals, without demanding and scoring entire portfolios. This allows the use of portfolio assessment on a large scale and still preserves the essential attribute of portfolios, which is a shared ownership of the assessment by teachers and students.

There are several concerns related to the use of portfolio-based information for the purpose of large-scale assessment. One is that schools and teachers might base their notions of classroom portfolio assessment on the model used for the larger assessment, and thereby limit the possibilities for portfolios in the classroom. A second, related concern is the tension between the need for teachers to develop their own understanding and use of portfolios over time, and the need for large-scale assessment programs to have some consistency and comparability — and to have them relatively quickly — in response to public demands for timely accountability. Another persistent problem is the achieving of comparability and consistency in assessment activities and scoring. Again, there is a tension between the leeway allowed teachers and students and the demands for publicly defensible assessment information. Schools and districts embarking on the use of portfolio assessment need to include time for teachers to understand the use of portfolios in contexts beyond the classroom and to be a part of the planning and development process.

Authenticity

Some of the assessments being developed for both state and national assessments are being designed with a clear commitment to reflecting good instruction and real-world reading activities. Some students taking the Maryland School Performance Assessment have an opportunity to select a short story from three or four possibilities and to answer several open-ended questions on the story. This reflects the world outside of the classroom and inside some classrooms, where students choose the literature they read. On the NAEP in Reading, students answer questions about directions for writing a résumé and then actually prepare a short résumé using the directions. The New Standards Project, which consists of several states working together to develop a nationwide assessment system, has been piloting reading tasks that are introduced by videos related to the readings and include small group discussions of selections.

States such as California, Kentucky, and Maryland have also been working on more authentic assessment tasks. For example, in Maryland one task integrated science, social studies, reading, and writing and required that students take and organize notes and write a report to be part of a health fair at the local mall. In Indiana, educators piloted complex problem-solving tasks that asked students to do research, organize information, and present a possible solution to a real-world problem such as the water shortage in some parts of the country. Students find these more authentic tasks engaging and challenging. Teachers find that they support generative classroom activities that require a wide range of thinking, creativity, and personal involvement on the part of students.

However, the use of these authentic tasks has raised some issues. The issues include:

- What is really authentic for students?
- Can we afford the time that these tasks are taking?
- Can we generalize about student performance based on tasks that are highly bound by context?
- Can we really obtain reliable, consistent scores or ratings of student performance?

In considering the first issue, it is important to realize that some tasks might be very related to the real world but not related to students' current experiences and developmental levels. For example, one large assessment piloted a task that asked fourth grade students to pretend they were park rangers and then to write a letter to their boss about a poem they had read. While it is important for students to have realistic audiences for their writing, the audience in this case was not appropriate on two counts. First, few of the fourth graders knew what a park ranger did, much less how such a person would write when addressing a boss. The task was not authentic given the experiences of fourth graders. Second, the task itself was not really very authentic; few park rangers write letters to their bosses about poems they have read. This task was a good example of efforts to use authentic, real-world tasks going awry.

Teachers involved in the development of the newer assessments find themselves involved in discussions that lead to insights about the activities of readers in the real world. For example, adult readers usually have choices about the literary reading they do. To reflect this, the NAEP includes blocks of open-ended items that can be answered by reading any one of seven stories. Students pick the story they will read for the assessment from a mini-anthology of the seven stories. The same assessment also includes questions about an actual public transportation schedule that was ordered in its original form from a metropolitan area. Another set of items culminates in twelfth grade students filling out an income tax form.

Teachers working on the development of assessment continue to struggle with the problem of what is authentic. We need some way to elicit and assess responses to literature, but in the real world we seldom answer other people's questions about what we read except for the general "What was it about?" and "Did you like it?" or "Was it like the author's other books/stories/poems?" Teachers and measurement staff on several assessment projects are struggling with the problem of how to develop assessments that are at the same time authentic, sound, and challenging.

The second issue, the amount of time required for students to complete authentic performances, has been raised by teachers in some instances of performance assessments. Currently, the state of Maryland assesses every student in grades three, five, and eight in mathematics, reading, writing, science, and social studies. The assessment takes 1½ hours a day for 5 days. The New Standards Project has been piloting reading and writing tasks that require 1½ hours a day for 3 to 10 days. These are substantial amounts of time. While these assessment tasks are engaging for students and reflect good instruction, they take time from other instructional activities that teachers might have chosen and students might have needed.

The third issue, the degree to which we can generalize about performance, is critical. Although reading a long passage and responding with more authentic tasks reflects real-world reading, it reflects only one small type of reading, about only one topic. A student might do significantly better in a different context, reading about a different topic. For example, a student might be given a passage on ecology, a topic of high interest to the student because of family discussions and projects. That student might perform very well on that reading task but show far less proficiency when asked to read a passage about village life in Russia. Consequently, interpretation of and generalization from individual data on newer large-scale assessments must be done with a great deal of caution.

The last issue, the reliability and consistency of scores on the newer assessments, is a continuing problem. Scores that fluctuate dramatically from scorer to scorer, or from year to year, are not very useful for accountability or assessment of individual achievement. Some states are experiencing this difficulty at this moment as they try to report and compare data from year to year. When administrators have a voice in choosing or designing the large-scale assessment by which the effectiveness of their schools or districts will be judged, they need to carefully weigh the reliability and consistency of the instruments being considered.

Increased Complexity of Assessment Tasks and Procedures

The newer assessments do not use simple excerpts of texts and simple questions. They employ texts that have been drawn from the real world: magazines, announcements, directions. These texts must be carefully screened for possible bias as well as age-appropriateness. The questions do not have simple right or wrong answers. Scoring of responses is based on several characteristics, not just the text information that the student provides. The scoring guide in Figure 10.1 shows one approach to scoring students' responses to reading.

Although other guides include different factors or do not include some of these aspects, there are important similarities across most scoring guides for extended written responses to open-ended reading questions. They usually examine several aspects of students' responses, and they focus on students' interactions with the text — interactions that can take many forms and can be from several possible perspectives. In preparing students to respond to the open-ended questions scored by these types of guides, teachers need to help students understand what makes a good response and give students opportunities to explore a range of ways of responding to questions about reading. One teacher developed a chart similar to the one in Figure 10.2 in order to guide discussions with her students about the quality of their responses.

The complexity of the newer assessments also challenges classroom organization. When assessment activities include student collaboration, classrooms need to be organized to support that collaboration on a regular basis — not just when students are being assessed. The use of multiple texts and activities with options for students requires that classrooms provide opportunities for students to relate to multiple texts and to choose from a variety of reading materials so that they are accustomed to those activities when they encounter them as part of an assessment.

Increased Involvement of Teachers in All Stages of Assessment

Past large-scale assessments were usually developed by measurement experts and commercial testing institutions and had little teacher input except perhaps for some review of items. The assessments being constructed today are being developed by teachers. In Maryland and Kentucky and on the New Standards Project, for example, teachers are part of the discussion of what to assess and how to do it. They are designing the tasks, developing the scoring guides, picking exemplary student responses, scoring responses, and helping to draft and deliver reports on the results of assessments. From identifying the outcomes to be assessed to speaking at the press conference on assessment results, teachers have had a voice in these assessments. This involvement has two important results.

First, the discussions and development activities provide staff development in the form of opportunities to reflect on and articulate what is important in curriculum, instruction, and student achievement. Teachers

Figure 10.1   Generic Rubric for Reading Activities

Note: The scoring criteria are applied as cued for or required by the activity. Not every activity cues for all the possible behaviors described in the generic rubric. Thus the scoring guide for specific activities can stop at different points.

0 = No evidence of construction of meaning.

1 = Some evidence of constructing meaning, building some understanding of the text. Presence of defensible, and possibly some indefensible, information.

2 = A superficial understanding of the text, with evidence of constructing meaning. One or two relevant but unsupported inferences.

3 = A developed understanding of the text with evidence of connections, extensions, or examinations of the meaning. Connections between the reader's ideas and the text itself are implied. Extensions and examinations are related to the text, but explicit references to the text in support of inferences are not present. When more than one stance is possible, the response may remain limited to one stance.

4 = A developed understanding of the text with evidence of connections, extensions, and examinations of meaning. Connections between the reader's ideas and the text are explicit. Extensions and examinations are accompanied by explicit references to the text in support of inferences. When possible, the response indicates more than one stance or perspective on the text; however, only one stance is substantially supported by inferences to the text.

5 = A developed understanding of the text with evidence of connections, extensions, examinations of meaning, and defense of interpretations. Connections between the reader's ideas and the text itself are explicit. Extensions and examinations are accompanied by explicit references to the text in support of inferences. When possible, the response indicates more than two stances, all substantially supported by references to the text.

6 = A complex, developed understanding of the text with evidence of connections, extensions, examinations of meaning, and defense of interpretations. Connections between the reader's ideas and the text itself are explicit. Extensions and examinations are accompanied by explicit references to the text in support of inferences. Responses indicate as many stances as possible based on the activity, all substantially supported by references to the text. These responses reflect careful thought and thoroughness.

Maryland State Department of Education
Maryland School Performance Assessment Program

Figure 10.2   Guide for Discussing Qualities of Good Responses

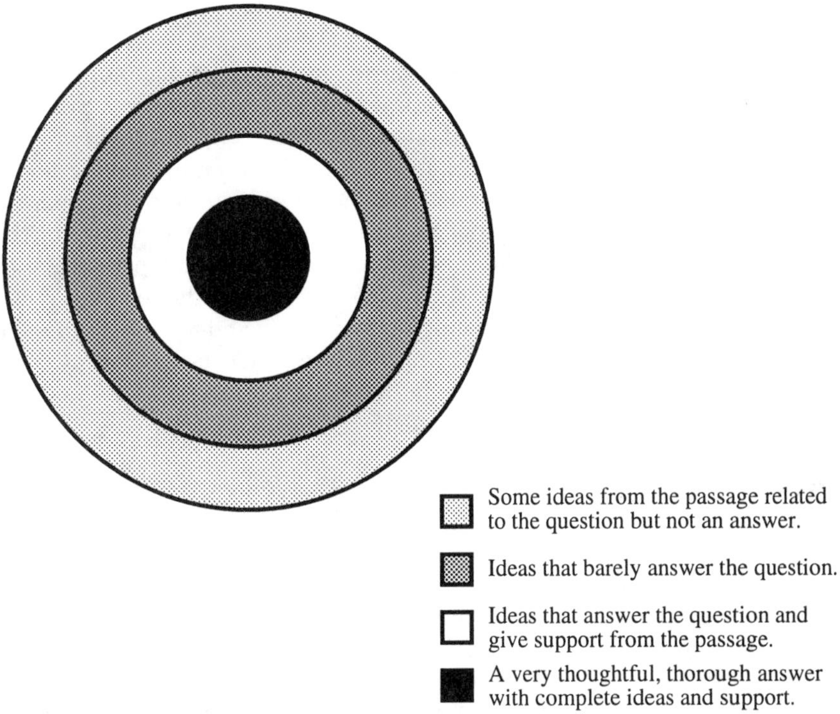

☐ Some ideas from the passage related to the question but not an answer.

▨ Ideas that barely answer the question.

☐ Ideas that answer the question and give support from the passage.

■ A very thoughtful, thorough answer with complete ideas and support.

have the opportunity to build clearer understandings of what they want to accomplish in their classrooms, how they might accomplish it, and how they will determine whether they and their students are successful.

The second result of teacher involvement in all the phases of the development and use of assessments is that they have a better understanding of the assessments and their purposes. With that understanding often comes support for the assessment and improved instruction. Teachers are not as likely to see assessment as something that is done to them, but rather as a tool for looking at their own effectiveness.

CLASSROOM ASSESSMENT

Some of the same trends evident in large-scale assessment are also found in current developing approaches to classroom assessment. It is not always clear which comes first, but it seems that while newer large-scale assessments are trying to capture the goals and approaches used in innovative, successful classrooms, classrooms are also being improved by the implementation of the newer assessments. For example, more traditional teachers working on or in preparation for newer large-scale assessments report that they are beginning to reflect on their own classroom practices in instruction and assessment, and often modify their approaches to reflect the assessment and in turn the innovative teaching and thinking about education on which the assessment was based. When these teachers provide information on the assessments or work on additional forms of the assessment, they provide insights based on their classroom experiences that are relevant to improving the design and content of large-scale assessments. That is, the improvement of instruction and assessment in the classroom is linked to improvements in large-scale assessment. Consequently, it is not surprising that the trends in classroom assessment are similar to those in large-scale assessment.

Authenticity

Classroom assessments are becoming increasingly authentic as instruction is focusing more on what readers need to be able to do in the real world. In addition, teachers are using separate assessment exercises less and less, and instead are using the products and observations of regular classroom activities to assess students' achievement. Teachers are also sharing the responsibility for assessment with students. The following interview questions and the answers of a primary student who is struggling to improve demonstrate this shared responsibility.

1. *What does someone have to do to be a good reader?* They have to write good. Good readers make good sentences. Good readers make mistakes and they fix them.
2. *How have you improved as a reader this nine weeks?* I go back to the beginning and start again. I try to read to the end. I think about the reading.
3. *What reading goal will you set for yourself for the next nine weeks?* I'll try to sound out the hard things I can't read.

On a bulletin board of Forest Edge Elementary
Fairfax, Virginia, January, 1989

Questions like these can document increased understanding of the reading process and growing ownership of their reading on the part of students.

Complexity

As teachers use a wider variety of assessment tools in their classrooms and as they assess more complex aspects of reading, they are challenged to bring it all together. Managing a classroom system of assessment can be as challenging as managing a statewide system. A classroom assessment system might include the following:

- Interviews of students about their progress
- Interviews of students about their reading preferences
- Observations of students discussing their reading
- Students' reflections on their discussions
- Reading response logs
- Samples of work picked by the teacher, the students, or both
- Special projects
- Students' reflections on their progress and their goals
- Notes on interviews with parents
- Notes from parents about students' reading habits or discussions at home

Managing all of these and weaving them into a coherent, meaningful description of the student as a reader is a challenge. One promising approach is the use of portfolios. The use of classroom portfolios is rapidly growing in popularity. However, there is also a great deal of misunderstanding about portfolios, as with many new popular movements. Teachers often believe that the collecting of students' work in some physical receptacle is the critical feature of using portfolios. As mentioned in an earlier section of this chapter, portfolios should allow for students and teachers to discuss and negotiate understandings of progress; in the classroom this conversation leads to the establishment of mutually accepted goals. This discussion and the focus on improvement over time are the essential ingredients in a portfolio approach in the classroom.

The process of examining progress with respect to goals and revising or reestablishing goals is at the core of portfolio use. Teachers need to have clear, challenging goals for their students that provide benchmarks for considering progress. For example, the following is a set of descriptors for an early stage of "developing reader." It is being piloted as a benchmark by teachers in a multistate project, the Primary Level Assessment System. The descriptors are based on materials used in the Upper Arlington schools in Ohio.

- Selects appropriate reading material with some support.
- Begins to keep a list of books read.
- Retells and discusses text with teacher support.
- Comments upon patterns, characters, plot, and setting with prompts. May compare or contrast his/her experiences with story.
- May make connections with other literature.
- Makes predictions using book language and story elements.
- Self-corrects most miscues that interfere with meaning.
- Able to problem-solve new words in a variety of ways: rereading the sentence, phrase, or preceding word, by analogy, sounding out, and so forth.
- Reads in multiple-word phrases.
- Beginning to read for longer periods of time on his/her own.
- Views self as a reader.

In using portfolios, teachers must be aware of their goals and keep them as a focus if they are to ensure students a reliable assessment of real progress. Without such focus, portfolios can support aimless education, unfocused activity, and even capricious evaluation.

Parents as Collaborators

Schools are becoming increasingly committed to forging partnerships with parents in the task of helping students become literate. Teachers are asking parents to provide information on home reading habits and discussion. When they meet with parents, they share portfolios or work samples, demonstrating specific areas of growth rather than reporting only numbers and scores as the source of evaluation. Parents bring as wide a range of backgrounds to conferences with teachers as their children bring to classrooms. However, there are many ways to involve parents in assessments and to inform them of the instructional program and its goals at the same time (see Chapter 11).

Constructive Learning and Activities

Classroom assessments are beginning to reflect a move toward constructivist classrooms where teachers and students are partners in the processes of learning and assessing. Teachers in these classrooms use assessment approaches that increase the understanding of students and themselves. For example, students might be asked to culminate a unit in geography by writing a reader-friendly article about the country or area studied, and to explain what characteristics of their text they believe will help their readers understand the ideas of the article. Such an activity allows students to apply their knowledge of reading, writing, and geography in complex and creative ways. The teacher will also learn about the students' understanding of reading, writing, and geography from the activity.

PUTTING IT TOGETHER IN A COHERENT PROGRAM

Assessment — large-scale as well as classroom — based mainly on commercial materials such as basal tests or norm-referenced tests is being replaced by newer tools and approaches more closely connected to good teaching and the ultimate goals of reading instruction. Not only are the characteristics of assessment changing, but the process by which assessment is developed is also changing. More interested parties, from students and parents to business leaders, are involved in the design of newer assessments. This means that the process of establishing or improving an assessment system for schools and districts requires time and resources as well as careful planning. An effective system must evolve; it cannot be laid in place overnight. The purposes and characteristics of each part of the system, from classroom-based evidence of growth to indications of program effectiveness, must be considered in building a related network of tools and approaches for assessment.

Educators as Meaning-Makers

Above all, as newer assessment approaches are developed and implemented, educators at all levels from national to the classroom are gaining insights into the goals of education and ways to reach those goals. Those insights must be developed by each person; they cannot be simply handed down by policymakers or administrators. This means that an approach like portfolios cannot really be set in place quickly through a district or state mandate. A cookbook for assessment is no more appropriate than a cookbook for instruction. Teachers need to be decisionmakers and problem-solvers in assessment as well as teaching. And teachers are not the only people who need to understand reading assessment. Educational leaders at all levels need to engage all the parties involved in education — students, parents, teachers, administrators, and policymakers — in the process of reflecting on the match among educational goals, instructional practice, and assessment approaches. A deep understanding and clarification of these areas on the part of individuals is necessary for successful evaluation. That increased knowledge cannot be simply transmitted but must be generated by individuals over time, experiences, and conversations. Administrators can provide the time, opportunities, and encouragement for the development of understanding necessary for successful assessment in reading programs.

RESOURCES FOR FURTHER READING

Atwell, N. (1987). *In the middle: Writing, reading, and learning with adolescents*. Upper Montclair, NJ: Boyton/Cook.

Au, K. H., Scheu, J. A., & Kawakami, A. J. (1990). Assessment of students' ownership of literacy. *The Reading Teacher, 44*(2), 154–156.

Barrs, M., Ellis, S., Hester, H., & Thomas, A. (1988). *The primary language record handbook for teachers*. Portsmouth, NH: Heinemann.

Clay, M. M. (1979). *The early detection of reading difficulties* (3rd ed.). Portmouth, NH: Heinemann.

Glazer, S. M., & Brown, C. S. (1993). *Portfolios and beyond: Collaborative assessment in reading and writing*. Norwood, MA: Christopher-Gordon Publishers.

Goodman, K., Goodman, Y., & Hood, J. W. (Eds.). (1989). *The whole language evaluation book*. Portsmouth, NH: Heinemann.

Harp, B. (Ed.). (1991). *Assessment and evaluation in language programs*. Norwood, MA: Christopher-Gordon Publishers.

Herald-Taylor, G. (1989). *The administrators' guide to whole language*. Katonah, NY: Richard C. Owen.

Herman, J. L., Aschbacher, P. R., & Winters, L. (1991). *A practical guide to alternative assessment*. Alexandria, VA: Association for Supervision and Curriculum Development.

Johnston, P. (1987). Teachers as evaluation experts. *The Reading Teacher, 40*(8), 744–748.

Meyer, C. A. (1992). What's the difference between *authentic* and performance assessment? *Educational Leadership, 49*(8), 39–40.

Pikulski, J. J. (1989). The assessment of reading: A time for change? *The Reading Teacher, 43*, 80–81.

Rhodes, L. K., & Shanklin, N. L. (1993). *Windows into literacy: Assessing learners, K–8*. Portsmouth, NH: Heinemann.

Taylor, D. (1990). Teaching without testing: Assessing the complexity of children's literacy learning. *English Education, 22*, 4–74.

Teale, W. H., Heibert, E. H., & Chittenden, E. A. (1987). Assessing young children's literacy learning. *The Reading Teacher, 22*, 4–74.

Tierney, R., Carter, M. A., & Desai, L. E. (1991). *Portfolio assessment in the reading–writing classroom*. Norwood, MA: Christopher-Gordon.

Valencia, S. (1990). A portfolio approach to classroom reading assessment: The whys, whats, and hows. *The Reading Teacher, 43*, 338–340.

Valencia, S. W., Hiebert, E. H., & Afflerbach, P. P. (Eds.). (1993). *Authentic reading assessment*. Newark, DE: International Reading Association.

Valencia, S., McGinley, W., & Pearson, P. D. (1990). Assessing reading and writing. In G. G. Duffy (Ed.), *Reading in the Middle School* (pp. 124–146). Newark, DE: International Reading Association.

Valencia, S. W., & Pearson, P. D. (1987). Reading assessment: Time for a change. *The Reading Teacher, 40*(8), 726–732.

Wolf, D. P. (1987, December/1988, January). Opening up assessment. *Educational Leadership, 45*(4), 24–29.

11 Community Outreach

ANTHONY D. FREDERICKS
York College

School personnel seeking to establish effective reading programs need to be cognizant of many factors that impact on the development and maintenance of those programs. Research suggests that dynamic reading programs emanate from strong leadership within the school as well as from sincere efforts by school personnel to reach out and involve all members of the family and community (Fredericks & Rasinski, 1990b; Fredericks & Taylor, 1985). In fact, reading programs that seek to establish a strong and positive partnership with parents and other community members are those that promote reading as more than just a school-related subject; students are provided with innumerable opportunities to make reading a very natural part of their everyday lifestyles.

If, as many educators contend, the school is a microcosm of the community it serves, then it seems logical to assume that scholastic affairs, including reading instruction, are a necessary interest of that community. Indeed, there is convincing evidence that when parents and community members are "recruited" as supporters and promoters of reading instruction and lifelong reading habits, then reading and learning become much more meaningful in children's lives (Fredericks, 1992). Critical factors that support a strong home/school/community relationship include: (1) regular and frequent communication between home and school; (2) the promotion of reading and learning as a natural part of everybody's lifestyle; and (3) systematic involvement throughout the entire school year (Fredericks, 1993). This chapter will deal with those issues in greater detail.

BACKGROUND ON COMMUNITY OUTREACH

The need to involve all family members in scholastic affairs is supported by both logic and a growing body of research that underscores the impact parents and others have on children's literacy development (Fredericks & Rasinski, 1990d; Mason & Au, 1986; Vukelich, 1984). While involving the entire family in a school's reading program would seem to be a naturally valuable extension of that program, past practices have not always subscribed to this notion. During the early part of this century, parents were admonished not to get involved in the scholastic affairs of their offspring. Many school personnel felt that the education of students should be left entirely to those formally trained to undertake such a task. In a sense, parents were systematically excluded from any and all educational matters (Vukelich, 1984). Some educators believed that parents would create unneeded conflict for youngsters by imposing inappropriate values or using unsophisticated teaching methods. Unfortunately, this isolationist policy persisted for many years, creating a "we-versus-them" attitude that, in many cases, threatened the fundamental tenets of American education.

Fortunately, the accumulation of a significant body of data in recent years has resulted in some rethinking for many school personnel. In one review of research related to parental involvement in education, Henderson (1988) reported a large body of evidence clearly indicating that parental involvement throughout the educational careers of youngsters can lead to impressive gains in achievement.

Fredericks and Rasinski (1990a, 1990b) also provide convincing evidence that the overall strength of a reading program can be predicted, in large measure, on the degree of parent and community involvement. Such involvement is structured on three vital elements woven throughout all dynamics of a planned or functioning reading program:

1. Parent involvement must be an *integral* part of the program, rather than a convenient "add-on."
2. Parent and community involvement must be conducted comprehensively — that is, it is an *investment* throughout the entire school year.
3. Parent and community involvement must be approached systematically and not as a "one-shot" effort by a few concerned educators.

The success of effective outreach efforts is often grounded on five critical criteria (Fredericks & Rasinski, 1990c). These criteria not only serve as "markers" for the successful program, but also provide guidelines for the maintenance of a program over time:

1. *Needs Assessment:* Programs built upon the expressed needs, wishes, and desires of parents, rather than the perceived issues of educators, have the greatest likelihood of success.
2. *Shared Responsibility:* A willingness on the part of both educators and parents to work together for the common good is a requisite element of successful outreach efforts.
3. *Decisionmaking:* Parents and community members need to have active opportunities to determine the scope and direction of outreach efforts.
4. *Constant Communication:* Lines of open and honest communication need to be established and maintained throughout the whole school year.
5. *Continuous Participation:* A long-term commitment to parents and the community sustains involvement and maintains interest.

URBAN–SUBURBAN DIFFERENCES

Although many schools are utilizing the power of parent participation within and throughout their reading programs, large numbers lack sufficient projects, most noticeably those in economically deprived neighborhoods. Lightfoot (1978) has noted that poor families are "excluded from life inside schools, and the extent of their participation reflects their social class, race, and ethnicity" (p. 38). She goes on to state that for too many economically deprived families, the school exists as a "frightening monolith, not only in the sense that the power of knowledge makes them feel inadequate . . . but because every bit of communication from the school comes as a negative appraisal of their child, a destructive comment about their lives" (Lightfoot, 1978, p. 36). Jenkins (1981) suggests that this distancing of poor families from the doors of the school is then perceived by educators to be a lack of parental interest — a factor that may contribute to the tacit assumption that poor families should not or cannot participate in school activities. This attitude is shown, in part, by data gathered from 3,698 elementary teachers in Maryland, which indicated that teachers frequently perceive less educated parents as unable or unwilling to carry out activities related to children's schoolwork at home (Becker & Epstein, 1982).

There are significant differences between suburban schools, which are typified by highly involved community outreach efforts and high levels of student achievement, and urban schools, typically characterized by low levels of participation and similarly low levels of achievement. These facts represent a considerable challenge for educators. In fact, many urban administrators are realizing that they may be neglecting a potent force for their reading program if they systematically exclude parents and the community at large. To be sure, urban parents, beset by a host of social and economic restraints, compounded by years of benign neglect, offer urban reading supervisors challenges not faced by their suburban counterparts.

Jenkins (1981) notes five considerations for urban administrators to think about as they design effective parent involvement programs:

1. Many urban schools fail as a result of ineffective leadership; that is, administrators are unwilling or unable to tap into the resources of the local community.
2. Class bias and racism remain entrenched in the public school system, a factor that can be moderated and ameliorated by the presence of parents in the school.
3. Urban schools remain mired in bureaucratic procedures that make the policymaking process inaccessible to parents; in short, parents are systematically excluded from the educational process.
4. Poverty and its effect on the urban poor leaves many parents emotionally unable to deal with the demands of their children.
5. The role of the parent in the development of the child's self-concept and motivation is vital and can be promoted through effective outreach efforts by the school.

A Model for Parent Involvement in the Urban School

One model designed by Jenkins (1981) is a five-level approach to parent involvement, beginning with informal contact and proceeding to structured participation in the decisionmaking process at the school level. Parents are encouraged to move through the levels or to remain at a level with which they are most comfortable. Jenkins's five levels are:

1. *Entry:* This first step is intended to interest parents in the life of the school. This may include, but not be limited to, afternoon teas, guidance meetings, home visits, telephone contacts, or a special "parent room" set up in the school. The object is to help parents feel comfortable with the school and its mission.
2. *Getting Involved:* The second level encourages parents to act as hosts for general parent activities such as family nights and open school days. This level may also involve parents in more formalized contacts with their children, such as contracts in which parents agree to read with their child for a minimum number of minutes a week.
3. *Curricular Participation:* At this level parents participate in workshops set up to acquaint them with the school's curriculum. Parents are provided with materials, games, and activities with which they can interact with their children at home—reinforcing math, reading, or science instruction.
4. *Self-Assertion:* At level four, parents learn to interpret their youngsters' behavior and provide appropriate parenting techniques to facilitate the development of self-concept and problem-solving skills. Parents share common problems with each other and a group facilitator to formulate new approaches to children's behavior, both academic and social. The goal is to bring about positive changes in parent behavior.
5. *Decisionmaking:* At the final level, parents are invited to participate with teachers and administrators in problem-solving sessions that focus on common educational concerns and issues. Parents are given an active role in these meetings, and their ideas are solicited and utilized. The object is to give parents a sense of ownership in the day-to-day affairs of the school and thus a personal stake in their children's education.

A Model for Urban Parent/School Interaction

Another model that has had a significant impact in helping urban parents become actively engaged in the affairs of the school is delineated by Rasinski and Fredericks (1989b). Their model, like Jenkins's, is a hierarchical structure that provides parents with four different levels of involvement and participation, but it also offers two parallel strands of involvement, one with a school orientation (parents become increasingly involved in the school community) and another with a home orientation (teachers become increasingly involved with their students' families). The four levels are:

1. *Monitor:* At this level teachers monitor students' completion of homework assignments as well as physical responses to classroom work. Parents monitor their children's emotional responses to the day's school activities as well as children's responses to home assignments from school. This is the critical stage in which parents and teachers communicate their feelings and thoughts with one another so as not to engender feelings of mistrust or an atmosphere of "checking up" on one another.

2. *Inform:* At the second level, teachers provide parents with regular and frequent communication, including telephone calls, newsletters, notes, and conferences relative to their children's academic progress. Parents offer teachers a variety of phone calls, notes, and messages relative to how the child is responding to reading assignments and activities completed at home.

3. *Participation:* At this level teachers actively solicit the physical participation of parents in school functions. Classroom aides, homework checkers, room mothers, tutoring, and the like are examples of this level of involvement. Teachers, on the other hand, primarily provide suggestions and training (e.g., how to read aloud, creating reading-related games, scheduling a family reading hour) to parents.

4. *Empowerment:* At this final level, strong bonds of respect and mutual accord have been built between parents and teachers. Empowered parents are provided with several opportunities to make instructional and curricular decisions that will affect their children. Teachers, too, feel empowered to ask parents for their support and direction. They also achieve a level of confidence that parents will want the best for their children, because teachers have been provided with opportunities to make appropriate decisions and follow through on those decisions.

Each model described above provides "room" for all parents in a school environment. Parents can "enter" at a level with which they feel most comfortable and "ascend" to a level commensurate with their interest, time, and commitment. Obviously, each model assumes that *all* parents can and should be part of the school community and that there are levels at which and through which they can demonstrate support of their children's education. Such a posture is a necessary element in any outreach effort, but particularly so for parents and community members in urban settings.

INTERGENERATIONAL PROGRAMS

One of the most exciting aspects of community involvement centers around intergenerational programs in which children have an opportunity to participate in literacy activities and events with older members of the community. Such events provide youngsters with wonderful insights into reading as a lifelong activity, an activity for all ages, and an activity that knows no limits of time, age, or circumstance. The result is not only a greater appreciation of reading by students, but an equally important appreciation of community members and the role of reading in their lives, too. The result is children and adults who are able to share a common bond and some common beliefs about education in general and reading in particular.

Rasinski and Fredericks (1991) present an intriguing overview of several different intergenerational projects for consideration by schools and teachers. These projects usually fall into one of two groups: those in which community members come into the classroom to share books, read favorite stories, or participate in any number of literacy activities (e.g., plays, puppet shows, readers theatre, etc.) with students; and those in which students participate in group or individual trips into the local community. The advantage of the group activities is that they allow children to interact with other adults in the community in a supportive and friendly environment, and children begin to understand the impact of reading in many individuals' lives. The second type, planned and regular visits to businesses or group homes, can offer valuable opportunities for students to learn about life in the community and to develop related literacy skills. An example of this type of program is when students are paired with residents of a local nursing home. Visits to the home allow children to read to the residents, share school experiences, learn about the "good old days," and converse in a friendly and meaningful way. Extensions of this kind of project can include the initiation of a pen pal program with the residents, taking and recording oral histories of the senior citizens, and developing appropriate journal activities over an extended period of time. The result is not only a sensitivity to the problems and conditions experienced by older people, but also an appreciation of literacy as a vehicle to learn more about a segment of the community.

In addressing the issue of involving parents and other community members in the dynamics of the classroom or school reading program, two questions surface: What materials and methods seem to be most effective in stimulating and maintaining parent participation? What factors are important in ensuring the success of these outreach efforts? The remainder of this chapter will focus on these issues.

EFFECTIVE STRATEGIES

Perhaps the most significant concern of administrators and reading supervisors deals with the methods and models proven effective in stimulating, promoting, and maintaining parent and community involvement. This section will address those methods educators have traditionally used, the data educators need to establish a viable home/school connection, and an effective model that ensures positive parent participation.

Assessing Traditional Methods

Over the years teachers have communicated with parents through a few established and universal methods. Becker and Epstein (1982) reported that almost 95 percent of the 3,698 teachers in their survey typically engaged in three types of parent contacts: sending notices home, talking with parents during open school evenings, and making occasional telephone calls. It also appears that this pattern of interaction is present in almost every school across the country. Vukelich (1984) has reported other media that teachers employ to establish an open dialogue with parents concerning their children's reading growth. Included in her list are booklets and handbooks, brochures or pamphlets, activity sheets, progress letters, notes and conferences, reading and shopping lists, courses and workshops, calendars of activities, and home learning kits. What is apparent in reviewing these parental contact methods is the fact that educators have a multiplicity of ways to reach out to parents and involve them in the dynamics of the reading program.

Just as the methods of sharing are diverse, so too are the types of information typically disseminated to parents. Vukelich's (1984) study, which involved a search of 37 references on parent involvement in reading, listed the following suggestions as those most frequently made to parents (listed in order of frequency): read to your child, be a good literate model, provide books and magazines for your child to read, build a reading atmosphere at home, talk and listen to your child, exemplify a positive attitude toward reading, provide a variety of experiences for your child, read environmental signs, provide children with paper and pencil, be aware of your child's interests, and point out similarities and differences in the environment. Various other kinds of information were shared with parents, but less frequently. It is interesting to note that while most educators would logically support these suggestions for parents, only one — "read to your child" — has been supported by any empirical research data (Vukelich, 1984).

Gathering Needed Information

Although we are aware of a plethora of ways to communicate with parents and of the types of information traditionally offered to parents, one major concern still remains: What kinds of information do educators need in order to plan, develop, and implement an effective outreach program? A study conducted among 75 reading educators (Fredericks & Taylor, 1984–1985) found that teachers and administrators are primarily interested in learning about (1) examples of materials for parent use, (2) parent participation in the home, (3) various models of parent involvement, and (4) methods of involving "absentee" parents. This study also found that most reading professionals are aware of the variety of ideas, suggestions, and information that could be shared with parents, but need an operational framework upon which to build a successful outreach program. While most educators have had little or no formal training in how to work with parents, they do, for the most part, have an intuitive knowledge of some communication methods and materials. What is lacking from their repertoire, however, is a systematic and easy-to-use network that facilitates outreach efforts and promotes family involvement as a positive extension of the school reading program.

Creating a New Model

With the exception of the two "urban" models presented above, there appears to be a dearth of available models for those seeking to establish successful family participation programs in all school settings. A cyclical paradigm, which provides an efficient and workable model for engaging parents in their youngsters' reading development, has been developed by Fredericks and Taylor (1985). It is based on the idea that most parent involvement programs in reading suffer because sufficient care was not taken in setting up a plan of action that takes into account community types, resources, needs, or long-term projections. The following four-stage model (known as the Parent Reading Engagement Profile, or PREP), however, provides a methodical approach to designing a successful involvement project. The four stages of the PREP model are as follows:

1. Needs assessment
2. Planning
3. Program implementation
4. Evaluation

Needs Assessment.   Outreach programs risk failure whenever they are predicated on ease of delivery rather than assessed needs. Parents will be more willing to participate in an outreach program when they know that the project is addressing their identified needs, more so than when the program is being set up at the convenience of the school or teachers.

PREP needs assessment procedures typically take two forms, formal and informal. Included among the formal methods are questionnaires, attitude scales, checklists, inventories, and self-evaluative scales. Informal methods can include individual conferences, small group discussions, telephone conferences, brainstorming sessions, and informal interviews (Fredericks & Taylor, 1985). It is crucial that a variety of assessment methods be utilized so that appropriate opportunities exist for parents and community members to voice their opinions.

Planning.   After parental needs have been assessed, it is vitally important that both educators and parents take sufficient time to analyze the results. In this way, necessary program goals can be established. While many concerns usually surface through the needs assessment procedure, any outreach effort must be careful to address only a limited number of needs, rather than tackle too many. The PREP model (Fredericks & Taylor, 1985) suggests that the planning group consider the following sequence of activities:

- Determine a few areas of greatest need.
- Establish priorities for those needs.
- Analyze the highest-ranked needs.
- Project a long-range plan (establish goals).
- Brainstorm for action.
- Outline a plan of action.
- Develop details for the plan of action.
- Develop a timeline.

Program Implementation.   Putting a program or project into place requires coordination of time and personnel tasks. While many outreach efforts may be simple in design, focusing on one class over a brief period of time, others may involve many elements of the school throughout the school year. Whatever programs are developed to reach into the community, it is vitally important that the individuals involved (educators, parents, students) all understand their roles and responsibilities. A program cannot exist on the whims or desires of a single individual; rather, it must be predicated on the combined efforts of all concerned.

Also, in timing the outreach program, administrators must consider the hectic schedules of both parents and teachers. In short, programs need to be built so that parents and teachers have a multiplicity of options by which to participate, in line with schedules that are constantly changing and evolving. Such decisions are not always easy, but demand that a flexible schedule of activities be designed to allow for the ebb and flow of time responsibilities for parents, educators, and students. In using the PREP model, implementation procedures must also ensure that both parents and educators are *aware* of program benefits, are *invited* to participate in the project, are *involved* throughout the duration of the proposed activities, and are *recognized* for their efforts to participate in and promote the program. With teacher and parent schedules often oversubscribed, it becomes necessary for the planning team to consider a multitude of scheduling options that maintain and preserve the program throughout its projected timeline.

Evaluation.   Designing and implementing a parent involvement project is one thing; knowing whether the project has made an impact on its intended audience is quite another. Unfortunately, some outreach efforts are developed with the simple goal of "making it to the end." The PREP model advises the effective administrator or reading supervisor to collect evaluative data that can lead to modifications or revisions during the course of the project and/or at its conclusion. This data collection must be both systematic and comprehensive so that intelligent decisions can be made as a project is in progress or is being considered for a "second round." As in the needs assessment stage of this model, a variety of evaluation techniques can be implemented (both formal and informal) that will provide the needed information. Of course, evaluation becomes particularly useful when it is keyed to the program goals established during the planning phase.

In sum, the PREP model provides a workable framework for any reading supervisor or administrator interested in soliciting parent support and participation within the school or district reading program. Its strength lies in the fact that it underscores the cooperative effort needed by both educators and community members to work together for the benefit of all students. Of course, as a model, PREP allows for necessary modifications according to the dynamics of individual schools or communities.

Suffice it to say, however, that working with parents is not a hit-or-miss proposition; rather, it requires an investment of time, talent, and energy on the part of many individuals in order to guarantee success.

GUIDELINES FOR SUCCESS AND SOME SUGGESTED PROJECTS

Without question, there is a wide diversity of outreach projects and programs that can be incorporated into the reading curriculum. Yet, regardless of the type of outreach program planned by administrators and/or reading supervisors, there are several guidelines against which a proposed project should be measured in terms of its potential impact. These guidelines, generated from an exhaustive survey of successful outreach projects, offer reading educators some practical considerations in planning effective parent/community involvement efforts (Rasinski & Fredericks, 1988, 1989a). Included with each of the following guidelines are some suggested parent involvement possibilities for the classroom, school, or district.

1. *Parents and children must have regular daily opportunities to share, discuss, and read together.*
Establish "reading contracts" with school families. Encourage families to read together on a regular basis every day. Ask parents to sign a contract that pledges them to make this a regular family practice. Special calendars can be prepared and distributed so that parents can check off appropriate reading times for all family members. Families who read together for a specified number of minutes each month can be awarded special certificates obtained from a local teacher supply store.

Community and neighborhood newspapers are always on the lookout for newsworthy items to put into their pages. Consider drafting a regular column on tips and ideas that parents can use in promoting the reading habit at home. This space can also be used to describe literacy-related events happening at school or to list recommended children's books.

2. *Purposeful activities need to be at the heart of the program.*
Children must be able to understand the relevance of reading-related activities (reading recipes, assembling a model, and so on) to their own growth as readers.

Develop and design a series of orientation programs for parents new to the school or district. It would be valuable to develop a slide program, a series of brochures, family guides, or other appropriate orientation materials to assist new families in learning as much as they can about purposeful activities in the reading curriculum.

Work with a group of parents to prepare a notebook of vacation home/community activities. Games, reading activities, places to visit, and sites to see in the community could all be included. These notebooks could be distributed to all families prior to a vacation period, especially summer.

3. *Children must be provided with regular opportunities to interact with good literature and well-written stories.*
Establish a lending library of resource materials and books for parents to check out and utilize at home. These materials can be purchased with school funds or by the local home and school organization. Also include a selection of educational games and activities for families to check out.

Periodically provide parents with various lists of recommended books. Work with the school librarian in distributing lists such as "The Supervisor's Top Ten Hits" throughout the year. Consider disseminating a list of books on child-rearing practices, as well as those containing reading-related activities. If possible, plan a few "share-and-discuss" sessions with groups of parents to talk over selected books.

Promulgate the benefits of public library membership to all families. Plan to work closely with the local public library to share information on the wealth of resources and information available to families in the community.

Ask parents and community people to list some of their favorite children's books, either those they read as children or those they are currently reading to their own children. Publish this list on a frequent basis and distribute it to all families.

4. *Projects should take into account not only specific needs of parents but the day-to-day needs of youngsters as well.*
Students' interests, hobbies, and free-time activities can be utilized in promoting the reading habit.

Distribute lists of recommended books to parents based on students' interests. Suggested readings on popular hobbies, arts and crafts projects, and playtime activities would be welcomed by parents. For example, families can be provided with book lists on how to create or practice a project or activity, along with names of books covering important personalities or discoveries in those particular areas. Encouraging families to bring and/or share their experiences with other students would also be appropriate.

5. *An outreach program should not attempt to turn parents into surrogate teachers, but rather should promote and extend the natural relationship between parent and child.*
Parenthood is not the easiest of jobs. It's one in which tolerance levels may be low and frustration ever-present. As such, any outreach effort must not

place any undue pressure on parents, but rather should subscribe to the notion that parent/child interaction time should be unhurried, pleasant for all parties, and tolerant of everyone's feelings.

Set up an exhibit in the local shopping mall, church, or synagogue that includes photos of parents and children reading together, tips for parent participation, and other reading-related activities. Engage children in designing and creating these displays, including their ideas for sharing the reading experience with the entire community.

Ask parents to keep special diaries or scrapbooks of family-related reading activities. For example, include books they have read and stories discussed, as well as photos of family members reading together. These can then be brought to school by students for special sharing.

6. *Parents should be provided with a variety of opportunities to support and encourage their children's growth as readers.*
Utilize the local media in disseminating information on how parents can and should become involved in their school's reading program. Public service announcements distributed to local television and radio stations, letters to the editor of the local newspaper on the value of community and parent involvement in the reading curriculum, or a monthly advice column in the Sunday newspaper can all be effective.

Invite parents and other community members to join a "reading curriculum council" to assist in the selection of new reading materials or to help establish guidelines and directions for the reading program throughout the year.

Establish an "open-door" policy with the community early in the school year. Parents need to feel comfortable in visiting their children's classrooms or schools. Frequent invitations from the administrator or reading supervisor are an important way of transmitting this philosophy. Also, invite parents and other community leaders to demonstrate their hobbies or favorite reading materials to groups of children. This reinforces the idea that all community members can and should enjoy reading as a lifetime pursuit.

Involve the community in establishing homework policies and practices. Homework continues to be the most traditional method of contact between home and school. By encouraging parental input in the design of an all-inclusive homework policy, schools can ensure the support they need.

7. *Although sufficient planning is the key to any elective program, informality needs to be the watchword.*
Offer parents and other community members a series of informal workshops throughout the year that focus on various aspects of the reading

curriculum. The workshops can address specific components of the school's reading program as well as ways and methods in which parents can help support teachers' instructional efforts.

Establish regularly scheduled informal meetings with parents throughout the year. These can be set up as brown-bag lunches with the building principal, a meeting over tea and coffee with the reading supervisor, or a "bring-your-own-dessert" gathering in the evening. The intent of these meetings should not be to provide instruction, but rather to give educators and community people an opportunity to meet informally and discuss common goals and objectives. If these meetings can be held in a neutral location, such as a church or YMCA, parents will be more inclined to come, particularly if the meeting is planned for the convenience of their schedules.

8. *A spirit of shared responsibility needs to be built into any outreach effort.*

Gather a coalition of parents, community workers, local businesspeople, and educators together to write a series of newsletters on suggested parent involvement ideas. Plan to have these distributed throughout the community in workplaces, office buildings, factories, and community centers.

Don't neglect grandparents and other senior citizens (see above). Many effective volunteer programs have relied on older people to provide innumerable reading services to the school. These can include listening to children read aloud, sharing childhood experiences with reading, and reading popular stories to classes of students.

Undoubtedly, no chapter can ever provide all the ideas or projects possible for a single community. It is hoped that ideas such as these will stimulate the creation of programs that reach far beyond the classroom walls and encompass the needs and desires of a particular community. The ideas just presented are only suggestions; what is needed is the creative vision generated when parents, community members, and educators come together for the mutual benefit of all students. Only then will a project or set of projects validate the positive relationship necessary for effective reading development.

REFERENCES

Becker, H. J., & Epstein, J. L. (1982). Parent involvement: A survey of teacher practices. *Elementary School Journal, 83*, 85–102.

Fredericks, A. D. (1992). *Involving parents through children's literature: Grades 1–2.* Englewood, CO: Teacher Ideas Press.

Fredericks, A. D. (1993). *Letters to parents in science.* Glenview, IL: Scott Foresman.

Fredericks, A. D., & Rasinski, T. V. (1990a). Involving the uninvolved: How to. *The Reading Teacher, 43*(6), 424–425.

Fredericks, A. D., & Rasinski, T. V. (1990b). Whole language and parents: Natural partners. *The Reading Teacher, 43*(9), 692–694.

Fredericks, A. D., & Rasinski, T. V. (1990c). Factors that make a difference. *The Reading Teacher, 44*(1), 76–77.

Fredericks, A. D., & Rasinski, T. V. (1990d). Involving parents in the assessment process. *The Reading Teacher, 44*(4), 346–349.

Fredericks, A. D., & Taylor, D. (1984–1985). Parent involvement in reading: What educators want to know. *The Reading Instruction Journal, 31*(2), 17–20.

Fredericks, A. D., & Taylor, D. (1985). *Parent programs in reading: Guidelines for success.* Newark, DE: International Reading Association.

Henderson, A. T. (1988). Parents are a school's best friends. *Phi Delta Kappan, 70,* 148–153.

Jenkins, P. W. (1981). Building parent participation in urban schools. *Principal, 61*(2), 21–23.

Lightfoot, S. L. (1978). *Worlds apart: Relationships between families and schools.* New York: Basic Books.

Mason, J. M., & Au, K. (1986). *Reading instruction for today.* Glenview, IL: Scott Foresman.

Rasinski, T. V., & Fredericks, A. D. (1988). School sharing literacy: Guiding principles and practices for parent involvement. *The Reading Teacher, 41,* 508–512.

Rasinski, T. V., & Fredericks, A. D. (1989a). Can parents make a difference? *The Reading Teacher, 43*(1), 84–85.

Rasinski, T. V., & Fredericks, A. D. (1989b). Dimensions of parent involvement. *The Reading Teacher, 43*(2), 180–182.

Rasinski, T. V., & Fredericks, A. D. (1991). Beyond parents and into the community. *The Reading Teacher, 44*(9), 698–699.

Vukelich, C. (1984). Parents' role in the reading process: A review of practical suggestions and ways to communicate with parents. *The Reading Teacher, 37,* 472–477.

Part IV

INTERCONNECTIONS

The reading program should not stand alone. Rather, it should be linked to other school programs that are concerned with literacy. First and foremost, current research has established that reading and writing are both active, constructive processes that are generated from schemata. Chapter 12 shows how the teaching of reading and writing can be connected with all learning. Current technology that offers new ways of communicating and graphically presenting information is a valuable tool that should be an integral part of any literacy curriculum. Chapter 13 demonstrates how administrators can promote the use of technology across the curriculum.

More and more children from diverse ethnic and linguistic cultures are entering our schools each day. Chapter 14 offers theoretical models for working with these diverse populations and practical ways of addressing their needs on a day-to-day basis.

The literacy program must not be focused only on the developmentally "average" child; it must provide for all children, including those who find learning to read and write difficult and those who are in special education programs. Chapter 15 reviews the literature on traditional and current approaches (pullout and in-class models) that deal with these special populations. Also, it describes new early intervention programs such as Reading Recovery and First Steps that are aimed at reducing remedial programs in the future. It closes with a set of 14 questions to ask about literacy programs for special needs children.

Because Part IV deals with these important links that must be made between and among literacy programs and other school programs, we have entitled it "Interconnections."

12 Connecting Reading, Writing, and Learning

JOAN T. FEELEY
William Paterson College of New Jersey

A fifth grade teacher in a midsized urban community in northern New Jersey began her two-hour language arts workshop by reading to her class a traditional version of the classic folktale *The Three Little Pigs.* Next, she shared Jon Scieszka's *The True Story of the Three Little Pigs* (1989). The latter is a "fractured" tale told from the wolf's point of view. In an amiable "tough guy's voice," the wolf explains that he never set out to eat the three pigs but that a series of unfortunate circumstances (such as his sneezing) caused the pigs' houses to be demolished and led to their eventual demise. He ate the dead pigs rather than waste the meat!

Next, the class helped to fill in a Venn diagram comparing and contrasting the two versions. They soon picked up the real difference. Although the characters and some events were similar, in the traditional version, the third pig told the story and the wolf was the villain, while in the retold version, the wolf told the story from his standpoint, portraying himself as a poor, misunderstood neighbor of the pigs who was merely trying to borrow "a cuppa sugar."

A student also shared another Scieszka book, *The Frog Prince Continued* (1991), which ended with a twist: instead of the frog turning into a prince, the prince and princess decide to remain frogs. Through these reading experiences, the class was effectively introduced to a special way of retelling traditional stories, the "fractured fairy tale."

After this reading workshop, in which these students took an incisive look at how authors can craft a story by playing off the familiar, they began their writing workshop by discussing in pairs a favorite tale they would like to retell à la Scieszka, usually by changing the voice and point of view: for example, *The Three Bears* from the Baby Bear's point of view, or *Cinderella* as told by one of the stepsisters. Eventually the room grew quiet as the children (and the teacher) wrote their first drafts. A genre study in reading had led naturally to writing in that genre.

* * *

Elsie Nigohosian, a kindergarten teacher in a New Jersey suburb, developed an ordinary science unit on animals into an extraordinary thematic study of endangered animals in Africa. After listening to chapters on African animals from *Grassland Animals* (Chinery, 1992) and *1000 Facts About Wild Animals* (Butterfield, 1992) and to an excellent concept book about endangered species, *Will We Miss Them?* (Wright, 1992), the children selected animals about which to collect more information. Six animals emerged for study. Some major books Elsie gathered for each were: *African Elephants: Giants of the Earth* (Patent, 1991); *Gordy Gorilla* (Irvine, 1990); *Manatee: On Location* (Darling, 1991); *Danger on the African Grassland*, about rhinos (Sackett, 1986); and Caroline Arnold's *Giraffe* (1987) and *Zebra* (1987).

After whole and small group reading/writing activities, the children made big books about their animals containing the following information: What does my animal look like? How does it move? Where does it live? What makes it special? Why is it endangered? To make some of these animals more personalized for her students, Elsie read aloud fictional picture books such as Anthony Browne's *Gorilla* (1983), about a lonely little girl, neglected by her father, whose toy gorilla becomes real for her; Howe's hilarious *The Day the Teacher Went Bananas* (1984), about a strange new substitute teacher (a gorilla); and Shel Silverstein's *Who*

Wants a Cheap Rhinoceros? (1983). Also, they shared Tomie De Paola's wordless picture book *The Hunter and the Hunted?* (1981) and William Steig's dreamlike fantasy *The Zabajaba Jungle* (1987). As postreading activities, the children retold the stories, advertised animals as being "good pets" through drawings, and reacted to the plots through art and writing.

Elsie introduced the children to social studies concepts by reading from the Cohens' *Zoos* (1992) and Curtis's *Animals and the New Zoos* (1991), which tell about the conversion of zoos into animal parks, preserves, and aquariums. She taught them about careers with animals by reading *The Work of the Zoo Doctors at the San Diego Zoo* (Irvine, 1991) and *I Can Be a Zoo Keeper* (Rowan, 1985). After a neighborhood vet had visited, the children wrote a class thank you note. Together they drew an outline map of Africa using yellow for deserts, green for grasslands, and blue for rain forests.

To introduce bar graphs in math, Elsie had the children conduct a survey among classmates on attitudes toward animal rights and graph their results. In addition, they made a class big book of animal word problems.

The endangered animals theme spread throughout the curriculum, and children learned about reading and writing as they were immersed in information presented in print, music, videos, and other technology (see Chapter 13).

*   *   *

These two vignettes illustrate how many of today's teachers are connecting reading, writing, and learning across the curriculum. Process (the "how") and product (the "what") are merging as classrooms become more child-centered, activity-oriented, and information-rich. How did this trend come about? Although we have seen integrated learning promoted before, I believe this current curriculum approach in the elementary school received its impetus from the writing process movement (writing workshop) of the 1980s, which led to the emergence of literature-based reading workshops, which have in turn spread to thematic teaching across the curriculum.

WRITING WORKSHOP

Until the last decade, we taught writing by using published workbooks and texts and assigning topics about which students were expected to write. Compositions were corrected mainly for spelling and mechanics, and the student's goal was to present an error-free end product. Because of initiatives such as the Bay Area Writing Project in California (Camp, 1982), Emig's (1983) study of the composing processes of twelfth graders in New Jersey, and research emanating from hundreds of National Writing Project centers across the country, we now know how writers write and how to teach writing. The National Writing Project researchers, who studied writers at work, described writing as a recursive process involving planning/prewriting, drafting, reading, revising, and editing. With real writers, content is always the most important element, and they compose from their own inner resources for an intended audience. The message for teaching was clear: Take the focus off the product and place it on the process. Consequently, the concept of writing workshop emerged; just as artists and actors learn in a workshop atmosphere, so students can learn to write in a writing workshop (Calkins, 1986; Graves, 1983).

Typically, in a writing workshop, students write on topics of their own choosing and read their drafts to their peers and/or teacher to get feedback on the content. This part of the process is called conferencing, and listeners tell the author whether or not the writing makes sense. Next comes revising, in which authors add, delete, or change text in response to suggestions offered in the conference. Editing, or fixing up the mechanics, comes last, and only if the piece is to be "published" in an individual or class book to be read by others. During this process, students begin to see themselves as authors and look forward to writing workshop (Feeley, Wahlers, & Jones, 1990). What a change from the old days, when writing was considered hard and relegated to Friday afternoon "composition" sessions!

The writing process researchers also added to our knowledge of how literacy (just like oral language) develops naturally (Calkins, 1986; Graves, 1983; Harste, Woodward, & Burke, 1984). Because they are immersed in language in meaningful situations, children learn to speak the language of their home. Adults don't directly teach; they just model language, give feedback, and praise early approximations such as "muk" for "milk" and "ba-ba" for "bottle." Yet when it came to writing, we didn't expect children to compose until they were well into first grade, and then we expected their writing to match adult, conventional standards!

We now know that children can write much earlier (Baghban, 1984; Bissex, 1980; Clay, 1975, 1993; Dyson, 1983; Ferriero & Teberosky, 1983; Harste, Woodward, & Burke, 1984) and that they go through stages just as they do when developing oral language. Temple et al. (1993) have found that young children who are encouraged to experiment with print will go from drawing and scribbling to adding random letters and eventually to "invented spelling," in which they first write prominent consonants and gradually add more consonants and vowels. These stages are readily discernible when one looks through writing workshop samples by four-, five-, and six-year-olds (see Chapter 3).

Writing workshop, which stresses a process approach to teaching writing, has become the accepted vehicle for developing writers in schools, pre-K to twelfth grade (Calkins, 1986; Fletcher, 1992; Graves, 1983; Karelitz, 1993; Moffett, 1992; Routman, 1991). Moffett (1981, 1992) has called the resulting curriculum changes the most important development in English education since World War II.

READING WORKSHOP

While some teachers always used literature as the content of their reading programs (Huck, 1977; Routman, 1988), most have relied heavily on published basal readers and anthologies, with their elaborate teachers' manuals and workbook aids. But as teachers became comfortable with writing workshop, which freed them from restrictive, tightly sequenced lesson plans for teaching writing, they became disenchanted with the prescriptive, skills-driven published systems used to teach reading. They soon realized that for their young writers to develop their craft, they would need exposure to the best of literature rather than to the abridged snippets, excerpts, and rewritten text found in most basals at the time. Gradually, they began to adapt writing workshop strategies to reading, and the concept of "reading workshop" emerged.

Many teachers are moving from being strict basal teachers to teachers who use basals plus literature and finally to teachers who use literature only in a reading workshop environment (Wepner & Feeley, 1993). For example, a basals plus first grade teacher uses her basal stories selectively (no workbooks) and organizes workshops around authors such as Mercer Mayer, Robert McCloskey, and Frank Asch. She starts her workshop by reading aloud as the children follow along in their copies, often joining her in chorus. The next day, the children read the same selection to her and to each other, often taping their reading. On the third day, they discuss the piece and finally write individual responses in their reading logs. And so the cycle continues.

A second grade teacher uses her basal materials selectively but switches off one week a month into reading an entire book with small groups or the whole class. They do a myriad of postreading activities, from puppetry to murals to writing inspired by the literature.

Some teachers have abandoned published programs entirely for full-blown reading workshops organized around literature (Wepner & Feeley, 1993). For instance, Janice Markovic introduces her kindergartners to reading and writing through shared reading experiences. Holdaway (1982) defines shared reading as literacy experiences in which teacher and children read together from enlarged print such as a big book, a chart, or an overhead transparency. Janice has collected over 40 big books from publishers such as The Wright Group, Rigby, and Scholastic. After she reads the story as they watch, the children read along with her; they use the text for many learning-to-read activities such as finding letters, words, and print conventions (left-to-right progression, punctuation, sound–symbol relationships).

Another second grade teacher's reading workshop revolves around her circulating class library of sets of books in a variety of genres (mystery, animals, adventure, classics, and nonfiction). Reading groups are made up of children who are reading the same book. Although the teacher selects the book at first, gradually she encourages the children to pick their own, just as children in writing workshops select their own topics. After a 20-minute silent reading time, the children form "literature circles" (Harste, Short, & Burke, 1988) to discuss their books.

Kathy Kelly, a fourth grade teacher, had started her literature-based reading workshop in a similar manner, with groups of students reading the same book. But after reading Atwell's *In the Middle* (1987), she decided to adapt the Atwell model; children select their own books, which they read every day for at least one half-hour both in school and at home. As they read, they write "literature letters" to their teacher and classmates in ringed notebooks called "dialogue journals." Kathy writes back to them and encourages classmates to respond, too (hence the dialogue).

Kathy's reading workshop starts with a mini-lesson on a reading strategy such as using the context to predict the meaning of an unknown word, or some aspect of literature such as the metaphor. This is followed by a period of silent reading in which Kathy models by reading also; then she circulates for one-to-one conferences to assess how students are progressing, do on-the-spot teaching, and record observational notes. On any given day, 20-plus different books are being read in her classroom representing authors from today (S. E. Hinton, Robert Lipsyte, Judy Blume, Paula Danziger, and Avi) to classic favorites such as Mark Twain and Hugh Lofting.

Most of the sampling of teachers described above began to change their approach to teaching reading from a three-group, basal reading program to a reading workshop — a place to learn a craft by experimenting with it — after experiencing a sense of ownership and success with teaching writing through a process-oriented writing workshop. While some are still using basals on their own terms (choosing specific pieces or skill work), all are using authentic literature in varying degrees. Workshop time is spent reading, responding, and sharing, with skills being taught within the context of real reading. The natural next step was to combine reading and writing workshops and to pursue a theme to offer integrated, connected learning. We saw this happening in our opening vignettes about a fifth grade study of a literary genre and a kindergarten study of African endangered species that eventually went across the curriculum.

THEMES IN LANGUAGE ARTS AND
ACROSS THE CURRICULUM

Schema theory is a way of explaining how knowledge is organized and stored in our brains. A schema (schemata is the plural form) represents all the information that summarizes what one knows about a concept (Anderson & Pearson, 1984). According to Mason and the Staff at the Center for the Study of Reading (1984), schemata come into play as readers interact with a text; comprehension depends upon having and activating appropriate schemata. Besides helping to explain the complex notion of reading comprehension, schema theory has implications for teaching and learning in general. Rumelhart (1980) suggests that we learn through: (1) *accretion*, or adding new information to existing schema; (2) *tuning*, or modifying existing schema; and (3) *restructuring*, or creating new schema from existing schema to further flesh out our cognitive network.

Thematic teaching is supported by schema theory. Connecting learning to read and write with the study of specific content makes much more sense than teaching reading and writing and the content areas as separate entities. In a discussion of why to use themes, Lipson et al. (1993) offer several cogent reasons. They say that a thematic approach provides a focus for classroom work that helps students to relate content and process, since they will be learning to read in order to learn specific content. It promotes the acquisition of an integrated knowledge base that results in faster retrieval of information and better concept transfer across content areas, thus enhancing learning. Also, besides encouraging depth and breadth in learning, it promotes positive attitudes toward reading and writing because students are engaged in authentic learning activities and have some choice in what they read and write. Finally, Lipson et al. (1993) say:

> Perhaps the most powerful, practical appeal of themes is that thematic teaching can provide time. By combining several separate curricular areas and reducing redundancy in the process, teachers and students should have not only *more time, but better quality* time that is less fragmented and available in larger blocks. Both are important to improved instruction. (p. 254)

In discussing the kinds of themes that teachers can pursue, Lipson et al. (1993) identify two broad categories. *Intradisciplinary* themes are designed to develop the language arts (reading, writing, listening, speaking) and are usually focused around selected literature. They may involve the study of an author, a genre, or a literary theme such as courage or survival. (The authors note that the current basals are doing a better job than basals of the past in presenting selections on coherent literary themes.) The fifth grade teacher in our first vignette was implementing an *intradisciplinary* theme on fairy tales in her combined reading–writing workshop.

On the other hand, *interdisciplinary* themes are intended to integrate content with the development of the reading and writing processes, to unify learning across several content areas as did Elsie Nigohosian in her African endangered species unit. Often the theme is drawn from one specific content area, yet extends into another. For example, one of my students who teaches eighth grade social studies and reading in a New York City middle school just completed a very successful unit on the Holocaust (Reistetter, 1993). While she taught two social studies classes through traditional text materials, she was able to extend the Holocaust theme into one group's reading class. The students who read, discussed, and wrote about several pieces of fiction, such as *Number the Stars* (Lowry, 1989), did significantly better than their counterparts who used only the text on both a school-developed test of content knowledge and a synthesizing essay. For a sustained period of time, they had become immersed in the topic through exposure to traditional texts, nonfiction, and fictional works, and they grew as readers, writers, and students knowledgeable about an important historical event.

Teachers who first espoused writing workshop and extended its philosophy and structure to teaching reading through reading workshop are now trying to teach reading and writing in blocks of time dedicated to the language arts with a literature or language focus, or, where possible, are combining reading, writing, and learning in an interdisciplinary across-the-curriculum theme.

HELPING TO IMPLEMENT CHANGE

How can supervisors and administrators help teachers move toward a more connected approach? We have identified three major ways in which change in schools can come about (Wepner & Feeley, 1993). When teachers lead the way, the bottom-up model is at work. In top-down models, change is instituted from above, usually by superintendents, principals, or curriculum coordinators. Sometimes it emanates from a state education department as in the case of Pennsylvania, described by Henk and Moore (1992) in the next section. In the best of both worlds, teachers and administrators work together to initiate change. In the current climate of empowerment, most agree that you cannot mandate change but must "invite" educators to become knowledgeable and reflective and to willingly buy into new ways of delivering literacy instruction (Ruth, 1991).

At the heart of the matter is helping teachers to change their belief systems about the culture of the classroom. Pahl and Monson (1992) call this a paradigm shift away from a transmission model, in which teachers dispense information to students, to a transaction model, in which students construct their own meanings by interacting with new ideas. The transmission model is skill-based, teacher-centered, and test-driven, reflecting the traditional view. The transaction model is process-oriented, student-centered, and concept-based, reflecting the current research on interactive, connected learning. A shift of this magnitude is not easy and requires much study, discussion, demonstration, reflection, and, of course, full support from administrators. But it appears to be the most important ingredient for promoting positive change (see Chapter 6 for further discussion of the transmission model).

Bottom-Up Initiatives

Bottom-up change comes through the grassroots, the teachers who have made the paradigm shift on their own. We saw this happen in many New Jersey districts. For example, after learning about teaching writing as process through the New Jersey Writing Project under Janet Emig at Rutgers University, Edie Ziegler and Lyn Stampa added writing workshop to their literature-based reading program in Closter, New Jersey. Edie continued her immersion in a connected, process approach by studying with Lucy Calkins at Columbia University's Teachers College (TC), eventually joining with several colleagues for weekly dinner meetings at which they shared what they were learning. This became their first network (Wepner & Feeley, 1993).

Through a TC teacher-researcher grant to study the effects of networking, the original network was expanded to include 16 teachers from the surrounding area schools that fed into a regional high school. They found that networking positively affected the behaviors and attitudes of the teachers involved. Network members began writing workshops in their classrooms and shared their experiences with other teachers, creating a ripple effect. As for attitudes, most began to make the paradigm shift from transmission to transaction models.

In the 1980s, the New Jersey Department of Education instituted the High School Proficiency Test (HSPT), a requirement for a high school diploma and taken in grade nine. Because the language subtest, influenced by the New Jersey Writing Project, included an essay worth 60 percent of the language subtest score, the cry went out for more writing in the elementary schools. Edie's group was enlisted to offer staff development in holistic scoring and conducting writing workshops; this eventually led to a new integrated language arts curriculum.

Now, Edie, Lyn, and Jim Klika teach a cross-graded group of second, third, and fourth graders and have shared their work with others through *Building Communities of Readers and Writers* (Klika, Stampa, & Ziegler, 1987), a publication funded by a Governor's Grant. They have also described their dynamic reading-writing workshop in detail in another publication (Ziegler, Klika, & Stampa, 1991).

The literature abounds with similar stories: for example, *The Author's Chair and Beyond: Language and Literacy in a Primary Classroom* (Karelitz, 1993); *A Door Opens: Writing in Fifth Grade* (Wilde, 1993); and *One Teacher's Classroom: Strategies for Successful Teaching and Learning* (Gordon, 1993). Supervisors and administrators can use teachers such as these as focal points for introducing new ways to develop literacy. At the very least, as in Closter, they can support these teachers with recognition and budgetary aid, and use them as resource teachers to help others who are willing to experiment with change.

Top-Down Initiatives

Top-down initiatives can come from the state, district office, or school principal. Henk and Moore (1992) describe Pennsylvania's efforts to implement its framework for curriculum construction, entitled *Reading, Writing, & Talking Across the Curriculum* (Lytle & Botel, 1988). An updated version of the Pennsylvania Comprehensive Reading Plan (PCRP), now called PCRP II, this new guide espouses a literature-based, process-oriented, integrated language arts approach. Initially it met with resistance because the state was still using a statewide test that assessed students' mastery of specific skills. Naturally, the teachers felt compelled to prepare students for the test, and this resulted in language programs that were fragmented and skills-dominated.

Recognizing that the test was driving instruction, Pennsylvania followed the lead of states such as Michigan and Illinois and created a different kind of state assessment that uses longer, authentic reading selections and taps higher-level thinking processes. It also includes a section that asks students about their reading attitudes and habits. The Department of

Education actively promotes PCRP II through workshops, consultant directories, school visitation opportunities, and an electronic communications network, and things seem to be moving ahead. As Henk and Moore (1992, p. 46) observe:

> The result of this ongoing commitment is that real changes have occurred in the way that reading is viewed and taught across the state. For example, most of Pennsylvania's school districts seem to have adopted to some extent the fundamental tenets of whole language not only by modifying their basic curricula accordingly, but also by instituting innovative organizational models at elementary through senior high schools (e.g., peer teaching, reading and writing workshops, and thematic content area instruction).

An example of a top-down initiative instituted at the district level is Leonia, New Jersey. Inspired by the work his wife Edie was doing in Closter, Deputy Superintendent Irv Ziegler wanted his teachers to try writing workshop, but at first the idea was not well received. Working with the most respected but most resistant sixth grade teacher, he modeled the approach by leading the workshop in her class for six weeks. From writing one piece per month, the students went to producing several "published" pieces and gained a real knowledge of the writing process. The teacher not only continued the workshop, but began a network in her district. Ziegler also took advantage of the state-mandated HSPT to offer district staff development on holistic scoring and the writing process, with a resource teacher to whom others could now turn for help. He also established the position of language arts coordinator, someone who was steeped in the process approach, to offer continued support and staff development to his teachers (Wepner & Feeley, 1993).

For an example of a principal who led the way, I will describe Peter Heaney, who arrived at P.S. 321, an urban Brooklyn school with students from a wide range of socioeconomic backgrounds, to find the primary grades using reading-writing workshops and a holistic approach but the middle grades still, except for one teacher, using basals and fragmenting the school day into discrete, skills-based periods (Feeley, 1991a). Having been a staff developer and teacher who was sold on the workshop approach, Heaney decided to dialogue with the middle grade teachers in a reading-writing-learning workshop held at lunchtime twice a month (he bought lunch, which also helped with attendance) and to use Laura Kotch, the one teacher who was using literature and workshops, as a model. First the teachers began using writing workshop; this need was identified early by the Program Improvement Committee, a site-based management team of teachers, parents, and administrators, and implemented with the aid of a consultant.

The noontime meetings gave the teachers a place to talk about their writing workshops and get help from each other. Next, they wanted to look at their reading program, so Heaney invited them to read Roald Dahl's *The Witches* (1983) with him and engaged them in various response activities so that they actually experienced a reading workshop for themselves. The modeling worked beautifully, and the entire staff voted to spend their textbook money on sets of trade books to be phased in and replace their basal program the next year. Laura Kotch and Leslie Zackman, a teacher resource center consultant, became in-house consultants, introducing literature through book talks and demonstrating and coaching whenever teachers asked for help.

Johnston and Wilder (1992) describe a similar approach to staff development in the Orange County, Florida, schools. Noting that one-shot lectures, conferences, and inservice workshops have poor payoff (only 5 % of these kinds of initiatives are usually actually implemented in schools), they set up Reading/Writing/Learning study groups for the 83 schools in their county. Teachers and principals volunteered to make a commitment to be leaders and learners in the study groups by reading professional literature, trying out new practices, and keeping journals on their reflections. Often principals became "head learners" and collaborated with the teachers to make curriculum change. They also arranged for teachers to visit other classrooms and supported them with adequate budgetary help.

The study groups began with book talks designed to broaden teachers' knowledge of children's literature and model how to use books with their students. Teachers and resource people demonstrated such practices as writing workshop, shared reading with big books, and using multiple copies of books. After the demonstrations and participatory sessions, the study groups would discuss the new practices and how they could apply them in their classrooms, often making appointments with resource teachers to visit their rooms to demonstrate further.

Because follow-up is so important to keep the momentum going, teachers kept journals on their experiences and reflections, sharing these at meetings and with the resource teachers at the end of the year. Also, as they planned for the following year, they were asked to complete a self-evaluation form on which they assessed their attention to such concerns as providing a print environment and time to read and write, implementing reading and writing workshops, reading aloud, and establishing portfolio assessment.

Orange County found the Reading/Writing/Learning study groups very effective in changing teachers' beliefs, attitudes, and classroom practices. They report that teachers who participated gained confidence as teachers who were willing to take a stand when they were asked to do things that did not fit with their new philosophy. It appears that they had effectively made the paradigm shift!

To bring about change, supervisors and administrators have to be a part of the initiative as were the deputy superintendent in Leonia, principal in New York City, and principals in the Orange County schools, who became learners along with their staffs in Reading/Writing/Learning study groups. In this way, they model the spirit of experimentation, simultaneously learn what the issues and problems are, and work with the teachers to solve them cooperatively. Top-down becomes invitational and cooperative, and has a much better chance of succeeding than a mandate to change with outside consultants hired to "inform" the staff. In effect, this traditional top-down model mirrors the transmission paradigm, whereas the newer study groups, networks, and teaching-learning workshops mirror the transaction paradigm.

Initiatives from Both the Bottom and the Top

Sometimes the impetus for change can come from one direction but gain fuel from the other. For instance, in River Edge, New Jersey, it was a reading teacher, Erika Steinbauer, who became aware of the process writing movement through TC's summer institute. After interesting some teachers in trying writing workshop, she asked Superintendent John LaVigne to help spread the practice throughout the school. He encouraged the small group of teachers to form a committee to sell the idea to the staff, board, and parents; consequently the Writing Process Committee was established and writing was made the focus of staff development for the year. Summer writing workshops were held and a new writing curriculum was developed (Feeley, 1991b).

Next LaVigne created the new position of Staff Developer and appointed Steinbauer to the slot. When the teachers realized that their basal reader was no longer adequate, the writing group became an enlarged Reading-Writing Committee, and Steinbauer led them in summer sessions that combined curriculum revision with the creation of guides for trade books and thematic units connecting reading, writing, and the content areas. Now the school's principal, Steinbauer continues to lead staff development workshops for a network of over 40 teachers from two districts. She feels she justly represents both the bottom and the top.

To promote change in the Kalispell, Montana, schools, Language Arts Coordinator Carol Santa (1991) began offering literacy workshops, summer institutes, and college courses in the district. While some teachers were "buying in," she became aware of an undercurrent of uneasiness in one school in which a second grade teacher who was still teaching traditionally with a transmission model began to complain openly about the first graders who were coming to him from a teacher using a literature-based approach, not knowing how to use worksheets, and writing in invented spelling. After meeting with the two teachers involved, Santa and the school principal took the problem to the language arts committee, composed of teachers and administrators from the whole district.

The committee undertook a yearlong study to develop a philosophy, and a curriculum assessment plan congruent with that philosophy. To arrive at a philosophy, Santa surveyed the teachers to learn their beliefs and "dreams" about literacy instruction. While the primary teachers believed in using a combination of basals and literature, the middle grade teachers wanted to teach mainly through literature. As for "dreams," few teachers at either level wanted a prescriptive basal driven by a publisher's scope and sequence chart; most wanted to expand their literature and writing programs. But assessment was a major concern, since all used basal assessment tests but were not satisfied with them.

Accordingly, after interviewing teachers for solutions, the committee decided that what Kalispell needed was its own scope and sequence chart of reading and writing behaviors that could be documented by products that would become the basis for their district portfolio assessment. Unlike the multitude of skill clusters found in basal readers, the scope and sequence array developed by Santa and the teachers contained only four categories of generally specified behaviors for each grade level. This provided a common strand for evaluation that teachers could use even if their philosophies differed. Santa (1991) said: "Because accountability was reduced to just a few things at each grade level, teachers felt free to move ahead" (p. 239).

In this instance, although change was initiated by the Language Arts Coordinator, she needed the collaboration of all the teachers to arrive at a philosophy and develop a curriculum and assessment procedure congruent with that philosophy.

Fair Oaks, a bilingual school in Redwood City, California, with 95 percent of its students coming from immigrant families living below the poverty line, has evolved from a school once targeted by the State Department of Education as needing to show improvement on state tests to a successful whole language school recognized as a model by others (Bird, 1989). Over the past decade, through the efforts of a resource teacher, its principal (Smith, 1989), superintendent (Hill, 1989), and significant others such as a school board member and several teachers, Fair Oaks has initiated an integrated reading-writing immersion program based on psycholinguistic principles (Goodman, Goodman, & Bird, 1991). To do this, the superintendent, principal, and teachers became learners together, visiting bilingual whole language schools in Phoenix to bring back ideas and engage in staff development on a continuous basis.

And their efforts paid off. The school has the highest attendance rate in Redwood City, and Fair Oaks students who are bilingual transfer to English instruction in grade three. While previously only 15 percent of its students passed the city Writing Proficiency Test, 82 percent passed after five years in the new program. Also, scores on the California Test of Basic Skills (CTBS) have been climbing, with those students in the program the longest showing the greatest gains (Smith, 1989).

Truly a top-down and bottom-up initiative, the Fair Oaks experiment worked because staff members were empowered by the district's site-based management program, and there was verification that the program, based on sound psycholinguistic research, really worked (Hill, 1989).

GUIDELINES FOR SUPERVISORS AND ADMINISTRATORS: CONNECTING READING, WRITING, AND LEARNING

Although change can come from the bottom or the top, collaborative initiatives appear to be the best for generating new approaches to literacy instruction that take root and flourish. With this in mind, the following guidelines are recommended:

1. For a start, support teachers who are experimenting with reading-writing workshops by recognizing their efforts, providing budgetary help to purchase trade books, and asking them to help you in your efforts to learn and to involve the rest of the school staff. Your inside innovators can be one of your best resources.
2. Learn how reading-writing classrooms work by visiting exemplary sites, networking with other administrators involved with holistic approaches, and reading the professional literature. I would recommend works that have most affected teachers, such as Atwell (1987), Calkins (1986), Graves (1983, 1991), and Routman (1988, 1991). To get schoolwide visions, read titles addressed more specifically to administrators, such as Bird (1989), Heald-Taylor (1989), Vacca (1992), Winograd (1992), and Yatvin (1992).

   Yatvin (1992) is particularly readable and helps one to understand some of the whole language terms within the reality of real classrooms. Through a question-answer format, she deals sensibly with issues such as materials, classroom environments, curriculum (yes, you need a curriculum), skills (yes, you teach skills), grouping patterns (most teachers can't handle a completely individualized pro-

gram; she suggests sets of books), the role of teachers, and the responsibilities that teachers have to each other across grade levels.

3. Try an approach to staff development such as the Reading/Writing/
Learning model offered by Johnston and Wilder (1992) as a good way
to get started with the whole staff. Through these informal study
groups, in which both teachers and administrators participate, all
involved can become more knowledgeable about the latest research
and practices through readings, demonstrations, simulations, and discussions about possible applications in your school. As seen in P.S. 321
(Feeley, 1991a) and Orange County, Florida (Johnston & Wilder,
1992), this models the workshop approach for educators and encourages them to experiment in their own classrooms. Also, by nurturing
the paradigm shift proposed by Pahl and Monson (1992), the Read-
ing/Writing/Learning study groups can lead to the development of a
consistent philosophy that is so important for goal-setting and future
curriculum, instruction, and assessment planning (see Chapter 9 for
other approaches to staff development).

4. If you cannot afford the time to lead the initiative yourself, appoint
an instructional leader to help teachers in their classrooms. While
some schools create full-time staff development positions, others provide staff members with release time for this purpose. It appears important to have a respected in-house resource person.

5. Provide teachers with observation opportunities and a professional
library. Henk and Moore (1992) suggest that besides visits to exemplary classrooms, teachers can learn much from videotapes. These can
be made locally or purchased from commercial sources. Videos are a
powerful tool that can reduce staff development costs. "A picture is
worth a thousand words."

Principals, curriculum coordinators, and supervisors should take an
active role in providing teachers with professional books, journals,
and research reports in the field of literacy instruction. Access to professional literature keeps the staff au courant and maintains the momentum begun in staff development initiatives.

6. Engage in curriculum review with your teachers. At the close of your
first set of Reading/Writing/Learning study group meetings, you can
survey your teachers to get a sense of how they think literacy should
be taught, and use the results to establish goals to guide your literacy
curriculum. Next, you or your instructional leader can work with a
committee of interested teachers to develop a flexible, broad-based
curriculum to carry out those goals (see the New York City guide,
Essential Learning Outcomes: The Communication Arts, 1988). At
the same time, consider assessment procedures that will be congruent

with your curriculum, as did Santa in Kalispell. To make connected, holistic learning work, you must deemphasize standardized testing, especially in the primary grades, and look into appropriate internal assessment tools such as portfolios. Essentially, your curriculum committee should draft a language curriculum and some ideas on assessment and call for response from the whole staff.

Yatvin (1992) suggests that each school have an oversight committee that guides and coordinates the entire program. This committee would do such things as establish the goals and philosophy, describe a general approach to teaching, secure and distribute funds, plan staff development, and help implement the new curriculum. A group from the district curriculum committee, it sees that things get started and move forward. Essentially, it oversees curriculum, instruction, and assessment planning and implementation (see Chapter 1).

7. Involve teachers more in the school budget process, as did Peter Heaney. Allow those who want to spend their allocations on trade books instead of basals to do so. As suggested in *Becoming a Nation of Readers* (Anderson et al., 1985), discourage the purchase and use of workbooks, and encourage teachers who want to stick with a basal to purchase only the student books and accessories that they really want to use.

8. Inform board members by having teachers report on innovations at board meetings. I remember once hearing a writing process teacher make a presentation of her students' "published" works at a school board session; the members were so impressed that they unanimously voted to fund staff development in the teaching of writing.

9. Inform parents by having staff members or consultants address PTA meetings, encouraging teachers to explain programs at back-to-school night, and sending home newsletters to disseminate information on new programs.

10. Establish networks with local colleges and universities. These resources can often provide consultants and access to well-known speakers through conferences and workshops. Becoming involved in consortia and networks can keep interest high and foster continued staff development.

CONCLUDING REMARKS

Moving from a transmission to a transactional model of teaching and learning takes time. More evolutionary than revolutionary, it involves changing philosophy, curriculum, instructional practices, and ways of assessing achievement. To work, it must be a collaborative effort, with supervisors, administrators, and teachers sharing in the transition process. Yatvin (1992) says:

> The most important aid to collegiality is an atmosphere of openness, unmarred by competition. Again, principals cannot decree an atmosphere; they can only set up favorable conditions and avoid unfavorable ones. An organizational system that provides for shared decision making and offers a multitude of opportunities for people to succeed tends to make people generous with their time and ideas. On the other hand, a school where teachers must compete for power and rewards encourages concealment, jealousy, and stinginess. In such schools, schoolwide programs exist on paper but rarely become part of the reality of teachers' lives. (p. 37)

REFERENCES

Anderson, R. C., Hiebert, E. H., Scott, J. A., & Wilkinson, I. A. G. (1985). *Becoming a nation of readers: The report of the Commission on Reading.* Champaign, IL: The National Academy of Education, The National Institute of Education, The Center for the Study of Reading.

Anderson, R. C., & Pearson, P. D. (1984). A schema theoretic view of basic processes in reading. In P. D. Pearson (Ed.), *Handbook of reading research* (pp. 255–291). New York: Longman.

Atwell, N. (1987). *In the middle: Writing, reading, with adolescents.* Portsmouth, NH: Heinemann.

Baghban, M. (1984). *Our daughter learns to read and write: A case study from birth to three.* Newark, DE: International Reading Association.

Bird, L. B. (Ed.). (1989). *Becoming a whole language school: The Fair Oaks story.* Katonah, NY: Richard C. Owen.

Bissex, G. L. (1980). *GYNS at WRK: A child learns to read and write.* Cambridge, MA: Harvard University Press.

Calkins, L. M. (1986). *The art of teaching writing.* Portsmouth, NH: Heinemann.

Camp, G. (1982). *Teaching writing: Essays from the Bay Area writing project.* Portsmouth, NH: Heinemann.

Clay, M. (1975). *Why did I write?* Portsmouth, NH: Heinemann.

Clay, M. (1993). *An observation survey of early literacy achievement.* Portsmouth, NH: Heinemann.

Dyson, A. H. (1983). The role of oral language in early writing processes. *Research in the Teaching of English, 17*(1), 1–30.

Emig, J. (1983). *The web of meaning: Essays on writing, teaching, learning, and thinking.* Portsmouth, NH: Heinemann.

Essential learning outcomes: The communication arts. (1988). New York: Office of Curriculum Development and Support, New York City Board of Education.

Feeley, J. T. (1991a). An urban school becomes a community of readers and writers. In J. T. Feeley, D. S. Strickland, & S. B. Wepner (Eds.), *Process reading and writing: A literature-based approach* (pp. 99–107). New York: Teachers College Press.

Feeley, J. T. (1991b). Transition in a suburban district: An interview with its superintendent. In J. T. Feeley, D. S. Strickland, & S. B. Wepner (Eds.), *Process reading and writing: A literature-based approach* (pp. 224–250). New York: Teachers College Press.

Feeley, J. T., Wahlers, G., & Jones, B. (1990, May). *Helping parents understand the writing process.* Paper presented at the International Reading Association Convention, Atlanta.

Ferriero, E., & Teberosky, A. (1983). *Writing before schooling.* Portsmouth, NH: Heinemann.

Fletcher, R. (1992). *What a writer needs.* Portsmouth, NH: Heinemann.

Goodman, K. S., Goodman, Y. M., & Bird, L. B. (Eds.). (1991). *The whole language catalog.* Santa Rosa, CA: American School Publishers.

Gordon, D. (1993). *One teacher's classroom: Strategies for successful teaching and learning.* Portsmouth, NH: Heinemann.

Graves, D. H. (1983). *Writing: Teachers and children at work.* Portsmouth, NH: Heinemann.

Graves, D. H. (1991). *Build a literate classroom.* Portsmouth, NH: Heinemann.

Harste, J., Short, K., & Burke, C. (1988). *Creating classrooms for authors: The reading-writing connection.* Portsmouth, NH: Heinemann.

Harste, J. C., Woodward, V. A., & Burke, C. L. (1984). *Language stories and literacy lessons.* Portsmouth, NH: Heinemann.

Heald-Taylor, G. (1989). *The administrator's guide to whole language.* Katonah, NY: Richard C. Owen.

Henk, W., & Moore, J. (1992). Facilitating change in school literacy: From state initiatives to district implementation. In J. Vacca (Ed.), *Bringing about change in schools* (pp. 44–48). Newark, DE: International Reading Association.

Hill, K. G. (1989). Nurturing a metamorphosis. In L. B. Bird (Ed.), *Becoming a whole language school* (pp. 123–128). Katonah, NY: Richard C. Owen.

Holdaway, D. (1982). Shared book experience: Teaching reading using favorite books. *Theory into Practice, 21,* 293–300.

Huck, C. (1977). Literature as the content of reading. *Theory into Practice, 16,* 363–371.

Johnston, J. S., & Wilder, S. L. (1992). Changing reading and writing programs through staff development. In P. Winograd (Ed.), *Exemplary practices in literacy development and instruction* (pp. 59–64). Newark, DE: International Reading Association.

Karelitz, E. B. (1993). *The author's chair and beyond: Language and literacy in a primary classroom.* Portsmouth, NH: Heinemann.

Klika, J., Stampa, M., & Ziegler, E. (1987). *Building communities of readers and writers.* Trenton, NJ: New Jersey State Department of Education.

Lipson, M. Y., Valencia, S. W., Wixson, K. K., & Peters, C. (1993). Integration and thematic teaching: Integration to improve teaching and learning. *Language Arts*, *70*, 252–263.

Lytle, S., & Botel, M. (1988). *Reading, writing, & talking across the curriculum, The Pennsylvania Comprehension, Reading and Communication Arts Plan II (PCRP)*. Harrisburg, PA: Pennsylvania Department of Education.

Mason, J. M., & the Staff at the Center for the Study of Reading. (1984). A schema-theoretic view of the reading process as a basis for comprehension instruction. In G. G. Duffy, L. R. Roehler, & J. Mason (Eds.), *Comprehension instruction: Perspectives and suggestions* (pp. 26–38). New York: Longman.

Moffett, J. (1981). *Coming on center: Essays on English education*. Portsmouth, NH: Boynton/Cook.

Moffett, J. (1992). *Active voice: A writing program across the curriculum*. Portsmouth, NH: Heinemann.

Pahl, M., & Monson, R. (1992). In search of whole language: Transforming curriculum and instruction. In J. Vacca (Ed.), *Bringing about change in schools* (pp. 6–12). Newark, DE: International Reading Association.

Reistetter, N. (1993). *Teaching social studies through literature*. Unpublished report, William Paterson College, Wayne, NJ.

Routman, R. (1988). *Transitions: From literature to literacy*. Portsmouth, NH: Heinemann.

Routman, R. (1991). *Invitations: Changing as teachers and learners K–12*. Portsmouth, NH: Heinemann.

Rumelhart, D. E. (1980). Schemata: The building blocks of cognition. In R. J. Spiro, B. C. Bruce, & W. F. Brewer (Eds.), *Theoretical issues in reading comprehension* (pp. 33–58). Hillsdale, NJ: Erlbaum.

Ruth, L. (1991). Who decides? Policymakers in English language arts education. In J. Flood, J. M. Jensen, D. Lapp, & J. R. Squire (Eds.), *Handbook of research on teaching the English language arts* (pp. 85–109). New York: Macmillan.

Santa, C. (1991). Cutting loose: A district's story of change. In J. T. Feeley, D. S. Strickland, & S. B. Wepner (Eds.), *Process reading and writing: A literature-based approach* (pp. 232–243). New York: Teachers College Press.

Smith, N. (1989). The view from the principal's desk. In L. B. Bird (Ed.), *Becoming a whole language school: The Fair Oaks story* (pp. 115–122). Katonah, NY: Richard C. Owen.

Temple, C., Nathan, R., Temple, F., & Burris, W. (1993). *The beginnings of writing*. Boston: Allyn and Bacon.

Vacca, J. (1992). *Bringing about a change in schools*. Newark, DE: International Reading Association.

Wepner, S. B., & Feeley, J. T. (1993). *Moving forward with literature: Basals, books, and beyond*. Columbus, OH: Merrill.

Wilde, J. (1993). *A door opens: Writing in the fifth grade*. Portsmouth, NH: Heinemann.

Winograd, P. (1992). *Exemplary practices in literacy development and instruction*. Newark, DE: International Reading Association.

Yatvin, J. (1992). *Developing a whole language program for a whole school.* Newark, DE: International Reading Association.

Ziegler, E. R., Klika, J., & Stampa, L. (1991). Triskadekaphobia and other uncommon nonfiction interests. In J. T. Feeley, D. S. Strickland, & S. B. Wepner (Eds.), *Process reading and writing: A literature based approach* (pp. 62–70). New York: Teachers College Press.

CHILDREN'S BOOKS CITED

Arnold, C. (1987). *Giraffe.* New York: Morrow.

Arnold, C. (1987). *Zebra.* New York: Morrow.

Browne, A. (1983). *Gorilla.* New York: Knopf.

Butterfield, M. (1992). *1000 facts about wild animals.* New York: Kingfisher Books.

Chinery, M. (1992). *Grassland animals.* New York: Random House.

Cohen, D., & Cohen, S. (1992). *Zoos.* New York: Doubleday.

Curtis, P. (1991). *Animals and the new zoos.* New York: Dutton.

Dahl, R. (1983). *The witches.* New York: Farrar.

Darling, K. (1991). *Manatee: On location.* New York: Morrow.

De Paola, T. (1981). *The hunter and the hunted?* New York: Holiday House.

Howe, J. (1984). *The day the teacher went bananas.* New York: Dutton.

Irvine, G. (1990). *Gordy gorilla.* New York: Simon and Schuster.

Irvine, G. (1991). *The work of the zoo doctors at the San Diego Zoo.* New York: Simon and Schuster.

Lowry, L. (1989). *Number the stars.* Boston: Houghton-Mifflin.

Patent, D. H. (1991). *African elephants: Giants of the Earth.* New York: Holiday House.

Rowan, J. (1985). *I can be a zoo keeper.* Chicago: Children's Press.

Sackett, E. (1986). *Danger on the African grassland.* Boston: Sierra Club/Little, Brown.

Scieszka, J. (1989). *The true story of the three little pigs.* New York: Viking.

Scieszka, J. (1991). *The frog prince continued.* New York: Viking.

Silverstein, S. (1983). *Who wants a cheap rhinoceros?* New York: Macmillan.

Steig, W. (1987). *The Zabajaba Jungle.* New York: Michael di Capua Books.

Wright, A. (1992). *Will we miss them?* Watertown, MA: Charlesbridge.

13 Using Technology for Literacy Instruction

SHELLEY B. WEPNER
William Paterson College of New Jersey

Dr. H. had been employed for the last 16 years as a reading supervisor for kindergarten through grade twelve in a large school district.
Because standardized testing hangs over teachers' heads like the sword
of Damocles, many teachers cannot part with the formulaic style of
their basal systems. Nevertheless, Dr. H. was proud of his efforts to get
teachers to use five trade books a year in lieu of a few stories from the
basal.

Within the last five years, he had initiated a plan for using computers
in reading/language arts instruction. However, don't think for a minute

that this was because of Dr. H.'s passion for technology. He had been badgered (to put it kindly) by his assistant superintendent, a staunch supporter of technology, to figure out ways to encourage teachers to use computers for reading and writing instruction. Because Dr. H.'s prior involvement with computers had been as far-reaching as his secretary's word-processing prowess (i.e., minimal) and as reinforcing as his abysmal failure at a programming course he took back in college, Dr. H. had been justifiably anxious about embarking on this new responsibility. Yet he knew that computers were quickly becoming an important new variable in the teaching of reading and writing, and that he would have to change his attitude.

Dr. H. did two things to initiate his plan to use computers. He appealed to a few of his reading specialists who already were using computers for just about every lesson, and he hired a consultant to help him create a five-year plan. His reading specialists, fervently dedicated to getting teachers in their buildings to use computers, had taken it upon themselves to learn as much as they could so that they could serve as resources to their teachers. They used whatever funds they had to order software. And they tried every piece of software with their own students before suggesting its use in the regular and special education classrooms.

The consultant helped by pushing Dr. H. to do a needs assessment in order to create a long-range plan for using technology. As a result, Dr. H. spent an agonizing year trying to figure out what had already been purchased for the district and what staff development efforts had taken place. A plan was created for slowly spreading the wealth of equipment and staff development. The consultant also spent about four months with a few teachers to help them see how specific pieces of software could enhance their instructional plans. While the consultant was there, things were beginning to hum. But the minute she left, the teachers, like rubber bands stretched to their limits, resumed their old instructional patterns.

*   *   *

Although the people are fictitious, the situation is real. Those in supervisory positions may find themselves coerced into becoming experts in educational computing. Often, because of their own fears and anxieties, they give lip service to mandates or, worse yet, never get off the dime with their technology plans. Yet instructional leaders such as Dr. H. are responsible for helping teachers to integrate computers into the curriculum. What can he and others like him do? This is the question addressed in this chapter.

WAYS TO GET STARTED

Today, with computers in just about every elementary classroom, teachers who reside in buildings with our technologically oriented reading specialists are using computers as naturally as they are using books and magazines. Teachers in buildings without an advocate for technology, however, are using them sparingly, if at all. They're a wonderful prop for Back to School night. In truth, these teachers do not have the support to help them see beyond what they think helps their students get ready for standardized testing. Yet when you ask them if they like computers, they respond affirmatively. And when you ask their students whether they like computers, they respond with a resounding yes!

Get Yourself Involved

If you don't understand or appreciate the value of technology, you're not going to advocate its use. That doesn't mean you have to be an avid user yourself; you just have to be aware of technology's integral position in our lives. A friend of mine who is a principal in a K–6 school admits that while she pushed computers in her school, she really didn't believe in the computer's ability to nurture critical and creative thinking until she was tutored privately by her computer teacher. After two hours of training, she discovered why people gravitate to computers for manipulating information beyond the literal level. Now her nudges to use computers are both ongoing and sincere.

Observe children as they work with computers to see how they get actively involved with software and with each other in collaborating about what's on the screen. One computer teacher tells the story of the day she cancelled her computer class with her first grade students. Somehow, through a series of miscommunications with the classroom teacher, the students didn't know this and went to the computer lab anyway. They opened up the file to the disk they had been working on and started to work together on their stories. When she entered the lab and saw what they were doing, she didn't have the heart to cancel class. Apparently the students wouldn't have noticed if she had!

Whether they're upwardly mobile kindergartners or poverty-stricken eighth graders, students enjoy working with computers. When I visited one kindergarten class where the teacher was sharing her students' written comments about what they liked in kindergarten for Back to School night, almost half of her students wrote, "I like the computer" (of course, with various spelling renditions). When I worked with barely literate eighth grade students in an urban school and surveyed them about their experiences with the computer, 84 of the 85 students said they liked to work with the computer all or most of the time (Wepner, 1990/1991).

Acknowledge that you need access, time, and training to really become proficient with the computer. As one principal, Nancy Letteney, bemoans, "I know that if I really want to know how to use a computer, I need to take time from other things to teach myself what to do. But first I have to get a computer in my office." While this principal spent time with a computer expert in her building, she never had the computer or the time to pursue it further. She knows that when she gets a computer on her desk, she has to make time to make it work for her. She already has spent a day with a principal in another district to learn about administrative software that can make her tasks easier. She took copious notes so that she can follow in this vein when her own computer arrives.

Get Others Involved

As you're helping yourself to learn and grow in this area, share your knowledge and ideas with others. When you read magazine and journal articles (for example, *Technology & Learning* or *The Computing Teacher*) and books (for example, Balajthy, 1989; Roberts et al., 1988; Whitaker, Schwartz, & Vockell, 1989), share your "finds" with teachers so that they're reading what you're reading. Use this reading matter as an opportunity to discuss how computers support your belief and knowledge about reading/language arts instruction.

Whenever you attend workshops to see what others are doing in their schools, or enroll in courses to better understand how computers can be integrated into the reading/language arts curriculum, arrange to have key teachers join you. Use your shared experiences to develop a focus and plan together ways in which computers can be reasonably incorporated into your school or district curriculum.

Establish a committee of key people who represent different constituencies in your school or building to take back the information to their colleagues. A computer teacher told me that when she was trying to sell the idea of working with technology to her classroom teachers, they began to grouse at the thought of yet another responsibility. One of the classroom teachers happened to be on the districtwide technology committee. Rather than let the computer teacher go it alone, the classroom teacher stood up and endorsed the mandate in colleague language, explaining that she, as their representative, promoted this charge on the districtwide committee. The classroom teachers immediately began to get involved with what the computer teacher had planned.

In the view of one administrator, if teachers are to be intrinsically motivated to incorporate software into their reading/language arts programs, they have to have a voice on what is done and how it is done. This administrator, who wishes to remain anonymous, believes that her role simply is to "dance around the rim of the cauldron stirring up the brew, even with the few vipers who are bubbling inside."

Even with the vipers, you still can find enough teachers who are motivated to find software packages that work with the curriculum. As long as they feel comfortable in knowing that they need not have all the answers with technology and that they have resource people to turn to who can help them find the answers, teachers will use technology as best they can.

Identify Significant Others Who Can Help You Move Forward

Just as teachers don't have to know everything in order to teach (and, in fact, it's better if they rely more on students' knowledge bases), administrators don't have to buy into the notion that change won't occur unless it's "from the top" (termed "top-down"). Often the most effective changes in the teaching/learning environment begin "from the bottom" (termed "bottom-up") of the educational hierarchy—the teacher (Wepner & Feeley, 1993). If technology still escapes you, look for others who are hellbent on using technology in the curriculum to get your school or district started with the process of change. Better yet, identify a teacher or two who know something about technology and work together with them to facilitate the process.

Here's an example of a bottom-up approach for helping technology find its way into an elementary school. Six years ago, kindergarten teacher Elsie Nigohosian decided to go for a master's degree in reading. During her three years at the college, and because of her professors' zealous belief in holistic approaches to teaching, Elsie came out of her own whole language closet. Much to the chagrin of her principal, Elsie began to change her classroom accordingly. She went from her ho-hum phonics worksheets to a thematic approach to teaching literacy across curricular areas. Her quiet, well-sequenced lessons turned into a satisfying buzz of student activity. Her final goal for herself was to figure out a way to use technology to enhance what she was already doing. Because she was working closely with a professor who was determined to excite teachers about the rewards of technology, the professor worked closely with Elsie, even supplying her with the software needed to help her integrate technology into one of her units. Unfortunately, Elsie did not have the equipment needed to work with the software. However, as with every other hurdle, she told her principal that she had to have the equipment in order to do justice to her unit.

Once Elsie began to work with the software, she discovered how it enriched everything that she was trying to do. Puppets could be made with *Puppetmaker* (available for Apple); music could be created with *Kidstime* (Macintosh). Students' math concepts and skills developed in the unit could be reinforced and extended with *Muppet Math* (Apple). Students' exposure to the different animals could be further developed with *The Treehouse* (Apple, Macintosh, & MS-DOS), since it included a module on animal classification.

After much ado, the principal became convinced of technology's usefulness. Elsie's colleagues began to ask questions about what they could do to model her initiatives. Of course, the best part was watching her students run to the computers during their free-choice time to work on their own with the software.

Here's an example of how a top-down decision to use technology turned into a combined top-down, bottom-up approach. Joanne Mullane, a K-8 computer teacher, knows that there is no administrator in her district who uses technology as frequently as she does. But it doesn't matter. The administrators were savvy enough to employ others who could accomplish their mission of creating a "technologically current learning environment." Her principal, the person in charge of technology for the district, is very enthusiastic about her use of technology to support a whole language learning environment. When you ask Joanne how she learns, she responds, "I take courses, I attend workshops, and I spend many hours on my computer." Is it worth it? In Joanne's eyes, nothing is more thrilling than to watch a group of her students come into the lab, even when they're scheduled to be someplace else, and work independently or in groups with one of the packages that she uses for instruction. Joanne is even more thrilled when she sees her teachers work along with the students in the lab and role reversal sets in: the students (often those with learning disabilities) assist the teachers in much the same way that the teachers help the students in the regular classroom.

What kinds of things is Joanne doing with her students during their weekly sessions? Since Joanne believes in the marriage of curriculum and technology, she tries to find ways to get children to work with software packages that support what the students are reading, either through on-screen text or word processing. When her kindergarten students read Mercer Mayer's (1983) *Just Grandma and Me*, a book about a critter's eventful day with his grandma at the beach, Joanne uses the computerized version of the same book to read along with her students. This software package (Macintosh & MS-DOS; requires CD-ROM player), available in three languages (English, Japanese, and Spanish), reads each page of the book in natural-sounding phrases that are highlighted as they are spoken in the selected language. Each screen contains dialogue between the critter and grandma, as well as animation of other animals and objects (Wepner, 1992). Once students read the book, they write a sentence or two that is a takeoff on the book, to contribute to a class book that they take back to their classroom library. They also use *Kid Works 2* (MS-DOS and Macintosh), a creativity software package that allows children to write, paint, illustrate, print, and hear the stories they create.

Her first and second grade students use *Kid Works 2* to capture the language and rhythm of patterned books and stories. For instance, to her first grade students she reads Maurice Sendak's (1963) *Where the Wild Things Are*, a book about mischievous Max, who, when he is sent to bed without any supper, vividly imagines that his bedroom turns into a forest inhabited by wild things. Then her students work in groups of five to word-process and illustrate their own versions, such as "Where the Good Things Are" or "Where the Funny Things Are." Big books are created for the regular classroom, the library, and her computer lab.

Joanne's fifth graders write autobiographies, replete with scanned photos of themselves, with *The Writing Center* (Macintosh), an easy-to-use word-processing program with two different formatting options (report/story/letter and newsletter) and multiple font options. It also contains a graphics library that can be used for page headings or within the body of the text. Her eighth graders use *HyperCard*, software that comes with the Macintosh, to create animated piles of cards containing information about the planets that they have researched. These stacks then are shared with the fourth grade classroom teachers when they study the solar system with their students.

Joanne's plans did not just happen. She works closely with her principal and the three other computer lab teachers in the district to plan for staff development and curricular integration. She spends much of her time working with her teachers to tie students' computer activities with their classroom units. Teachers who feel comfortable with technology will bring ideas to her. Teachers who still are skittish about computers wait for Joanne to come up with something clever and useful to do.

Joanne hopes her teachers will respect and understand technology enough to feel the excitement of it as an educational tool, so that they will link it with the curriculum. Her wish for her students is that they have computers available to them for the entire day so that they become more active learners, take more responsibility for their learning, and generate a greater feeling of self-worth.

Professionals such as Elsie and Joanne feel the excitement of teaching with technology. Yet it doesn't take a classroom teacher or a computer resource teacher to get you started. It can be a library media specialist.

Or, as with Dr. H., it can be a reading specialist. It can also be one of your special education teachers. One of my favorite special education whole language/technology teachers is Jane Beaty, an Apple Classrooms of Tomorrow (ACOT) teacher who, out of sheer frustration with her inattentive teenage special education students, turned to technology to see if she could get them to attend to a task for more than five minutes at a time. After burning the midnight oil for more nights than she cares to admit, Jane got up to speed with the tool-based software that she thought would inspire her students. Apple Computer learned about her initiatives and invited her to experiment with their products. Today, after many (and she means *many*) fits and starts with her literature-based technology plans, Jane is quite expert on using technology to support just about everything she does. More importantly, her interest in technology has spread throughout her building and her district.

A FRAMEWORK FOR USING TECHNOLOGY

As soon as you have some appreciation of technology's potential role in literacy instruction, you should create a vision for how you want technology to be used. Along with creating this vision is the need to establish what it is you have and what it is you need. Four questions, used cyclically to extend the lifespan of your technology plan, can be used to help you with your curricular decisionmaking: Where are we? Where do we want to be? How do we get there? How do we know we are there? These questions emanate from a model, RECAP (REading/Computers Assessment Plan), that was used to help two school districts move forward with their technology plans in reading/language arts. I am sharing an adapted version of the model, based on what I have learned from my experiences and interactions with administrators and teachers. (See the first edition of this book for the original model.)

Phase 1: Where Are We?

Before you create a plan, consider what you already have in place. First and foremost, you need to identify the teachers, administrators, parents, and community members who have supported and will continue to support your initiatives. Who can help you with curricular decisions? Who can help you with staff development? Who can help you technically? Analysis of your personnel support will help you to decide how much you can accomplish and how long it will take. Second, assess your material resources — hardware and software — and their location. Figure 13.1 pro-

Figure 13.1   Questions to Be Addressed in Phase 1

CURRICULUM

1. How is technology being used for reading/language arts (e.g., skill development, word processing, desktop publishing, basal-based reading, literature-based reading)?
2. For which grade levels?
3. For which students (e.g., regular classroom, basic skills, gifted and talented)?

HARDWARE

4. What hardware is available to teachers and where is it located?
   Elementary
   _____ School: Number _____   Type _____
   Location _____
   Secondary
   _____ School: Number _____   Type _____
   Location _____
5. How often is the hardware used during the school day?
   0–25% of the time _____   25–50% _____   50–75% _____
   75–100% _____

SOFTWARE

6. What software exists in the district?
   Elementary
   Name (Publisher) _____   Number _____
   Location _____
   Secondary
   Name (Publisher) _____   Number _____
   Location _____
7. What licensing agreements exist?
   Software (Publisher) _____
8. Does a software inventory exist? If yes, what information does it include (e.g., annotations) and to whom is it distributed?
9. Is software coordinated with your curriculum? If yes, who does it? How is it done?

STAFF DEVELOPMENT

10. Identify the type of staff development that has been offered:
    Date: _____
    Topic: _____ Number Involved: _____
11. How are teachers implementing what they learned from staff development?
12. What type of staff development is needed?

vides a list of questions organized around four areas for Phase 1 of the RECAP model. Responses to these 12 survey questions will help you identify existing technology efforts so that you know how to plan.

Curriculum.   This is probably the most difficult area to address, since you need to examine, through discussion, interviews, and surveys, what is being done to support students' literacy development. Are teachers using technology as a gamelike "reward" for completing one's "real" work? Are teachers using technology as a glitzy substitute for a series of workbook pages? Or are teachers using technology to support students' trade book–related reading and writing activities? Often technology use depends on teachers' instructional philosophies. By analyzing who is working with technology and the kinds of activities in which students are engaged, you will get a better understanding of the role that technology plays in your school or district.

Hardware.   Assessing hardware availability, location, and usage is essential for planning future acquisitions. For example, you may have one school that has computers located in every classroom but that are used by only 25 percent of the teachers. Yet these teachers are using them for just about every instructional plan and are frustrated because there are too few computers in their room. Or you may have a lab that is excruciatingly quiet from lack of activity. While the former scenario may prompt you to move some of the computers into technologically active classrooms until your other teachers are ready to take the plunge, the latter scenario may prompt you to move computers into a few interested teachers' classrooms or, better yet, create a staff development plan that prompts teachers to use the lab.

Software.   As with a hardware inventory, a software inventory can be painstaking, time-consuming, and frustrating. Yet, as with books, magazines, and other materials used for literacy instruction, it's important to know what you have in order to help teachers figure out what can be used and when it should be used. Recently a curriculum coordinator new to a district called me to brainstorm ways to help her teachers integrate software into the curriculum. As we were talking, she realized that the reason she couldn't help them was because she didn't even know what software the district owned. Once she took the time to do the inventory and study the software, she felt better equipped to offer suggestions. Before you begin, find out if a software inventory already exists and how current it is. If an inventory does exist, examine the information included (for example, subject area, description, rating), and decide how you want to keep your own inventory.

As you gather information for your own software inventory (after all, if you're taking the time to do this, you might as well formalize your list), examine each piece for its primary use, for example, drill and practice, word processing, holistic applications, or record-keeping. Identify whether any licensing agreements exist for certain packages or with certain companies. (Licensing agreements are contracts between software vendors and, in this case, school districts, enabling districts to legally make and use multiple copies of specified software at reduced rates.)

Staff Development. Staff development is probably the most overlooked yet essential component for implementing technology. Exposure is simply not enough. Teachers need time to develop "automaticity" in the technical aspect of working with the hardware so they can focus on the content of the software. It's not only important to identify the type and frequency of staff development offered, but also the degree to which teachers have applied what they've learned in their classrooms. This analysis will help determine the type of staff development that is needed to help teachers feel secure in working with technology.

As so many administrators learn, often a bit too late, fully equipped schools are useless without a critical mass of computer users. Here's an example of the frustration felt by Ruth Murphy, principal of New Hope School in Chapel Hill, North Carolina. Ruth knows that her school is sitting on a hardware gold mine. Because her K–5 nongraded, literature-based school was created to be a world-class school to demonstrate best practice, and because there was a community-based technology committee that had included corporate heavyweights, IBM contributed $1.4 million to help create a state-of-the-art technology environment. Imagine this: Every classroom has six computers that are networked. Computers are stationed in each of the three teachers' rooms for teachers to use during their planning time. The classrooms are wired for telecommunications and interactive media. And her software inventory is equally plentiful, since IBM contributed its company-published software to the school.

So when you ask Ruth Murphy if she's satisfied with what is happening with technology in her school, she admits that while she has the necessary hardware and enough good software packages, she still does not have a necessary ingredient for technology integration: teacher competence and confidence with technology. Even though she knows that her school is suffering from a high-class problem of resource overload, she nevertheless recognizes that her teachers cannot move forward with technology as naturally as they are progressing with other learning tools until they know what can be done and how to do it. She has IBM knocking on her door to assess technology's role in her school, yet she has her teachers choking from confusion about what to do with all their equipment. Ruth Murphy knows that her school's technology wonderland will remain idle until her teachers have the right kinds of staff development opportunities.

Phase 2: Where Do We Want to Be?

Where do you want your school or district to be with technology three years from now? What do you need to do to get your teachers to use technology to support literacy instruction? This phase helps you to answer these two questions by setting goals for what you want to happen and how you want it to happen. The key to this phase is to involve a committee of representative teachers, administrators, and parents who take ownership for these goals. If you are forming a districtwide committee, it should consist of teachers and administrators from different schools and grade levels so that it embodies districtwide needs (Strickland, Feeley, & Wepner, 1987). As shown in Figure 13.2, the same four areas that are assessed during Phase 1 are used for creating goals during Phase 2.

If your district has done little in the area of technology, you will want to start small. Examine your reading curriculum, focus on those areas that may be problematic, and investigate what technology can do to help. One district, intent on helping teachers to simply feel comfortable in using the machines, identified software that went along with their basal reading program to support the skills addressed. Another district, determined to help its students to pass the statewide literacy test, decided to examine how computers might assist them in addressing statewide reading objectives. They began to look for software that pertained to those objectives causing their students the most difficulty. A third district, committed to getting teachers to integrate computers into their whole language reading program, decided to help teachers use technology along with their literature-based reading program.

So much depends on where teachers are with their literacy instruction. Edicts from above don't work (Doyle, 1993), as I know from first-hand experience. A few years ago, I asked a reading supervisor if I could field-test a series of literature-based technology plans with a few teachers. He was quite amenable to my idea and identified a school whose principal would be willing to work with me. The principal, in turn, identified a group of teachers to field-test these plans. Little did I know that the teachers almost never used computers and, worse yet, had no interest in putting aside their basals and concomitant skills for this new program. To add insult to injury, the amount of staff development allocated for helping

Figure 13.2   Chart for Developing Long-Term Goals in Phase 2

	Where do we want to be in year:				
	1	2	3	4	5
CURRICULUM					
Elementary					
Classroom teachers					
Chapter I					
Gifted and talented					
Special education					
Other					
Secondary					
Developmental reading					
Remedial reading					
Language arts teachers					
HARDWARE/PERIPHERAL ACQUISITIONS AND LOCATION					
Type/memory					
Budget (district/external)					
SOFTWARE					
Type					
Licensing					
Budget (district/external)					
STAFF DEVELOPMENT					
Type					
Person(s) responsible					
Participants					
Time frame					

teachers to feel prepared was, at best, insufficient. I spent the year apologizing for my existence. In truth, these teachers should not have been selected to participate in this program because they were not psychologically or professionally ready for this dramatic change. Needless to say, they felt as much ownership toward this program as the Jim Crow loyalists felt toward the civil rights movement in the 1960s. Teachers need to be involved in decisionmaking from the outset to garner acceptance for change (Barnard & Hetzel, 1986; English, 1975; Likert, 1969). The stronger their feelings of ownership for technology goals, the more motivated the teachers will be to implement change (see Veatch & Cooter, 1985–86).

As you consider your goals, identify simultaneously where your school or district is headed with literacy instruction. Dagmar Durish, K–12 language arts district supervisor, explains that while her district is moving toward a whole language model, they're only using skill-exercise software packages with limited-choice answers. She wants her teachers to have software that supports students' trade book reading. She also wants to work with her Advisory Council for Curriculum and Instruction to figure out ways to use technology across the curriculum. Once curricular goals are set, hardware/software acquisition and staff development goals must be established and documented.

Phase 3: How Do We Get There?

A plan of action, with a time frame, must be created by the same goal-setting committee for each of the four areas in Figure 13.3. Your curriculum goals should form the basis for your plan. If, for example, your teachers are already using cross-curricular thematic units for instruction at the elementary level, work with them to help them identify software that supports the unit. If your teachers are working on report writing at the secondary level, help them to identify tools (e.g., word-processing packages, multimedia tools, encyclopedic databases, tutorials for report writing) to support their instructional efforts.

Hardware and software accessibility must be considered. Plan to work immediately with the teachers who have at least one computer in their classroom or access to a computer lab so that they can use the available software. At the same time, strategically plan for future hardware and software acquisitions so that teachers who are willing to work with technology have access to what is needed. Technology plans are for naught if teachers do not have access to computers. Ruth Murphy, the principal of New Hope School, believes that teachers need to have a computer at home or, at the very least, in the classroom, where they can practice with software on their own or apply what they learn from staff development sessions. According to Chira (1990), in an article in the *New York Times*, if teachers are ever going to move beyond seeing computers as substitutes for skill books, they must have access to a variety of hardware and software to experiment with different uses.

Yet hardware and software access is just the beginning. Staff development must be planned so that teachers know what to do with what they have. In addition to access, teachers need training and time to become

Figure 13.3   Chart for Developing the First-Year Plan in Phase 3

Year 1: _____ to _____

Instructions: Specify how you intend to accomplish each goal for the first year. For example, in the area of curriculum, your specific objective might be to help fourth grade teachers use one piece of software with each trade book. You identify the need for a committee, including your fourth grade teachers, to accomplish this objective. You decide on specific tasks, a budget, and a time frame to accomplish each of the curricular objectives listed.

CURRICULUM

    Specific objectives
    Tasks required
    Task assignments
    Time frame
    Budget

HARDWARE

    Purchase plan (new or trade-in): type, quantity, features, cost
    Peripherals (e.g., printers, CD player, speech synthesizer)
    Network/cable requirements
    Location
    Budget for purchase (district and external funds)

SOFTWARE

    Type
    Quantity
    Hardware required
    Budget

STAFF DEVELOPMENT

    Person(s) responsible
    Purpose
    Participants (teachers and others)
    Schedule
    Location

---

versatile computer users (Wepner & Feeley, 1993). According to Chira (1990), teachers take at least five years to learn how to use computers creatively and effectively.

As one teacher of the gifted and talented bemoans, "No one really knows how to use technology in my building because there has been no guidance or encouragement." When she received a computer in her room, someone said to her, "Here are the manuals. Figure out what to do." Although software was purchased, no one was using it. Until a few years ago, when she had to do a project for a learning technologies course that she was taking, she didn't even know that the software existed. Although she decided to "take the risk" with technology and all its electronic nuances, she was one of the few who persisted. Because most of the teachers in her building were trained halfheartedly, they opted to ignore technology for less anxiety-producing tasks. When you listen to such tales of frustration about administrators' laissez-faire attitudes toward technology, you understand why many teachers continue to do business as usual.

"Training" in the form of two-day workshops just won't work. As Joanne Mullane, the computer teacher mentioned earlier in this chapter, says, "Teachers won't follow through in using technology if they do not have the training and time to become comfortable with it." She believes that teachers should receive a semester's worth of staff development that is equal in credit to a college course, so that they internalize how computers can help them professionally and personally. They need to see and use software that supports the grade-level and content areas they teach, to understand how technology works together with other resources to support, for example, a unit on Africa or a unit on the solar system.

If properly exposed to technology and guided along the way, teachers will use the computer as a teaching and learning tool. Your staff development plans will be successful if you: (1) start small so that it is digestible; (2) show teachers that technology is not yet another demand on the curriculum but rather can be a valuable tool and an integral part of the existing curriculum; and (3) expect teachers to be responsible for doing something by the end of the series of staff development sessions so that they participate fully.

The following is an example of a seven-step staff development program to help elementary teachers use software along with their literature-based plans. This plan assumes that the necessary hardware is available in teachers' classrooms:

Step 1: Identify a resource person who knows software. It can be you, another classroom teacher, a reading specialist, a media specialist, or a parent in the community.

Step 2: Convene a committee with your resource person and grade-level teachers to identify the trade books and concomitant activities, strategies, and skills that will be incorporated into their literature-based plans. For example, if you are working with fourth grade teachers, they may be using John Reynolds Gardiner's (1980) *Stone Fox*, a book about 10-year-old Willie, who discovers that his ailing grandfather's potato farm will be taken away if Willie doesn't earn enough money to pay back taxes. Willie decides to enter a dog-sled race with his dog Searchlight, and soon discovers that he will be competing with the legendary racer Stone Fox. Teachers might have students do a problem–solution activity in which they identify the main character's worries and the ways in which he tries to resolve them (Wepner, Layton, & Beaty, 1992). They also may use the same problem–solution format to analyze their own worries. Teachers might have students study Willie's relationship with his grandfather as a stepping-stone for writing a biography about one of their own grandparents.

Step 3: Have your resource person bring in one or two pieces of software that fit with a book. Once your resource person demonstrates the software, have your teachers work with it so that they truly understand its purpose and feel comfortable using it. You, too, should work with the software, to show your teachers that you're not afraid to take risks either. Teachers might work with a reading package and a writing package for *Stone Fox*. The reading package, *Reading Realities Elementary Series* (Apple and MS-DOS), contains, among 45 stories related to real-life issues, a passage entitled "Worries," about a group of students who talk to each other about their various worries. Since discussion and creative writing questions prompt students to discuss worries, this software package could be used to help introduce *Stone Fox*. Teachers also might work with *The Children's Writing and Publishing Center* (Apple and MS-DOS) or *The Writing Center* (described earlier in this chapter). Students can use this software package after they read the book, to summarize how Willie dealt with his worries. Students then can use this same package to generate a class-generated interview form to use with their grandparents, and use the information gleaned from the interviews to write biographies with the same package again (Wepner, 1992).

Step 4: Before your teachers decide how and when to use the software, have them identify why it should be used. How will the students benefit? What can be eliminated from the traditional plan? Then have your teachers work together to create a plan of action that delineates daily lessons.

Step 5: Meet periodically as a committee to determine what is working and what is not. Encourage your resource person to visit your teachers to help them with any concerns. Make sure that someone is available for technical troubleshooting if your resource person cannot serve in this capacity.

Step 6: Once the plan has been implemented, meet again as a committee to assess the plan's strengths and weaknesses vis-à-vis the marriage between the trade book activities and the software's support of these activities. Plan for another set of literature-based technology plans that include "used" and new software packages.

Step 7: Use this type of format to extend to other grade levels and special areas. Plan to set aside half a year for each grade level.

Phase 4: How Do We Know We Are There?

The last phase of RECAP helps you to determine the degree to which your goals are being achieved in order to make adjustments. Figure 13.4 lists factors to consider. For example, a school that used parts of the aforementioned seven-step plan included teachers and students for its *evaluation sources.* Teacher observations and conferences, teacher journals, standardized test data, and student surveys were used for its *evaluation techniques.* Since teachers had adequate hardware in their classrooms, teachers focused on staff development, the curriculum, and the software for the *contents of evaluation.* The teachers, the resource person, and the supervisor used the data collected to evaluate the plan and to recommend, for *follow-up,* how the program could be maintained, expanded, and monitored the next year.

Figure 13.4   Factors to Consider in Phase 4

Evaluation techniques	*Contents of evaluation*
Teacher observations and conferences	Curriculum
	Hardware
Review/analysis of standardized and informal test data	Software
	Staff development
Informal student assessments	Facilities
Interviews	
Communication with board and community	*Follow-up*
	Recommendations from evaluation
Survey questionnaires	Program maintenance and expansion
	Monitoring plan
Evaluation sources	Continued communication
Administrators	
Teachers	
Students	
Community	
Outside consultants	

Although data gathered during this phase may not indicate dramatic improvements in academic achievement, using a variety of informal measures will allow you to document subtle changes that may otherwise have gone unnoticed.

A key element to this phase is a plan for follow-up so that pilot programs expand to include more students and teachers, and full-fledged programs evolve to satisfy those involved. Or, as I discovered in one district, this phase helps you to realize that a project may need to be aborted in favor of something more realistic. With any scenario, ownership for follow-up needs to come from the teachers, so that a program's lifespan extends beyond its initial phase. At the same time, teachers need to know that the use of technology is an expectation that will be supported and monitored. Once you and your staff have worked through this phase, you will better understand what your school or district is willing and able to do to bring technology into students' lives.

SUMMARY

Sometimes, when we think of integrating technology into our school's or district's curricular plans, we may be reminded of the White Queen in Lewis Carroll's *Through the Looking Glass*, when she says that sometimes she's believed as many as six impossible things before breakfast; we can't imagine having all the ingredients in place, and in the right places, and, to boot, having our teachers so entrenched with technology that they automatically know what to do and how to do it. Time and money seem to get in the immediate way of anything that we attempt to do. Yet, when we sit down and analyze how change occurs, we realize that, as with the fermentation of wine, the implementation of technology takes time and patience. The RECAP framework presented in this chapter helps you think about what needs to be done for curriculum, hardware, software, and staff development, and how to go about doing it. And while it is merely one way to sit down and plan for yourself, it is a way to get started in making the seemingly impossible become probable.

REFERENCES

Balajthy, E. (1989). *Computers and reading: Lessons from the past and the technologies of the future*. Englewood Cliffs, NJ: Prentice Hall.

Barnard, D. P., & Hetzel, R. W. (1986). *Principal's handbook to improve reading* (2nd ed.). Lexington, MA: Ginn.

Chira, S. (1990, September 5). Making computers better teachers. *The New York Times*, p. B7.

Doyle, D. P. (1993). A study in change: Transforming the Charlotte-Mecklenburg schools. *Phi Delta Kappan, 74*, 534–539.

English, F. W. (1975). *School organization and management*. Worthington, OH: Charles A. Johnes.

Likert, R. (1969). The nature of highly effective groups. In F. D. Carver & T. J. Sergiovanni (Eds.), *Organization and human behavior: Focus on schools* (pp. 360–361). New York: McGraw-Hill.

Roberts, N., Carter, R. C., Friel, S. N., & Miller, M. S. (1988). *Integrating computers into the elementary and middle school*. Englewood Cliffs, NJ: Prentice Hall.

Strickland, D. S., Feeley, J. T., & Wepner, S. B. (1987). *Using computers in the teaching of reading*. New York: Teachers College Press.

Veatch, J., & Cooter, R. B. (1985–1986). Suggestions to school administrators for involving teachers in the selection of reading programs: The California study. *National Forum of Educational Administration and Supervision Journal, 3*(1), 1–6.

Wepner, S. B. (1990/1991). Computers, reading software, and at-risk eighth graders. *Journal of Reading, 34*, 264–268.

Wepner, S. B. (1992). Technology and textsets. *The Reading Teacher, 46*, 68–71.

Wepner, S. B., & Feeley, J. T. (1993). *Moving forward with literature: Basals, books, and beyond*. Columbus, OH: Merrill/Macmillan.

Wepner, S. B., Layton, K., & Beaty, J. (1992). *Stone Fox: Literature lesson links*. Gainesville, FL: Teacher Support Software.

Whitaker, B. T., Schwartz, E., & Vockell, E. (1989). *The computer in the reading curriculum*. Watsonville, CA: Mitchell Publishing.

TRADE BOOKS CITED

Mayer, M. (1983). *Just grandma and me*. Racine, WI: Western.

Gardiner, J. R. (1980). *Stone Fox*. New York: HarperCollins.

Sendak, M. (1963). *Where the wild things are*. New York: Harper & Row.

SOFTWARE CITED

Broderbund. (1992). *Just grandma and me*. Novato, CA: Author (500 Redwood Blvd., Novato, CA 94948-6121, USA; 1-800-521-6263).

Davidson & Associates. (1992). *Kid Works 2*. Torrance, CA: Author (19840 Pioneer Ave., Torrance, CA 90503, USA; 310-793-0600).

Gardner, R., & Gardner, D. (1988). *Kidstime* (rev. ed.). Scotts Valley, CA: Great Wave Software (5353 Scotts Valley Drive, Scotts Valley, CA 95066, USA; 408-438-1990).

Grimm, L., & Kirkpatrick, L. (1991). *The treehouse*. Novato, CA: Broderbund (500 Redwood Blvd., Novato, CA 94948-6121, USA; 1-800-521-6263).

The Learning Company. (1988). *The children's writing and publishing center*. Fremont, CA: Author (6493 Kaiser Drive, Fremont, CA 94555, USA; 1-800-852-2255).

The Learning Company. (1991). *The writing center*. Fremont, CA: Author.

Stanger, D. (1991). *Puppetmaker*. Pleasantville, NY: Sunburst Communications.

Stanger, D., Hermann, M. A., & Cerf, C. (1991). *Muppet math*. Pleasantville, NY: Sunburst Communications.

Wepner, S. B. (1989). *Reading Realities Elementary Series*. Gainesville, FL: Teacher Support Software (1035 NW 57th Street, Gainesville, FL 32605-4486, USA; 1-800-228-2871).

14 Literacy Development for Students of Diverse Populations

JUNKO YOKOTA

National-Louis University, Evanston, IL

One reason that educators of today will find it important to consider issues related to students of diverse populations is the tremendous change in school population during recent years. In the five years between 1986 and 1991, the elementary and secondary school populations showed gains for all ethnic groups except the white group, which showed a 3 percent decline from 70.4 percent to 67.4 percent. In future years, there will be even higher numbers of people from diverse backgrounds. In some areas, it is already difficult to identify a "mainstream population." In states such as

New Mexico, California, and Texas, the Hispanic population alone accounts for 45.3 percent, 35.3 percent, and 34.4 percent of the total school population respectively (National Center for Educational Statistics, 1993).

Another reason that literacy development of diverse learners is in need of close attention is that differences in the performance of mainstream students and their peers of diverse backgrounds is evident by the early elementary years, and the gap widens as students move through the grades. Although ethnic, cultural, and linguistic variances are not automatic determinants of academic performance, there is much evidence that these factors are often part of the profile of students who have low levels of school success (for example, Au, 1993; Pallas, Natriello, & McDill, 1989).

TYPES OF DIVERSITY

When identifying students who are different from the mainstream population, we frequently identify three types of diversity: ethnic, cultural, and linguistic. A brief description of each type of diversity is provided below. These descriptions are followed by a summary of what educators need to understand about these types of diversity.

1. *Ethnic Diversity*. Ethnicity basically refers to ancestral roots. But, more importantly, ethnicity is the core by which people often share a sense of belonging to a group. Ethnic group membership implies a shared history that affects the way in which people live today (Gollnick & Chinn, 1990). It is usually best to identify ethnicity as specifically as possible. For example, students should be referred to as being Japanese, Cuban, or Navajo rather than merely being categorized into major groups such as Asian, Hispanic, or Native American. One issue that remains unresolved is that the acceptable name for some ethnic groups is based on highly individual preference. For example, depending on individual preference, a student of Mexican descent living in the U.S. may prefer to be called Mexican-American, Latino/a, Hispanic, or Chicano/a.

2. *Cultural Diversity*. Culture is defined as a system of values, beliefs, and standards that guides people's thoughts, feelings, and behavior. Culture is not static, but a dynamic process by which people make sense of their lives. Cultural understanding is learned and shared by members of the cultural group (Au, 1993). Values and behaviors shared by cultural groups are adapted by subgroups and individuals, but often hold a common basis from which these values and behaviors stem. The boundaries by

which cultures are defined are sometimes based on ethnicity, religion, philosophy, geographical region, or other common ground.

3. *Linguistic Diversity.* Two types of linguistic diversity can be identified: multilingualism and dialect differences. Multilingualism refers to the ability to speak in more than one language. Dialect differences are variations of the English language. Linguistic factors such as these often play a critical role in school learning because uses of language by different groups of people can result in miscommunication due to differences in interpretation. When mainstream, "standard" rules of communication are imposed on all, students from nonmainstream backgrounds often feel a sense of denial, since language is so much a part of one's identity.

Understanding these different types of diversity is important foundational knowledge that can help educators develop ethnosensitivity, a critical disposition for having success in reaching diverse populations. Although it may be unintentional, most educators in this country have been made to believe that the cultural and linguistic norm of their mainstream background is to be upheld, and they interpret the actions and speech of their students according to those norms (Farr, 1991). Such ethnocentrism needs to be replaced by an ethnosensitivity that takes into account an understanding that all students are competent in the language and culture in which they were raised. When students possess a cultural background or linguistic pattern that is different from that of the mainstream, it should not be considered a deficit, but rather a difference (Au, 1993; Farr, 1991). For many students of diversity, there is often a mismatch between the experiences they have in their homes and the experiences they have at school (Rueda, 1991). It becomes problematic when these differences come into conflict with what is expected in schools, and therefore are interpreted by educators as deficits to be overcome. A priority need, then, is to bring about the understanding that cultural and linguistic variation is natural, and that prejudices against such variation should be eliminated.

MODELS OF ADDRESSING DIVERSE POPULATIONS OF STUDENTS

Beyond an understanding of the types of diversity, there is a need to consider various models for how to address culturally diverse populations. Numerous models have been proposed, and terms used to describe these models are varied. The various models can be sorted into two main ways in which issues of diversity are dealt with in schools today. I have chosen to use the terms identified by Au (1993): *transmission model* and *social constructivist model*.

Transmission Model

Transmission models are based on the belief that all students learn in the same manner, and "absorb" knowledge that is transmitted to them. The emphasis in this model is on learning skills in small units, presented in a predetermined sequence. The belief here is that learning parts leads to understanding the whole; learning a sequence of skills leads to ability to read and write. This belief is put into practice when students are taught to read by first learning the letters of the alphabet, then letter–sound correspondence, then combining sounds until they make words, and gradually combining a few words to make sentences; the underlying philosophy is that students cannot possibly learn to read unless they progress successfully through each step of this process. Tasks are assigned to the students, often in the written form of worksheets or workbooks focused on isolated skills. There is a sense of organization and orderliness; all students are given the same set of instructions and the same tasks to be completed. The perceived reason why students complete assignments may be because they were instructed to do so by the teacher, and they are complying (Langer, 1991). Students in the transmission model tend to view reading and writing as skills that are required for the purpose of advancing in school, and often do not make the connection of the role of literacy development to their lives.

Transmission models tend to reflect the teacher's background experiences, which are often largely based on mainstream values. The transmissions are better received by students who are from a background similar to the teacher's. Students of diversity, however, may feel the imposition of the dominant group's expectations, or may not be able to interpret the transmission as intended. When failure of literacy learning occurs in this situation, sometimes the remedy has been to place students in highly structured remedial programs. The problem is compounded as students get a heavier dose of what they have already experienced as failure.

Social Constructivist Model

This model is based on the understanding that all learners come to school with literacy knowledge of some type, but the kind of literacy knowledge each learner has and the way in which each learner develops literacy differ (Erickson, 1991). In the most basic sense, "constructivism" (for example, the works of Dewey, Piaget, and Vygotsky) in literacy learning refers to the understanding that meaning is created through the interaction of reader and text.

Learners in the social constructivist model are active participants in constructing their own learning, based on their own backgrounds and interests. Students set their own goals and determine their own paths for literacy learning. The teacher's role is to guide and to provide support for students so that they may successfully pursue their literacy acquisition. This support includes instruction and mini-lessons in specific areas of literacy development.

Literacy is seen as embedded in social contexts. Learners are aware of the many functions of literacy and how it connects to their everyday lives and their backgrounds. The instruction the teacher provides is contextualized and meaningful to students.

An example of a classroom employing the social constructivist model is one in which the teacher creates an ethos that is supportive and nurturing, and students take ownership of their learning. Teachers provide students with opportunities to make choices about their own learning. The teacher fills the role of "facilitator," assisting and guiding students in their own search for making the learning experiences personally meaningful. Students are actively engaged in planning and carrying out their own learning. A visitor to such a classroom may feel the level of active student participation to be rather chaotic. But instead there is structure and organization to the variety of reading/writing activities occurring and in the materials being used by students.

1. Why does the social constructivist model work for students of diversity?
The social constructivist model defines literacy learning by considering how people think and construct knowledge in the various social contexts in which literacy is used. Because of their variety of social and cultural experiences with literacy prior to schooling, students of diversity inevitably have varying understandings of literacy and ways of thinking about it. The social constructivist model endorses literacy instruction that takes such backgrounds into consideration, makes connections, and builds literacy based on the backgrounds students already have (Langer, 1991). Specific reasons why the social constructivist model is particularly well suited to students of diverse background include:

- Students can select some of their own reading material.
- Students can write and speak on topics of their choice.
- Students have the opportunity to select some of the types of literacy activities in which they wish to participate.
- Literacy-related skills are contextualized in meaningful ways.

When students of diverse backgrounds have choices regarding their reading materials, topics for writing and speaking, and literacy activities, then the opportunity to tap their individual backgrounds becomes an option. It will be more likely that students will be able to make meaningful connections between their backgrounds and literacy learning in schools.

2. What precautions should be taken when employing the social constructivist model for students of diversity?

Clearly, the constructivist model has many advantages for students of diversity, as well as for mainstream students. There are potential pitfalls that should be avoided when employing the social constructivist model for students of diversity. Students from mainstream families acquire the basic codes of literacy at home and put them into practice at school. However, students who have acquired their literacy from a code other than standard English may need explicit instruction to acquire the skills expected. In order to have lifetime access to the expectations of the culture of power, all students must be able to communicate in standard English. Explicit instruction is often the most effective and efficient method of explaining how and why things work the way they do. For example, suppose that an educator goes to Japan and purchases a kimono to wear. Based on previous experience with other robelike closures of clothing, she crosses the right side over the left. Would it be more efficient to explain explicitly to this newcomer that crossing a kimono right-over-left is only appropriate when dressing the deceased who is to be cremated, or to see how long it would take her to notice and realize that everyone else in Japan crosses kimonos left-over-right? Explicit instruction may seem to conflict with the role of teachers as facilitators. But a facilitator meets the needs of students, and students cannot be held accountable for knowledge that has never been made available to them. This does not imply that direct instruction of skills in isolation is advocated. Delpit (1988) cites Siddle in stating that mini-lessons taught in the context of meaningful activities are most effective.

While the value of emphasizing the process of learning is without question, there is also a need to emphasize product. Ultimately, it is the product that society will judge (Delpit, 1988). And many times it is the standards of mainstream culture that are used to make these judgments. Teachers will differ in the ways that they help students achieve these end goals and the processes by which they achieve them.

Most literacy-related components of the social constructivist model are supportive of diversity in learners. However, not all activities appropriate for the mainstream population within the constructivist model are also to be assumed appropriate for the diverse population. For example, Reyes (1991) studied the use of dialogue journals and literature logs in a sixth grade bilingual classroom. While the students were able to communicate effectively with their teacher, gains in mastering the conventions of standard English writing were not made as rapidly as could be accomplished through direct instruction. Such activities should not necessarily be dropped as inappropriate, but instead altered to fit the differing needs of students of diversity.

Another example of the differing roles for teachers who teach diverse students is the need for explicit teacher assistance when students are unable to make choices on their own (Reyes, 1991). An example cited by Au (1993) is that of a student who is asking for help in selecting a library book, and told by the teacher to continue looking alone. Failure to find an appropriate book is interpreted as a lack of motivation. What is interesting is that the selection of a book is viewed as requiring less guidance than some other choices to be made. Children are generally given much guidance on how to select the proper foods in order to have a balanced meal. Parents would not consider allowing a child to eat only sweets all day, but would insist on the child making more nutritious choices. An analogy of how it feels to be a child who is having difficulty making a book selection alone will be made by comparing it to a situation that we, as adults, can imagine for ourselves. Imagine entering a foreign restaurant for the first time, being offered any choice on a menu in a foreign language, and trying to select a meal among dishes you have never tasted. Most adults would ask for assistance or recommendations from anyone who seems to have more knowledge about the choices we are presented. Likewise, children who have limited background in making personal book selections may seek the assistance of those they perceive as having the expertise and experience in making such choices. When there are opportunities in school for students to discuss authors, illustrators, and topics of study as found in books, students are likely to consider these factors in their book selection (Hiebert, Mervar, & Person, 1990).

EDUCATIONAL IMPLICATIONS: GUIDELINES FOR PRACTICE

The discussion of an appropriate model for the literacy education of diverse populations has important implications for classroom climate and educational activities. First, educators must acknowledge diversity as a factor that can enrich students' literacy development. Next, while many similarities between literacy development for mainstream populations and students of diversity exist, there must be an understanding that there will be some differences. An attitude of willingness to understand these differences will be reflected in the effectiveness of instruction.

The following paragraphs discuss eight specific ways in which literacy needs of diverse student populations can be effectively met, followed by a classroom example of each.

1. Create a culturally responsive language and literacy environment.

A culturally responsive classroom environment provides an ethos that is conducive to advancing students' literacy learning while recognizing and supporting diverse backgrounds. Students of diverse backgrounds live in a different world at home than that which exists in the community. When going from home to school, they must change from one world to another (Phelan, Davidson, & Cao, 1991). Au (1993) suggests that students will better be able to manage this boundary crossing if they become active and constructive participants in their literacy instruction.

A classroom that has a culturally responsive language and literacy environment is one in which there is an ethos of support, cooperation, and collaboration. All languages and dialects spoken by students are respected and, when possible, represented in the materials and activities available to students.

2. Connect student background to literacy instruction.

While this statement is true for all students, it is especially important to give recognition to those of culturally diverse backgrounds because their background knowledge and experiences may be perceived by others as being irrelevant or deficient. There are two aspects to connecting student background to literacy instruction and activities. First, there is a need to make connections between literacy materials and activities and the background knowledge and experiences of students, since it is more likely that print materials encountered in schools will relate to the background knowledge and experiences of the mainstream population. Educators could include materials that relate to the backgrounds of diverse students, or make the connections of other materials more explicit. An example of such a connection is made in the book *Molly's Pilgrim* (1983), by Barbara Cohen. Molly is a recent immigrant from Russia, and prior to Thanksgiving is assigned to make a pilgrim doll at home to bring to school. This very American holiday and the concept behind it are made applicable to Molly's heritage when her mother makes a Russian pilgrim doll that represents her own journey to America in search of freedom. Making connections between school instruction and students' background makes learning more personally important.

The next aspect, basing literacy growth on students' background, goes beyond the initial connection made. Literacy-related activities should have a basis in the cultural background held by the child. Encouraging students to tell stories from their own background can be one way to accomplish this. Books that are strongly rooted in culturally based experiences can provide good reading materials as well as serving as the springboard for speaking and writing experiences. *Family Pictures* (1990) by Carmen Lomas Garza is a bilingual book reflecting a Mexican-American family's experiences. Other books to pair with this one could be *The Relatives Came* (1985) by Cynthia Rylant, about an Appalachian family's reunion, or *Bigmama's* (1991) by Donald Crews, about an African-American family reunion. After reading the variety of books on family gatherings, students could interview family members, tell or write about their own family experiences, and even create their own album of remembered family gatherings.

3. Recognize the first language and add English as another language.

There are three positions regarding language policies: eradication, biloquialism, and appreciation of dialect differences (Fasold & Shuy, 1970). Advocate biloquialism — teaching mainstream linguistic patterns as an addition to what students already have in their linguistic repertoires, rather than as a replacement. This "additive approach" recognizes the worth of the first language and adds English as another language for communication. The value of continuously maintaining the first language should be made clear to students. Students also need to understand that effective communication in the language of the mainstream is important for success in many situations. Some believe that diversity in dialect should be accepted; others argue that this denies some students access to the language of power (Delpit, 1988).

Students entering school with a non-English language as their first language may find that English is the exclusive language developed in school. In such cases, the native language does not become developed in a formal sense. Consequently, students may never learn to improve that first language to the extent of using it effectively for full communication in their adult lives. A point for consideration: What happens during the time period before English becomes proficient enough to become the language in which content learning can take place?

Bilingual education is an enormous field of study by itself. There is much researched and written on the topic; however, because these issues go beyond the scope of this chapter, they will not be discussed here. The main issue that educators need to keep in mind is that whenever possible, students should be supported in continuing to learn their first language.

McLaughlin (1992) prepared a set of statements regarding the myths and misconceptions held about how children acquire a second language. The myths that he debunks are:

- Children learn second languages quickly and easily.
- The younger the child, the more skilled in acquiring a second language.
- The more time students spend in a second language context, the quicker they learn the language.
- Children have acquired a second language once they can speak it.
- All children learn a second language in the same way.

4. Provide assessment that accurately reflects students' strengths and weaknesses.

Traditional assessment practices do not necessarily reflect the true strengths and weaknesses of students from diverse populations. This may lead to teachers locating problems in the students, labeling, and segregation. This then leads to the "gatekeeping" function of allowing some to have entry into educational experiences but not others. In addition, it allows for the tracking system, in which students, once labeled, tend to stay in a particular track for the rest of their school careers. When administrators and supervisors look at their own schools, they should see if the percentage of students of diversity who are in remedial programs parallels the ethnic balance of the school as a whole. There is a need to consider advocacy-oriented assessment that locates the problems in the social and educational context and seeks to change the instructional situations (Allington, 1991). One example of the need for assessment to match student background is evident from a study by Applebee (1991). He cites statistics that indicate that students tend to fare better on testing that reflects their particular ethnic background. The example cited is that when responding to a question on Langston Hughes's poetry, 53 percent of the African-Americans answered the question correctly, in comparison to 35 percent of the white students and 27 percent of the Hispanic students.

5. Establish strong home/school/community connections.

The importance of a strong home/school/community connection is virtually without debate. However, there is a misconception that when the home and community differ from the mainstream population, there is little interest or willingness for home or community involvement. Rather, there are factors that inhibit the participation of homes and communities of diversity. When these factors are addressed and the reasons for their hesitation dispelled, then families and communities find themselves very actively involved in their neighborhood schools. Typically, parents and the community are asked to provide support for the instructional program in ways identified by the school. When Keenan, Willett, and Solsken (1993) invited community participation, they changed the focus so that the school looked for ways to change and support families. They identify four ways in which such change can occur: discovering parents' talents and teaching capabilities, overcoming fears of difference, trusting curriculum to emerge through conversation, and constructing equitable relations with parents.

In Japan, nearly all mothers are members of parent/teacher organizations and operate an extensive volunteering network. The same mothers, when coming to the United States, are usually not involved in PTAs. Causes cited for not being involved in the U.S. PTAs include a sense of not "belonging" due to cultural and linguistic barriers, a lack of understanding about how American schools operate, and not being solicited for assistance. When asked about their interest in being involved in their children's schools, the mothers expressed interest and willingness, provided that the barriers cited be removed.

6. Include multicultural literature as reading material in the classroom.

Multicultural literature, when culturally authentic, provides an insight into how cultures function. Students from the cultures represented feel a sense of self-esteem as they see their lives reflected in literature. Through reading, students from other cultural groups can gain insight into cultures and their values and beliefs. Regardless of their backgrounds, all students will gain from the broadening of the literary canon to include multicultural literature that reflects a diversity of views. This should include books about ethnic groups in the U.S., as well as books entirely set in foreign countries and about other distinct cultural groups.

Applebee's 1989 survey of the literature being read in schools today found that high school students today are required to read basically the same books that were required nearly a hundred years ago—works by white, male Anglo-Saxons—when literature was seen as a vehicle to reduce diversity and promote a common set of values. But if literature is to be regarded as having power not only to influence the values of individuals but to "redirect the course of society as a whole" (1991), then the need for diversity of literature is clear. Rosenblatt's (1938) belief that literature provides access to the feelings, beliefs, and values that help individuals make choices in developing their personal philosophies also calls for the dignification, through inclusion in the curriculum, of the literature that reflects the lives of students of diversity.

When including multicultural literature in the classroom, some considerations are important to keep in mind (Yokota, 1993):

- Include multicultural literature in all aspects of the curriculum.
- Include a diversity of cultural groups, ethnic, linguistic, and so forth.
- Include a balance of genres: folklore, poetry, historical fiction, informational, contemporary fiction, biography, and picture books.
- Include a balance of books set in other countries, as well as those about diverse groups in the United States.

Literature that has text in a language other than English holds an important place among books made available to students of diverse backgrounds. When a bilingual book or two versions of a book in different languages is made available to students who are bilingual, they see both of their languages represented and have the opportunity to comparatively study the two languages. Translated literature originally published in a non-English language offers a different opportunity. It presents a culture and language natively depicted by people from the original country of publication; then the English translation makes it available to a wider audience. Students may be able to read a book that originated in the country of their own heritage, or from that of their classmates.

7. Read literature as a catalyst for discussions of diversity.
    In addition to the values of multicultural literature previously discussed, another way in which it can be used is as a catalyst for discussions of diversity. Often, multicultural literature has characters who face the same issues that students of diversity face. Through such literature, both students of diversity and students from the mainstream population can vicariously experience these lives. Thus, multicultural literature serves as a catalyst for discussions of the many issues that students of diversity face. One book that naturally leads into discussions of what characters of diverse backgrounds face is Sonia Levitin's *The Golem & the Dragon Girl* (1993). Laurel Wang's Chinese heritage and Jonathan's Jewish heritage seem to be very different backgrounds. Initially, readers may find many ways in which these two cultures experience contrasting beliefs. However, there are many parallels that exist: Saturday Chinese school/Hebrew school, great-grandfather's spirit/golem, the influence of elderly relatives, and the ways in which both Laurel and Jonathan realize the meaning of their heritage. Through literature of this type, readers will have the opportunity to discuss issues regarding how diversity affects the lives of characters.
    An example of how linguistic diversity is viewed by speakers of more than one language is found in Laurence Yep's (1991) *The Star Fisher*. The Chinese-born mother repeatedly tells her American-born children to

"speak only Chinese" in the home. She supports their success in learning English at school, but fears that her children will not retain their family's home language. The mother expresses concern that as the children's English improves, their Chinese will diminish, and she will no longer be able to communicate effectively with her own children. This does not arise from lack of desire to learn English on the mother's part, but rather from fear of losing higher levels of verbal communication between parent and child. This fear is very real and valid not only in this story, but also among bilingual people today. For example, I have been raised with Japanese as my first and home language, but with English as my school and adult language; my mother and I cannot communicate as well on some difficult issues because our stronger language is not the same. This perspective of bilingualism, as presented in *The Star Fisher*, is one that adult readers will understand. On the other hand, students who read this book may instead empathize with the children in the story, who are told they must always speak to each other only in Chinese when they would prefer to use the language of school instruction, and what it is like to have parents rely on children when English communication for parents is difficult. Educators reading books such as Yep's *The Star Fisher* will find themselves empathizing with the characters' dilemma, taking a different stance than wondering at each conference time, "Why can't a parent who has lived in this country for [x] years communicate at a child's conference in English?"

8. *Provide extensive staff development and support in issues related to ethnic, cultural, and linguistic diversity.*
    Ongoing staff development is necessary to support educators who are working to meet the literacy needs of students of diversity. When backgrounds differ from the educators' backgrounds, there is need for additional support in learning about these differences and how to best support literacy learning in each case. It is necessary for teachers to be provided with appropriate materials that connect to experiences of students of diversity.

CONCLUDING REMARKS

Administrators and supervisors play a critical role regarding how issues of diversity are addressed in the classroom. Being well informed about the various issues surrounding the education of students from diverse populations allows administrators and supervisors to take a leadership role in the decisions that must be made. This chapter's purpose has been to introduce some of the issues, briefly discuss their educational implications, describe examples, and offer recommendations. Most importantly, administrators and supervisors should advocate an open discussion of these issues among teachers, parents, and students.

One issue that administrators and supervisors need to consider carefully is that of how various policies and mandates affect the literacy learning that goes on in classrooms. The interpretation of state legislation and district mandates may leave little room for negotiating the implementation of such decisions. Therefore, those who are in positions of influencing such policymaking and implementation need to have a thorough understanding of literacy development that is responsive to diversity (Hiebert, 1991).

After reading the other chapters in this book, it is probably obvious that there are many recommendations made by others that are true for students of diversity as well. Recommendations for improving the literacy learning of students of diverse backgrounds are specifically geared to meet their needs. However, many of the principles are also applicable to mainstream students and can be helpful to all, regardless of their background. It should be noted that although all students deserve the best literacy instruction possible, at present there is a notable difference in the quality of instruction offered (Allington, 1991). The additive stance (Cummins, 1986) implies that the home language and culture are not replaced, but broadened, so that students will be able to function in both the home and their ethnic community as well as in the mainstream culture.

REFERENCES

Allington, R. L. (1991). Children who find learning to read difficult: School responses to diversity. In E. H. Hiebert (Ed.), *Literacy for a diverse society: Perspectives, practices, and policies* (pp. 237–252). New York: Teachers College Press.

Applebee, A. N. (1991). Literature: Whose heritage? In E. H. Hiebert (Ed.), *Literacy for a diverse society: Perspectives, practices, and policies* (pp. 228–236). New York: Teachers College Press.

Au, K. H. (1993). *Literacy instruction in multicultural settings.* Fort Worth: Harcourt Brace Jovanovich College Publishers.

Cummins, J. (1986). Empowering minority students: A framework for intervention. *Harvard Educational Review, 56*(1), 18–36.

Delpit, L. D. (1988). The silenced dialogue: Power and pedagogy in educating other people's children. *Harvard Educational Review, 58*, 280–298.

Erickson, F. (1991). Foreword. In E. H. Hiebert (Ed.), *Literacy for a diverse society: Perspectives, practices, and policies* (pp. vii–x). New York: Teachers College Press.

Farr, M. (1991). Dialects, culture, and teaching the English language arts. In J. Flood, J. M. Jensen, D. Lapp, and J. R. Squire (Eds.), *Handbook of research on teaching the English language arts* (pp. 365–371). New York: Macmillan.

Fashold, R. W., & Shuy, R. W. (Eds.). (1970). *Teaching standard English in the inner city*. Washington, DC: Center for Applied Linguistics.

Gollnick, D. M., & Chinn, P. C. (1990). *Multicultural education in a pluralistic society* (3rd ed.). Columbus, OH: Merrill.

Hiebert, E. H. (1991). *Literacy for a diverse society: Perspectives, practices, and policies*. New York: Teachers College Press.

Hiebert, E. H., Mervar, K. B., & Person, D. (1990). Research directions: Children's selection of trade books in libraries and classrooms. *Language Arts, 67,* 758–763.

Keenan, J. W., Willett, J., & Solsken, J. (1993). Focus on research: Constructing an urban village: School/home collaboration in a multicultural classroom. *Language Arts, 70,* 204–213.

Langer, J. A. (1991). Literacy and schooling: A sociocognitive perspective. In E. H. Hiebert (Ed.), *Literacy for a diverse society: Perspectives, practices, and policies* (pp. 9–27). New York: Teachers College Press.

McLaughlin, B. (1992). *Myths and misconceptions about second language learning: What every teacher needs to unlearn*. Santa Cruz, CA: National Center for Research on Cultural Diversity and Second Language Learning.

National Center for Educational Statistics. (1993). *Digest of Educational Statistics*. Washington, DC: U.S. Department of Education.

Pallas, A. M., Natriello, G., & McDill, E. L. (1989). Changing nature of the disadvantaged population: Current dimensions and future trends. *Educational Researcher, 18*(5), 16–22.

Phelan, P., Davidson, A. L., & Cao, H. T. (1991). Students' multiple worlds: Negotiating the boundaries of family, peer, and school cultures. *Anthropology & Education Quarterly, 22*(3), 224–250.

Reyes, M. de la Luz. (1991). A process approach to literacy instruction for Spanish-speaking students: In search of a best fit. In E. H. Hiebert (Ed.), *Literacy for a diverse society: Perspectives, practices, and policies* (pp. 157–171). New York: Teachers College Press.

Rosenblatt, L. (1938). *Literature as exploration*. New York: D. Appleton Century.

Rueda, R. (1991). Characteristics of literacy programs for language-minority students. In E. H. Hiebert (Ed.), *Literacy for a diverse society: Perspectives, practices, and policies* (pp. 93–107). New York: Teachers College Press.

Yokota, J. (1993). Issues in selecting multicultural children's literature. *Language Arts, 70,* 156–167.

CHILDREN'S BOOKS CITED

Cohen, B., illus. by Michael J. Deraney. (1983). *Molly's pilgrim*. New York: Lothrop, Lee & Shepard Books.

Crews, D. (1991). *Bigmama's*. New York: Greenwillow.

Garza, C. L. (1990). *Family pictures/Cuadros de familia*. San Francisco: Children's Book Press.

Levitin, S. (1993). *The golem & the dragon girl*. New York: Dial.

Rylant, C., illus. by Stephen Gammell. (1985). *The relatives came*. New York: Macmillan.

Yep, L. (1991). *The Star Fisher*. New York: Morrow.

15 Special Initiatives for Special Needs

DIXIE LEE SPIEGEL
University of North Carolina at Chapel Hill

The first 14 chapters in this book have shown how to develop and administer the very best reading programs. However, even an exemplary program will rarely succeed with all children. Some children come to school at risk for falling behind in literacy for a variety of reasons. Other children have difficulty in attaining full literacy once they enter school. For these special children, special initiatives are needed. In this chapter I review traditional responses to children with special needs, including pullout remedial reading programs, special education programs, and programs for children with limited English proficiency. Next I describe some promising new interventions that fit well within the framework of more traditional programs. Last, I provide a set of guidelines to serve as a lens through which readers might wish to examine programs, either for modification or adoption.

TRADITIONAL SCHOOL-BASED RESPONSES
TO SPECIAL LITERACY NEEDS

In spite of nearly three decades of concerted efforts to wipe out illiteracy, United States schools are still graduating too many marginally literate young adults. In addition, the dropout rate, which hovers around 30 percent in some states, virtually ensures that large numbers of young people are leaving school without even functional literacy. This situation is especially alarming for minorities. Sticht (1987) reports that as many as 40% of minority adults are unemployable or only marginally employable due in part to poor literacy skills. Thus it would seem that traditional responses to children at risk for literacy failure have had at best limited success. An examination of these traditional programs is in order, to determine the nature of these programs and the degree to which they are meeting children's literacy needs.

Pullout Remedial Reading Programs

The most common special placement for children experiencing trouble with literacy is a pullout remedial reading program. In these programs children leave their regular classroom and go "down the hall" to the reading teacher's room, where they receive instructions in small groups, usually on a daily basis. Many of these pullout programs are funded by Chapter 1; therefore, data about Chapter 1 programs and non–Chapter 1 pullout programs will often be combined in this review.

The extent of Chapter 1 funding provides a sense of the magnitude of special efforts for children with reading problems. Ninety percent of school districts, over 14,000, receive Chapter 1 funds, serving about 15 percent of American elementary school children (Cooley, 1981; Savage, 1987). The 1993–1994 Chapter 1 budget was $6.1 billion (LeTendre, 1991).

One would expect that such an infusion of funds and effort would have positive results. However, most reviews of research have concluded that Chapter 1 programs have had at best a "positive but marginal impact" on achievement (Fagan & Heid, 1991). Children in Chapter 1 programs have often made more progress than at-risk children not receiving services, but overall, Chapter 1 children remain behind their grade-level peers. There is little progress toward closing the achievement gap, they just don't fall as far behind as children not served (Bean et al., 1991; Fagan & Heid, 1991; Slavin, 1987). For example, the average gain in reading for Chapter 1 students in 1987–1988 was a modest three normal curve equivalents, or NCEs (Fagan & Heid, 1991). Furthermore, gains shown by spring achievement tests do not appear to last, often disappearing as early as the following fall (Slavin, 1987), with no lasting discernible effects of participation in Chapter 1 showing by junior high school age (Carter, 1984; Kennedy, Birman, & Demaline, 1986). Another depressing finding is that Chapter 1 programs generally are most effective with children with only minor to moderate reading disability (Carter, 1984; Kennedy et al., 1986).

An examination of research about Chapter 1 and pullout remedial reading programs provides insight into their modest success. When one compares what typically happens in these programs with what we know about effective reading instruction, it is not surprising that children do not progress more rapidly. One important factor is the amount of reading instruction provided. Chapter 1 programs are specifically funded to provide supplemental instruction. Therefore, one would expect that when the amount of instruction in the regular classroom is combined with the amount of instruction in the Chapter 1 classroom, Chapter 1 students would receive more instruction than children not receiving special services. Unfortunately, observation does not confirm this expectation (Carter, 1984; Johnston & Allington, 1991; Ligon & Doss, 1982; Rowan & Guthrie, 1989). Thus, there is not the increased opportunity to learn that is needed for children to make the accelerated progress necessary to catch up with their peers (Allington, 1983).

Research has indicated that other factors related to achievement in literacy are frequently not present in pullout programs. Instruction often focuses on fragmented skills taught and practiced in isolation (Allington et al., 1986; Rowan & Guthrie, 1989), with little or no attention to transfer to real texts (Allington et al., 1986; Bean et al., 1991). In fact, children in remedial reading programs get few opportunities to practice their strategies with authentic, connected text, and instead spend their time completing worksheets (Bean et al., 1991).

One would also expect that instruction in small pullout programs would be individualized so that every child got the program he or she needed. Sadly, little evidence of individualization has been found (Allington & McGill-Franzen, 1989; Allington et al., 1986; Bean et al., 1991). Small groups of students often get a group lesson, and groups at the same grade placement may get the same lesson on a given day, that is, "the third grade lesson." One especially dangerous result of this lack of individualization is that students are often given materials not at their instructional level that are too hard for them, and with which they cannot successfully practice strategies they are learning (Johnston & Allington, 1991).

Another aspect of individualization is monitoring and reinforcement of student efforts. This, too, does not seem to occur in many pullout programs (Allington et al., 1986; Bean et al., 1991), although Carter (1984) concluded after reviewing Title I research that compensatory classrooms did provide "higher quality cognitive monitoring" than did regular classrooms (p. 5). More typically, the monitoring that does take place is feedback on the accuracy of children's responses and not on the appropriateness of the strategies used (Allington et al., 1986; Johnston & Allington, 1991). Even more damaging, responding to the correctness of student responses frequently is given in the absence of direct instruction. That is, all too often direct instruction in what a strategy is, why it might be useful, and how that strategy is carried out is not provided (Allington & McGill-Franzen, 1989; Allington et al., 1986; Bean et al., 1991). Children are simply given worksheets and workbooks to complete with little or no teacher input. They are told to do a task, but not told how or why.

Another extremely important factor to consider in the success of pullout programs is the degree to which they are congruent with regular classroom programs. Children targeted for special help through pullout programs are generally having difficulty learning one literacy curriculum. If they are placed in a pullout program that offers a different curriculum, these at-risk children are forced to try to learn two (sometimes incompatible) curricula (Allington & Broikou, 1988; Johnston, Allington, & Afflerbach, 1985). Unfortunately, research has not found a high degree of congruence between pullout programs and classroom programs (Allington et al., 1986; Bean et al., 1991; Carter, 1984; Johnston et al., 1985).

Special Education Programs

Many children with special needs are served through special education programs, typically through pullout programs in resource rooms. Literacy instruction in special education resource rooms unfortunately mirrors instruction in pullout remedial reading programs. There is little individualization in either amount or nature of services (Allington & McGill-Franzen, 1989; Haynes & Jenkins, 1986; Ysseldyke et al., 1989). Monitoring of student responses is infrequent, and generally limited to marking papers right or wrong (Haynes & Jenkins, 1986). Strategies are seldom explicitly taught, and when they are, children receive few opportunities to practice them in extended, authentic text (Allington & McGill-Franzen, 1989; Haynes & Jenkins, 1986). As in Chapter 1 pullout programs, congruence is rarely found between special education pullout programs and the regular education curriculum (Haynes & Jenkins, 1986; O'Sullivan et al., 1990).

Overall, attendance in special education resource rooms does not guarantee that special education children get more reading instruction than regular education students. Some research has found that special education students often receive more reading instruction in their pullout programs than do Chapter 1 students (Allington & McGill-Franzen, 1989), although other research has found little reading instruction in resource rooms (Haynes & Jenkins, 1986). Observations consistently show that special education children get less reading instruction and opportunity to learn in their regular classrooms than do nonhandicapped children (Allington & McGill-Franzen, 1989; O'Sullivan et al., 1990). Thus, even when reading instruction is taking place in the resource room, the overall reading instruction provided special education students is not greater than or even equal to that of children in regular education settings. Furthermore, Haynes and Jenkins (1986) found that the amount of services scheduled by special education had only a weak relationship to the severity of the child's need. Thus, say Haynes and Jenkins, it is not surprising that children rarely "get out" of special education, because at best comparable services are provided, and comparable services do not allow for accelerated progress.

Pullout versus In-Class Models

Research on traditional pullout programs, whether remedial reading or special education classes, is not encouraging. One alternative increasingly recommended is that of the in-class or "push-in" model. The reading specialist or special education teacher works within the regular classroom, often as a tutor who assists target children in completing assignments given by the regular classroom teacher. Theoretically, in-class models should provide more congruence between special and regular curricula. This, along with no time lost traveling between regular and special classrooms, should provide at-risk children with increased opportunity to learn.

Unfortunately, research does not support this optimism. Allington and Shake (1986) did not find a greater degree of congruence between regular and special classroom curricula with in-class models. Archambault (1987) and Rowan and Guthrie (1989) found few differences between pullout and in-class settings. Bean et al. (1991) did find some differences, but did not find that these differences gave in-class programs an advantage over pullout. In fact, Bean et al. suggested that in-class programs may generate a whole new set of problems, such as surprisingly large amounts of time with no interaction between the reading specialist and students, or inappropriate instructional tasks set by the classroom teacher with which the reading specialist was to assist learners.

Research on traditional programs for children with literacy problems is not encouraging. At best, some children in these programs make normal progress, but as a group they do not catch up with their peers. One possible explanation for the minimal results is the failure of these programs to implement effective instructional practices. Fortunately, some recent early intervention efforts show great promise, both because research shows that served children can catch up and because these programs do provide sound instruction.

EARLY INTERVENTION PROGRAMS

Early intervention programs are designed to prevent problems from arising in the first place. Traditional school-based literacy intervention programs, such as most Chapter 1 and special education programs, are often reactive; they respond to the needs of children who have already begun to fall behind in literacy acquisition. Early intervention programs are proactive; they seek to identify children at risk for literacy failure prior to or at the very beginning of formal literacy training, and to work with them before the cycle of failure begins. Children identified as at risk are placed in an intensive one-to-one or small group program that provides strategy training, immediate reinforcement, and corrective feedback. In other words, these programs utilize effective instructional practices. Three early intervention programs will be described here: Reading Recovery, First Steps, and Early Intervention in Reading.

Reading Recovery

Reading Recovery, originated by Marie Clay (Clay, 1987) in New Zealand, is the most widespread first grade tutorial intervention program in the United States. The U.S. training and dissemination site is Ohio State University.

Reading Recovery teachers complete a rigorous yearlong training program with a certified Reading Recovery teacher trainer. The children are selected from the lowest 20 percent of first graders, based on teacher judgment and performance on the Observation Survey, Reading Recovery's screening measure. Children who have been identified as special education students are eligible (Lyons, 1989, 1991). Selected children then work with a Reading Recovery teacher on a one-to-one basis for 30 minutes a day in order to improve the child's "in-the-head processing" during reading and writing (Clay, 1987, p. 49). Emphasis is on the development of metacognition and strategy usage. Children are "discontinued" when they meet two criteria: they are able to work in the middle reading group in their own classroom, and they have developed a self-improving system through which they learn more about reading by themselves every time they read (Clay & Cazden, 1990).

The general Reading Recovery lesson framework has four parts:

1. The child rereads one or more familiar books in order to practice strategy use and gain fluency.
2. The child reads a new book and the teacher keeps a "running record" that describes the child's strategy use with that text.
3. The child writes and then reads a one- or two-sentence message, with assistance as needed from the teacher. The child and the teacher use this message to explore letter-sound relationships.
4. The child reads another new book, which becomes the "new book" for the first part of the next day's lesson.

During each part of the lesson, the teacher responds to the child's attempts in ways that will strengthen appropriate strategy usage and replace ineffective practices (Pinnell, DeFord, & Lyons, 1988).

Research with Reading Recovery has shown high success rates for the program. For example, during the first three years of the Ohio State project, the percentage of children successfully discontinued was 73%, 82%, and 86% (Pinnell et al., 1988). Two-thirds of the children in the second state cohort and 74 percent in the third cohort had text reading scores equal to or exceeding the average band (plus or minus .5 standard deviation) of scores of a randomly selected group of first graders (Pinnell et al., 1988). NCE reading comprehension gains of 9.6 and 7.0 were found for the second and third cohorts respectively (Pinnell et al., 1988), compared to an average NCE gain of 3 for Chapter 1 children (Fagan & Heid, 1991). Longitudinal data suggest that at least two-thirds of discontinued children make accelerated progress, are able to perform within the average range for their classes, and continue to make progress for at least two more years after intervention has stopped (Pinnell, 1989). Combining the most conservative of these figures, one can infer that if 73 percent are successfully discontinued and 67 percent of these now perform at least at average level, then Reading Recovery's "recovery rate" is about 50 percent. That might not seem impressive until one remembers that these children were in the lowest 20 percent of their classes.

First Steps

First Steps is also an individual tutoring program for at-risk first graders and has much in common with Reading Recovery (Morris, 1993). The lowest-achieving first graders are selected and the lesson framework is similar to that of Reading Recovery. However, both Chapter 1 reading teachers and first grade teachers are trained to tutor, with the Chapter 1 teacher working with three or four children daily and the classroom teacher tutoring one child from his or her classroom. Another difference is in tutor training, which is somewhat abbreviated from the Reading Recovery model. Training begins with the trainer explaining the process. Next, tutors observe the trainer via video implementing the process. Then tutors observe the trainer with a child, followed by a debriefing session. Next, tutors implement the process under the trainer's observation, followed by a debriefing session to jointly plan the next lesson. In addition, tutors attend 15 evening inservice sessions, mostly in the first semester. Also, the trainer continues to observe the tutors at work throughout the year and provide feedback.

First Steps has been implemented at only a few sites, but preliminary data are encouraging (Morris, 1993). Compared to low-reading first graders from two previous years who had no intervention, more First Steps children were able to read 75 percent of the basal primer words than comparison children (50% vs. 7%, respectively). Further, 76 percent of First Step students could read the primer text with 90 percent accuracy at the end of first grade in three of the four schools, and 38 percent could read at the first grade–second half level (Morris, 1993). As with Reading Recovery, these data reflect the progress of children deemed most at risk in their classrooms.

Early Intervention in Reading

Early Intervention in Reading (EIR) is another program in which the most at-risk children are served, in this case the lowest-achieving five students in a classroom. First grade teachers are trained through a one-day summer workshop and inservice training after school to work with these groups of five for 15 to 20 minutes daily (Taylor et al., 1992; Taylor, Strait, & Medo, 1994). EIR sessions follow a three-day cycle that begins with the teacher reading a picture book to the entire class and then a summary of that book to the EIR group. Over the next two days, repeated readings and other interactions with the book summary help children develop use of context, phonemic awareness, writing and spelling abilities, sight vocabulary, and a working knowledge of phonics. The teacher uses records of children's strategy usage to plan lessons. In addition to the small group work, each child works for 5 minutes a day individually with a trained teacher aide or for 10 minutes in a group of two.

As with First Steps, preliminary EIR data show promise. Fifty percent of EIR children could read at least the first grade–second half level at the end of first grade, compared to 20 percent of the control group of 30 low achievers from other first grade classes and 55 percent of 30 average-ability children in their own classes (the comparison group) (Taylor et al., 1992). Follow-up data showed that at the end of second grade, without further intervention, 98 percent of EIR children could read at the second grade level (Taylor et al., 1994).

QUESTIONS TO ASK ABOUT A READING PROGRAM FOR SPECIAL NEEDS CHILDREN

This review of existing programs has presented both good news and bad news. The bad news is that traditional programs often have only limited success. The good news is that new initiatives in early intervention show much promise, probably because they implement effective instructional practices. The very good news is that traditional programs are amenable to change and modification. They can be made better. Research about effective instructional practices, both within the developmental reading program and in programs for at-risk children or children who have already fallen behind, can inform these modifications, just as they have informed the development of the early intervention programs described in this chapter. The following questions have been extracted from that research, in the hopes of providing educators a lens through which to view their current special reading initiatives or through which to select a program.

Real Reading

1. *Is reading instruction focused on comprehension of connected text, not on the fragmented study of isolated skills?* Real reading involves comprehension of connected text for authentic purposes. Secondly we teach children to read in order that they can do real reading, so that they can read to find information they need, entertain themselves, and broaden their understanding of the world. Unfortunately, the ways in which we go about teaching children to read are often antithetical to these goals. This is especially true for poor readers, who receive instruction based on fragmented skills with tiny pieces of text, often single words and sentences

(Allington, 1983; Allington et al., 1986; Gambrell, Wilson, & Gantt, 1981; Rowan & Guthrie, 1989). Clay and Cazden suggest a persuasive rationale and a clear guideline: "For all children, the larger the chunks of printed language they can work with, the richer the network of information they can use, and the quicker they learn. Teaching should dwell on detail only long enough for the child to discover its existence and then encourage the use of it in isolation only when absolutely necessary" (1990, p. 207).

2. *Do children spend time reading?* Practice may not make perfect, but in reading practice, spending time reading does have a positive relationship with achievement (Anderson, Wilson, & Fielding, 1986). It is through practice that learners try out new strategies, develop fluency, and begin to experience the rewards of reading. However, in many remedial and resource rooms students have few opportunities to practice learned strategies by applying them to real text (Bean et al., 1991; Haynes & Jenkins, 1986). Instead, they spend their time completing worksheets.

Opportunity to Learn

3. *Do students have the opportunity to learn?* Students have the opportunity to learn when time is both allocated to and actually provided for a task, and when students are on task or engaged. A review of research on instruction for good and poor readers (Allington, 1983) found that good readers have more opportunity to learn to read because they spend more time engaged in the task of reading. Gambrell et al. (1981) suggest that because poor readers are often assigned tasks that are too difficult, they are more frequently off task than good readers and therefore have decreased opportunity to learn.

Another aspect of opportunity to learn is the actual amount of instruction provided. Research has often found that special programs do not ensure that children receive additional reading instruction (Allington et al., 1986; Haynes & Jenkins, 1986; Hiebert, 1983; Johnston & Allington, 1991). One problem is that special needs children often get substantially less instruction in the regular classroom than other students; thus even if they do receive reading instruction in their special classes, the combined amount does not equal that of nontargeted children (Haynes & Jenkins, 1986; Hiebert, 1983).

4. *Are the goals of instruction clear to both students and teachers?* If the goals of instruction are not clear to the learners, then they may focus

on other issues. For example, poor readers are often given tasks that focus on accurate decoding, not comprehension, whereas good readers are given comprehension-based tasks (Allington, 1983). Therefore, it is not surprising that some poor readers may view reading as pronouncing words correctly, not comprehending (Gambrell & Heathington, 1981) or that they cannot express the purposes of the activities they are completing (Johnston et al., 1985). Conversely, if the goals of instruction are not clear to teachers, they too may focus on other issues. Research by Allington et al. (1986) concluded that teachers often do not have clear goals for individual students, nor do they have long-term plans for their students.

5. *Is the special reading program congruent with the classroom reading program?* As discussed earlier in this chapter, research on both Chapter 1 and special education settings in the 1980s and early 1990s rarely found congruence between either pullout or in-class models and regular classroom programs (Allington et al., 1986; Bean et al., 1991; Carter, 1984; Haynes & Jenkins, 1986; Johnston et al., 1985; O'Sullivan et al., 1990).

6. *Are learners given materials at their instructional level?* When a reader can decode with approximately 95 percent accuracy and comprehend about 70 to 90 percent of what was read, that individual is said to be reading at the instructional level. This is the level at which the learner is challenged but not overwhelmed (Morris, Shaw, & Perney, 1990), the level at which the learner can profit from instruction. Unfortunately, both Gambrell et al. (1981) and Johnston and Allington (1991) concluded that poor readers often are assigned materials with which they cannot succeed, that is, at their frustration level.

7. *Is instruction individualized?* In spite of lower student–teacher ratios than in regular classrooms, most special initiative classrooms show little individualization (Allington & McGill-Franzen, 1989; Allington et al., 1986; Bean et al., 1991; Haynes & Jenkins, 1986; McGill-Franzen & Allington, 1990).

Direct Instruction

8. *Is direct instruction a part of the program?* Through direct instruction a teacher explains, models, or discusses what is to be learned, why it is important, and how to apply what is learned. Direct instruction acknowledges that many children cannot infer strategies, their impor-

tance, or the situations in which they might be used (Adams, 1990; Ehri & Wilce, 1985). Direct instruction is especially important for children targeted for special initiatives because children from low-income families (Calfee & Piontkowski, 1981) or minority backgrounds (Delpit, 1988) have been found unable to discover reading strategies without some guidance. Unfortunately, direct instruction is not found in many remedial reading or special education classes (Allington & McGill-Franzen, 1989; Allington et al., 1986; Bean et al., 1991; Haynes & Jenkins, 1986).

9. *Are children's attempts to make meaning of text monitored and reinforced?* Through monitoring and reinforcement, teachers reassure students when they are using strategies appropriately and make suggestions for alternatives when ineffective strategies are used. However, in general, teachers in traditional pullout programs (both Chapter 1 and special education) have not been found to provide much monitoring or reinforcement of student efforts (Allington et al., 1986; Bean et al., 1991; Haynes & Jenkins, 1986).

The Content of Programs

10. *Are children taught strategies and how to transfer strategies to new situations?* Strategies are complex "in-the-head" processes (Pinnell, 1989, p. 166) and are consciously selected to solve a problem. Skills, on the other hand, are taught as entities of value in themselves and are used without thought, in a reflexive manner.

For strategies to be useful, they must be taught in such a way that learners can generalize the usefulness of the strategy beyond the immediate context (Johnston et al., 1985). For this to happen, a real-world use for the strategy must be clearly delineated. However, observation of remedial classroom has found little or no attention to transfer (Allington et al., 1986; Bean et al., 1991). Too often the student's goal is to finish the assigned worksheet or to read aloud without embarrassing mistakes, not to learn a strategy that can be of value elsewhere to solve a problem.

11. *Is writing an integral part of the program?* This is especially important for a beginning reading program because of the reciprocal nature of reading and writing for developing an awareness of the sound–symbol relationship of the language (Clay & Cazden, 1990). When emergent writers try JKLT for *chocolate*, they are breaking words down, isolating sounds, attempting to match letters with sounds, and blending it all back together again. This playing with sounds to spell helps learners in the task of playing with sounds to read.

12. *If this is a beginning reading program, is phonemic awareness part of the curriculum?* Phonemic awareness is a *consciousness* of sounds as entities that can be blended and taken apart and manipulated. Phonemic awareness includes the ability to *use* sounds. It is different from *knowing about* sounds, which may be what is taught in a traditional phonics program.

From her massive study of beginning reading, Adams (1990) concluded that familiarity with the letters of the alphabet and phonemic awareness "are very strong predictors of the ease with which a child will learn to read" (p. 7). Clay and Cazden (1990) suggest that phonemic awareness is an outcome of learning to read and write rather than a prerequisite for learning to read. It is by using sounds, by "trying them out" in reading and writing, that children develop phonemic awareness.

The Quality of Instructional Personnel

13. *Are children most at risk taught by the best teachers?* Sadly, research clearly indicates that for many special initiatives for special needs children, the answers to quite a few of questions 1 through 12 should be "seldom" or at best "sometimes." Therefore, one logical inference may be that children in these programs are not taught by the most effective teachers. Stanovich (1986) warns of the Matthew Effect: Learners who need the most and best instruction too often get the least and the worst (Allington & McGill-Franzen, 1989). One salient example of the Matthew Effect is the common practice of using federally funded aides, who may not be certified teachers, to work with poor readers (Johnston & Allington, 1991). Another example is the tendency for students from advantaged backgrounds to attend schools rich in resources and vice versa (Carter, 1984). At-risk children must be given the best, not just what is available or left over.

Accelerated Progress

14. *Will this program help children who have fallen behind make accelerated progress?* Traditional programs for children who have fallen behind are not helping them close the gap, in Chapter 1 programs (Fagan & Heid, 1991), preschool intervention programs like Head Start (Scott-Jones, 1992), or special education (Haynes & Jenkins, 1986). Although in some instances programs have helped children who have fallen behind to make normal progress, normal progress is not enough. They need to make accelerated progress in order to catch up with their peers. Therefore, equivalence of services is insufficient. Children with only the same oppor-

tunities to learn as their peers who are on grade level cannot make accelerated progress (Allington, 1983). O'Sullivan and colleagues (1990) ask: "Does it make sense, at the elementary school level, that the same amount of time is spent in reading instruction time for students who are good readers as for students who are poor readers?" (pp. 144–145).

SUMMARY

Special needs children must have special initiatives. And "special" should mean the very best. We know, from research on effective literacy education, many of the factors related to literacy success. We know from research on traditional intervention programs that many programs do not implement effective practices. Literacy administrators, supervisors, and teachers need to ensure that our at-risk children receive the instruction they need to make accelerated progress. Fortunately, the first grade intervention programs highlighted in this review are a big step in this direction.

REFERENCES

Adams, M. J. (1990). *Beginning to read: Thinking and learning about print.* Cambridge: MIT Press.

Allington, R. L. (1983). The reading instruction provided readers of differing reading abilities. *Elementary School Journal, 83,* 548–559.

Allington, R. L., & Broikou, K. A. (1988). Development of shared knowledge: A new role for classroom and specialist teachers. *The Reading Teacher, 41,* 806–811.

Allington, R. L., & McGill-Franzen, A. (1989). School response to reading failure: Instruction for Chapter 1 and special students in grades 2, 4, and 8. *Elementary School Journal, 89,* 529–542.

Allington, R. L., & Shake, M. C. (1986). Remedial reading: Achieving curricular congruence in classroom and clinic. *The Reading Teacher, 39,* 648–654.

Allington, R. L., Stuetzel, H., Shake, M., & Lamarche, S. (1986). What is remedial reading? A descriptive study. *Reading Research and Instruction, 26,* 15–30.

Anderson, R. C., Wilson, P. T., & Fielding, L. G. (1986). *Growth in reading and how children spend their time outside of school* (Tech. Rep. No. 389). Urbana: University of Illinois, Center for the Study of Reading.

Archambault, F. X. (1987). *Pullout versus in-class instruction in compensatory education.* Paper presented at the annual meeting of the American Educational Research Association, Washington, DC.

Bean, R. M., Cooley, W. W., Eichelberger, R. T., Lazar, M. K., & Zigmond, N. (1991). Inclass or pullout: Effects of setting on the remedial reading program. *Journal of Reading Behavior, 23,* 445–464.

Calfee, R. C., & Piontkowski, D. C. (1981). The reading diary: Acquisition of decoding. *Reading Research Quarterly, 16*, 346–373.

Carter, L. F. (1984). The Sustaining Effects Study of compensatory and elementary education. *Educational Researcher, 12*, 4–13.

Clay, M. M. (1987). Implementing Reading Recovery: Systemic adaptations to an educational innovation. *New Zealand Journal of Educational Studies, 22*, 35–58.

Clay, M. M., & Cazden, C. B. (1990). A Vygotskian interpretation of Reading Recovery. In L. C. Moll (Ed.), *Vygotsky and education: Instructional implications and applications of socio-historical psychology* (pp. 206–222). New York: Cambridge University Press.

Cooley, W. C. (1981). Effectiveness of compensatory education. *Educational Leadership, 38*, 298–301.

Delpit, L. D. (1988). The silenced dialogue: Power and pedagogy in educating other people's children. *Harvard Educational Review, 58*, 280–298.

Ehri, L. C., & Wilce, L. S. (1985). Movement into reading: Is the first stage of printed word learning visual or phonetic? *Reading Research Quarterly, 20*, 163–179.

Fagan, T. W., & Heid, C. A. (1991). Chapter 1 program improvement: Opportunity and practice. *Phi Delta Kappan, 72*, 582–585.

Gambrell, L. B., & Heathington, B. S. (1981). Adult disabled readers' metacognitive awareness about reading tasks and strategies. *Journal of Reading Behavior, 13*, 215–222.

Gambrell, L. B., Wilson, R. M., & Gantt, W. N. (1981). Classroom observations of task-attending behaviors of good and poor readers. *Journal of Educational Research, 74*, 400–404.

Haynes, M. C., & Jenkins, J. R. (1986). Reading instruction in special education resource rooms. *American Educational Research Journal, 23*, 161–190.

Hiebert, E. H. (1983). An examination of ability grouping for remediation instruction. *Reading Research Quarterly, 18*, 231–255.

Johnston, P. H., & Allington, R. L. (1991). Remediation. In R. Barr, M. L. Kamil, P. B. Mosenthal, & P. D. Pearson (Eds), *Handbook of reading research: Volume II* (pp. 984–1012). New York: Longman.

Johnston, P. H., Allington, R. L., & Afflerbach, P. (1985). The congruence of classroom and remedial reading instruction. *Elementary School Journal, 85*, 465–477.

Kennedy, M. M., Birman, B. F., & Demaline, R. E. (1986). *The effectiveness of Chapter 1 services*. Washington, DC: U.S. Department of Education, Office of Educational Research and Improvement.

LeTendre, M. J. (1991). Improving Chapter 1 programs: We can do better. *Phi Delta Kappan, 72*, 577–580.

Ligon, G. D., & Doss, D. A. (1982). *Some lessons we have learned from 6,500 hours of classroom observations* (Publication no. 81.56). Austin, TX: Office of Research and Evaluation, Austin Independent School District.

Lyons, C. A. (1989). Reading Recovery: A preventative for mislabeling young "at-risk" learners. *Urban Education, 24*, 125–139.

Lyons, C. A. (1991). Reading Recovery: A viable prevention for learning disability. *Reading Horizons, 31*, 384–408.

McGill-Franzen, A., & Allington, R. L. (1990). Comprehension and coherence: Neglected elements of literacy instruction in remedial and resource rooms. *Journal of Reading, Writing and Learning Disabilities, 6*, 149–181.

Morris, D. (1993). *First Steps, an early intervention program.* Manuscript submitted for publication.

Morris, D., Shaw, B., & Perney, J. (1990). Helping low readers in grades 2 and 3: An after-school volunteer tutoring program. *Elementary School Journal, 91*, 133–150.

O'Sullivan, P. J., Ysseldyke, J. E., Christenson, S. L., & Thurlow, M. L. (1990). Mildly handicapped elementary students' opportunity to learn during reading instruction in mainstream and special education settings. *Reading Research Quarterly, 25*, 131–146.

Pinnell, G. S. (1989). Reading Recovery: Helping at-risk children learn to read. *Elementary School Journal, 90*, 159–181.

Pinnell, G. S., DeFord, D., & Lyons, C. A. (1988). *Reading Recovery: Early intervention for at-risk first graders.* Arlington, VA: Educational Research Service.

Rowan, G., & Guthrie, L. F. (1989). The quality of Chapter 1 instruction: Results from a study of twenty-four schools. In R. E. Slavin, N. L. Karweit, & N. A. Madden (Eds.), *Effective programs for schools at risk* (pp. 195–219). Boston: Allyn and Bacon.

Savage, D. G. (1987). Why Chapter 1 has not made much difference. *Phi Delta Kappan, 68*, 581–584.

Scott-Jones, D. (1992). Family and community interventions affecting the development of cognitive skills in children. In T. G. Sticht, M. J. Beeler, & B. A. McDonald (Eds.), *The intergenerational transfer of cognitive skills. Volume I: Programs, policy, and research issues* (pp. 84–108). Norwood, NJ: Ablex.

Slavin, R. E. (1987). Making Chapter 1 make a difference. *Phi Delta Kappan, 69*, 110–119.

Stanovich, K. E. (1986). Matthew effects in reading: Some consequences of individual differences in the acquisition of literacy. *Reading Research Quarterly, 21*, 360–407.

Sticht, T. G. (1987). *Functional context education: Workshop resource notebook.* San Diego, CA: Applied Behavioral and Cognitive Sciences.

Taylor, B. M., Short, R. A., Frye, B. J., & Shearer, B. A. (1992). Classroom teachers prevent reading failure among low-achieving first grade students. *The Reading Teacher, 45*, 592–597.

Taylor, B. M., Strait, J., & Medo, M. A. (1994). Early intervention in reading: Supplemental instruction for groups of low-achieving students provided by first grade teachers. In E. H. Hiebert & B. M. Taylor (Eds.), *Getting reading right from the start: Effective early literacy intervention* (pp. 107–121). Needham, MA: Allyn and Bacon.

Ysseldyke, J. E., Christenson, S. L., Thurlow, M. L., & Bakewell, D. (1989). Are different kinds of instructional tasks used by different categories of students in different settings? *School Psychology Review, 18*, 98–111.

Epilogue:
Connections and Directions

SHELLEY B. WEPNER
JOAN T. FEELEY
William Paterson College of New Jersey

DOROTHY S. STRICKLAND
Teachers College, Columbia University

As with the first edition of *The Administration and Supervision of Reading Programs*, this second edition is about making connections among administrators, teachers, parents, and students; between recent research and current practices; and between professional relationships and theoretical conceptions.

While the contributors wrote about particular topics, a common philosophy has emerged about their beliefs, practices, and ideals. What they communicated is an *esprit de corps* for finding ways to connect the educational research of the last few decades with the realities of today's supervisory responsibilities. For example, even as they grappled with unresolved issues, they never let go of their holistic perspective on reading. It is clear that reading, as described throughout this text, is a functional, constructive process that must be *used* — not simply taught — in order to be developed for lifelong literacy. Instant formulaic answers to the many complex queries surrounding reading supervision are neither sought nor offered. Rather, numerous research-based guidelines for productive supervisory practices are presented.

What follows here is a summary of the themes that recur throughout the text. Restated as connections and directions, they represent the key ideas presented in this book.

CONNECTIONS

1. *Reforming school reading programs is a systemic, ongoing, collaborative process.* In order for change to occur, it is essential that key participants be involved — reading specialists, reading coordinators, reading

supervisors, teachers from appropriate subject areas and grade levels, building and district-level administrators, school board members, and parents.

Committees or site-based management teams must be responsible for assessing the district's or school's status, planning accordingly, implementing a plan, and evaluating for future program decisions. Fact-finding visits to other districts and schools, workshops, coursework, interviews, and independent reading research will give committee and team members the knowledge needed to make informed decisions and sound judgments about the proposed program changes. Teachers and others directly or indirectly involved with the team's work will develop a sense of ownership in program change and serve as collective agents for change in the school or district.

2. *Sound instructional reading programs are created at the school and district levels, not purchased.* In order to build an atmosphere for success, respect, and individuality, we must build instruction on what children know. We must be sensitive and responsive to children's diverse backgrounds and unique needs for learning so that we seek materials that match their abilities and skills. We also must have our own vision of what reading is so that we know how to best develop sound instructional programs. Moreover, we must view assessment as an opportunity to promote good teaching and high achievement rather than as a mechanism for stratifying students.

We need to recognize that the role of the teacher is to create, in collaboration with the learner, an environment that encourages active reading and researching. Since teachers are the key to successful reading programs, we need to provide opportunities for teachers to talk about their teaching and classroom-based research so that they can reflect on ways to best provide instruction for their students. We need to help teachers bridge the gap between the habit of transmitting information and the practice of negotiating concepts and ideas. In helping teachers to establish favorable conditions for learning, we need to help them understand how to select and use suitable texts and activities within and across curricular areas.

As initiators and leaders, we need to help our administrator and teacher colleagues evolve in their understanding of reading as a process for communicating with authors from a variety of vantage points. We need to help them recognize that sound instructional programs are woven with a blend of school-related and community-based factors. We need to help them tap into what exists so that they know how to move the school or district forward in its commitment to literacy as a lifelong habit rather than as a skill purchased from a set of materials.

3. *Communication and collaboration among colleagues and with the community are essential.* If change is to occur in our schools and ourselves, we must collaborate regularly with our colleagues to better understand and plan for the varied complexities of our reading programs. This allows us to take stock of our successes and failures with our students, and the conditions that surround each. It also provides for better coordination between and across grade levels, and between regular and special programs.

   Similar collaboration should exist with the community so that parents are an integral part of the reading program, from helping to select materials to working with their children at home. The more open and receptive we are to feedback, the more likely we are to engender positive feelings toward the change we want to promote.

4. *Realistic expectations inspire productive supervision.* As educational leaders, we cannot expect to be expert in everything related to our discipline. What we can expect of ourselves is that we take the responsibility to be informed decisionmakers. We should continue to learn about current research, newly developed theories, and applied practices. We also should keep abreast of national trends, statewide initiatives, and local changes. Finally, we should recognize that there is no best program for all learners at every level, nor at any level; nor is there any best way to supervise under all circumstances.

   If we realize our strengths and limitations and know how to connect with the appropriate people and resources in order to become better informed, we can begin to create a balance between our role responsibilities, our characteristics, our ideals, and the realities of our individual situations.

DIRECTIONS

As more and more connections are made between what we know and what we seek to learn, our understandings are fused into a fluid network for change. This second edition of *The Administration and Supervision of Reading Programs*, written five years after the publication of the first edition, contains 10 directions that have a different twist from the first edition because of the research-based shifts in thinking about teaching and learning.

1. Those in the position to initiate change—politicians, state boards of education, building- and district-level administrators, and school board members—will support the restructuring of reading programs because of their improved understanding of the nature of the reading process.
2. Teachers will take more ownership in evaluating their classroom practices through their own self-reflective analysis of the conditions they are creating for reading and writing.
3. Teachers, as members of site-based management teams, will participate with other teacher and administrator colleagues to make decisions about programs, personnel, instruction, and resources.
4. Teacher evaluation practices will change (e.g., use of portfolios for teaching assessment) to reflect the progress with instructional practices.
5. Greater collaboration will exist among universities, school districts, and businesses to support professional development and assess the value of innovative programs.
6. Improved large-scale and local assessment practices that focus on real-world reading practices will positively impact on the way in which reading is taught.
7. Instructional practices and materials will be more obviously responsive to the ethnically, culturally, and linguistically diverse student populations in our classrooms.
8. Early intervention programs for students with special needs will become more widespread as success rates for preventing reading failure become more evident.
9. Technology will become part of the panorama of available materials that support process-oriented, literature-based instruction.
10. Community outreach efforts that include the media will focus on involving parents from urban areas to get them involved in cultivating their children's reading habits.

Even as we look toward the future, we realize how critical our current initiatives are. As we continue to be informed by the best thinking available, we can continue to sharpen our vision for carving out future directions in literacy development.

About the Contributors

Kathryn H. Au is an educational psychologist responsible for development of the language arts curriculum at the Kamehameha Elementary Education Program (KEEP) in Honolulu, Hawaii. A former classroom teacher, her research interest is the school literacy learning of students of diverse backgrounds, and she has published a book, *Literacy Instruction in Multicultural Settings*, as well as many articles on this topic. She has served on the editorial advisory boards of *The Reading Teacher*, *Reading Research Quarterly*, and *Journal of Reading Behavior* and as a column editor for *Language Arts*. She has been a vice president of the American Educational Research Association and a board member of the National Reading Conference.

Rita M. Bean is Professor of Education at the University of Pittsburgh and Associate Dean of Research and Development. Before coming to the university, she taught elementary school and served as a reading specialist and reading supervisor. Her publications include research and applied articles specifically focused on the role of the reading specialist, instructional procedures for teaching individuals with reading problems, and comprehension instruction. Professor Bean has served on many editorial advisory boards, including *Reading Research and Instruction* and *The Reading Professor*. She currently directs a school restructuring effort in the Western Pennsylvania region, Project Read/Inquiring School, that promotes critical literacy as the primary focus of elementary school instruction. For the past several years she has also directed state projects investigating Chapter 1 reading programs: specifically, the nature of the instruction, the preparation of reading specialists, and the relationship between Chapter 1 reading programs and pre-referral programs for students with reading difficulties.

Mark W. Conley is Associate Professor of Teacher Education at Michigan State University. He received his Ph.D. in reading education at the Syracuse University Reading and Language Arts Center. Along with coursework in reading and teacher education, Dr. Conley teaches English and mathematics to eighth graders at Holt (MI) Junior High School. His publications include research and applied articles related to school/ university collaboration and content reading instruction. He is the author of *Content Reading Instruction: A Communication Approach* and, with

Donna Alvermann and David Moore, coeditor of *Research Within Reach: Secondary School Reading.*

Joan T. Feeley was Coordinator of the graduate reading program and Professor in the Department of Curriculum and Instruction at William Paterson College, Wayne, New Jersey, where she taught undergraduate courses in emergent literacy and graduate courses in research and psycholinguistics. Beginning her career as a high school teacher of English and French, she also taught in elementary schools in New York City and suburban New Jersey. Besides articles and reviews for journals such as *The Reading Teacher, Journal of Reading,* and *Language Arts,* she has co-authored a chapter, "Research on Language Learners: Development in the Elementary Years," in *The Handbook of Research on Teaching the English Language Arts.* Her books include *Using Computers in the Teaching of Reading, The Administration and Supervision of Reading Programs, Process Reading and Writing: A Literature-Based Approach,* and *Moving Forward with Literature: Basals, Books, and Beyond.* A past president of the North Jersey Council of the International Reading Association, she received the Distinguished Service Award from the New Jersey Reading Association.

Anthony D. Fredericks is Associate Professor of Education at York College, York, Pennsylvania. He earned his Ed.D. in reading from Lehigh University. A former classroom teacher and reading specialist, he is a recipient of the Innovative Teaching Award from the Pennsylvania State Education Association. He is the author/coauthor of more than 25 teacher resource books, including *Thematic Units: An Integrated Approach to Teaching Science and Social Studies, Frantic Frogs and Other Frankly Fractured Folktales for Readers Theatre,* and the *Involving Parents Through Children's Literature* series of books. A frequent presenter at inservice meetings and teacher workshops throughout North America, his interests include parent involvement, creative uses of children's literature, and thematic teaching.

Holly Genzen is a classroom teacher in the Lorain, Ohio, schools. She has taught in traditional, continuous-progress, and math intervention classes. She received her Ph.D. in educational administration from Kent State University and has particular interests in leadership, supervision, and the teacher as researcher. She has done research on women in leadership positions and on the position of the principal in site-based management and shared decisionmaking.

Bill Harp is Professor of Language Arts and Literacy in the College of Education, University of Massachusetts-Lowell. His Ed.D. is from the University of Oregon where he focused on curriculum and supervision with an emphasis on reading education. Dr. Harp has been an elementary classroom teacher and principal. His extensive publications include *Reading and Writing: Teaching for the Connections*, coauthored with Jo Ann Brewer, and two recent edited titles: *Assessment and Evaluation in Whole Language Programs* and *Bringing Children to Literacy: Classrooms at Work*.

Barbara A. Kapinus is currently a senior program coordinator at the Council of Chief State School Officers. In that role she works with several state consortia on the development of improved assessments. She has been a junior high school classroom teacher, a school-based reading specialist, and a district instructional specialist. She worked as the state reading specialist in Maryland. She coordinated the consensus process for designing the 1992 National Assessment of Education Progress in Reading, served on the National Steering Committee for the International Literacy Assessment, and has recently worked on the New Standards Project, a multistate effort to develop assessment systems. Barbara received her Ph.D. in Reading from the University of Maryland and has taught graduate courses at Johns Hopkins University and Western Maryland College. She has served on the editorial board of *The Reading Teacher* and the *Journal of Reading* and as coeditor of the assessment column of *The Reading Teacher*.

Carole S. Rhodes is Assistant Professor of Reading/Language Arts in the Department of Curriculum and Instruction at William Paterson College, Wayne, New Jersey. She earned a Ph.D. in curriculum and instruction from New York University, where she was awarded the Pi Lambda Theta Award. Dr. Rhodes is currently a consultant and staff development specialist for several urban and suburban school districts. As a classroom teacher and reading specialist in the New York City public schools, she has worked with students in the primary grades through high school. Dr. Rhodes is particularly interested in teachers as agents of change.

Nancy E. Seminoff is the Dean of the School of Education at William Paterson College in Wayne, New Jersey. She received her Ed.D. from Wayne State University. She was a classroom teacher and reading consultant before teaching at the university level. A former member of the Board of Directors for the International Reading Association (1986–1989), Dr. Seminoff has written widely about topics related to comprehension, teacher preparation, and the use of magazines and technology for instruction. She is author of *Using Children's Magazines in the K–8 Classroom* and served as a consultant in reading and questioning strategies for Holt's *Elements of Literature* program, grades 7–12. She is coauthoring a software package on writing and children's literature.

Dixie Lee Spiegel is a Professor of Education and Associate Dean for Students at the University of North Carolina at Chapel Hill. She holds a

Ph.D. in curriculum and instruction with emphasis in reading from the University of Wisconsin at Madison. She is a former third grade classroom teacher and a former elementary grades reading teacher. Dr. Spiegel is particularly interested in applying research in reading and writing to classroom practice. She is the author of a monograph on recreational reading as well as several research and applied articles and a reading methods textbook.

Dorothy S. Strickland is the State of New Jersey Professor of Reading at Rutgers University. Formerly the Arthur I. Gates Professor of Education at Teachers College, Columbia University, she has been a classroom teacher and reading specialist. Her publications include *Family Storybook Reading*; *The Administration and Supervision of Reading Programs*; *Emerging Literacy: Young Children Learn to Read and Write*; and *Language, Literacy and the Child*. She is past president of the International Reading Association and a member of the Reading Hall of Fame.

JoAnne L. Vacca is a Professor and Department Chairperson of Teaching, Leadership and Curriculum Studies at Kent State University, Kent, Ohio. She received her Ed.D. from Boston University. Professor Vacca taught at the middle school level and was a consultant with the Illinois Office of Education. She is the author of articles, reviews, and chapters, and coauthor of *Content Area Reading* (4th ed.) and *Reading and Learning to Read* (3rd ed.). She is interested in staff development and leadership and applications of qualitative research design.

Richard T. Vacca is Professor of Education at Kent State University. He completed his doctoral studies at Syracuse University and has been an instructor at Northern Illinois University and the University of Connecticut. Dr. Vacca has taught reading and writing at the junior high and high school levels. He is the coauthor of *Content Area Reading* (4th ed.) and *Reading and Learning to Read* (3rd ed.). Dr. Vacca has been elected president of the International Reading Association in 1996.

Shelley B. Wepner is Assistant to the Dean for the School of Education at William Paterson College, Wayne, New Jersey. She received her Ed.D. from the University of Pennsylvania. She held various public school positions in New Jersey, including Supervisor of Curriculum and Instruction. Her books include *Using Computers in the Teaching of Reading*; *The Administration and Supervision of Reading Programs*; *Process Reading and Writing: A Literature-Based Approach*; and *Moving Forward with Literature: Basals, Books, and Beyond*. Her award-winning software includes *Reading Realities*, *Reading Realities Elementary Series*, and *Read-A-Logo*. She is a former editor of *Reading Instruction Journal* and a former department editor of the "Technology Links to Literacy" column for *The Reading Teacher*.

Lee Williams is a teaching fellow at Kent State University, where she is currently completing her doctoral dissertation. Previously she taught English in the middle and high school, as well as composition and developmental reading at the college level. Her articles and reviews on secondary school reading have appeared in *English Leadership Quarterly* and *English Journal*. Her research interests include the social dimensions of literacy and classroom discourse.

Junko Yokota is Assistant Professor of Reading/Language Arts and Children's Literature in the Department of Curriculum and Instruction, National-Louis College. She received her Ph.D. from the University of North Texas. She has been an elementary classroom teacher and an elementary school librarian. She has written a chapter on Asian and Asian-American literature for *Multicultural Literature and Literacies: Making Space for Differences* as well as journal articles on multicultural literature. Her research interests center on issues regarding multicultural literature and literacy development for multicultural populations.

Index